Understanding Cultural Diversity in the Early Years

Peter Baldock

Los Angeles | London | New Delhi
Singapore | Washington DC

SAGE Publications Ltd
1 Oliver's Yard
55 City Road
London EC1Y 1SP

SAGE Publications Inc.
2455 Teller Road
Thousand Oaks, California 91320

SAGE Publications India Pvt Ltd
B 1/I 1 Mohan Cooperative Industrial Area
Mathura Road
New Delhi 110 044

SAGE Publications Asia-Pacific Pte Ltd
33 Pekin Street #02-01
Far East Square
Singapore 048763

Library of Congress Control Number: 2009935102

British Library Cataloguing in Publication data

A catalogue record for this book is available from the
British Library

ISBN 978-1-84860-986-0 (hbk)
ISBN 978-1-84860-987-7 (pbk)

Typeset by C&M Digitals (P) Ltd, Chennai, India
Printed in Great Britain by CPI Antony Rowe, Chippenham, Wiltshire
Printed on paper from sustainable resources

For Tempest and Maija

Contents

About the author

Peter Baldock

After working as a teacher and as one of the members of staff at the HQ of an international organization, Peter Baldock worked for more than twenty years in community development, always with a particular interest in early years projects. Later he worked in registration and inspection of early years services and as an associate lecturer of the Open University. His publications include three books on early years services. He is a member of the management committee of two voluntary organizations and he has served on one of the boards of Sheffield's Children and Young People Partnership.

Acknowledgements

Some of the material in this book first appeared in slightly different form in a series of articles I wrote for *Nursery World* in 2005 and 2006, and I am grateful to the editor for her generous permission to use it again here.

I have been for some time a member of the management committee of a voluntary organization called the Development Education Centre for South Yorkshire DEC(SY) and since 2004 I have had particular responsibility for the organization's work in the early years field. That work has been undertaken primarily by a group of staff called 'cultural mentors'. Many of the ideas in this book have come out of the work of that team and I want to acknowledge in the fullest possible terms my debt to the staff in DEC(SY) who been involved in that work over the last few years: Hlabera Chirwa, Valerie Garvey, Duraiya Kupasi, Rimas Tankile Morris and Rob Unwin. (One of the appendices gives a brief description of the work of DEC(SY) and its Cultural Mentor Service.)

I am also grateful to other friends and colleagues who contributed ideas and information, or who provided me with useful comments on earlier drafts. My thanks, therefore, to Sharon Curtis, Helen Griffin, Celia Mather, Glòria Rubiol, Judy Thompson and Janet Uwins who have helped to make this book better than it would otherwise have been. I remain, of course, responsible for the book itself.

Preface

Walk into any early years setting in the United Kingdom and you will not be surprised to see a notice in Reception bidding you welcome in several languages, a wok in the home corner, a copy of *Handa's Surprise* on the book shelf or evidence that the setting is planning for Divali. The celebration of cultural diversity is pretty standard now, recognized by staff as part of daily practice, expected by childcare inspectors and others in authority.

When something is part of the routine it is always a good idea to pause in order to question why this is the case and how things are working out in practice. Even if you end up continuing to support the objective and taking a positive view of current activity, critical examination will help you think more clearly on how an issue is being tackled. This book is intended to encourage you to re-examine your commitment and that of your setting (if you are currently working in one) to cultural diversity. It is important to do this not only because it is always a good idea to review what may be in danger of becoming routine, but also because the commitment to celebrating diversity is under attack in the wider world, with many assertions in the media that 'multiculturalism' has failed.

It is useful to remember that this commitment to cultural diversity is relatively recent in the early years professions and is a reflection of wider changes in British society. The origins can be sought in measures taken towards the end of the 19th century. At that time the largest immigrant communities in Britain were those of Irish Catholics and East European Jews. The leaders of those communities were often concerned that the new services for children that were developing (the universal school system, children's homes and adoption agencies, pioneering early years services) would drag the children of their communities into Protestant Christianity. They argued successfully for measures that would protect the wishes of parents in such matters as religion. Acceptance of this principle became part of further legislation on work with children. When the Conservative government reformed several services in their 1989 Children Act they consolidated this aspect of the law, making it a requirement that those who provided services for children gave 'due consideration ... to the child's religious persuasion, racial origin and cultural and linguistic background'.

This fairly straightforward re-framing of the law took place, however, in the context of a particular political situation. People from South Asia or the Caribbean had first arrived in the UK in large numbers in the 1950s and 1960s. By the 1970s they were becoming much more assertive in their resistance to racism and were winning support in the professions of the welfare state. At the same time there seemed to be a real threat that economic and political instability were encouraging the growth of organizations of the far right. Those engaged in the regulation of early years services or with training and development extended in practice the implications of the clauses in the 1989 Act. They argued that practitioners should not be content with being sensitive to the needs of the individual child from a minority culture whose parents were making use of a service. They should be helping all children to learn how to live in a multicultural society. This approach was endorsed when Ofsted took over the task of regulating early years services in England. In 2001 the promotion of equal opportunities was made one of the national standards for early years providers. This development was, of course, part of a broader move to promote multiculturalism by the Labour Party, which had come to power in the general election of 1997.

The new emphasis was underpinned by two kinds of publication for early years practitioners. On the one hand, there were books that spelled out the damage done by racism and the action that could be undertaken to tackle it in early years settings. Many of these were produced in the period when the Labour government was beginning to put its strategy on early years services into place. Leading examples were Brown (1998), Lane (1999) and Siraj-Blatchford (2000). Their advocacy of explicitly anti-racist strategies was underpinned by earlier research demonstrating that discriminatory behaviour by staff in early years settings was often more frequent than they themselves recognized. (See, for example, Ogilvy et al., 1990, cited in Siraj-Blatchford, 1994, pp.43–4.)

Texts such as these provided a valuable service, but their impact was sometimes to unnerve practitioners who became more conscious of what they might get wrong than confident they knew how to get things right. One response to this was the production of books and films offering practical suggestions on relevant activities, particularly the celebration of the festivals typical of various communities. These were also useful. However, there was always the risk that, where children were celebrating festivals from communities other than their own, what was happening would simply be a form of tourism, looking at exotic cultures from the outside. It could be entertaining and, perhaps, encourage a positive view of those communities. It might, nevertheless, do comparatively little to foster real understanding and communication (Derman-Sparks, 1993).

Now seems a good time to address the issue again. There are several reasons for this:

- We have had several years' experience of attempting to respond to cultural diversity in early years settings. It is time to review how that is going.
- The cultural mix in the UK has become even more complicated with increasing numbers of people from black Africa and Eastern Europe joining the longer established and larger communities from the Caribbean and South Asia. Some of those who have come here recently are migrant workers entitled to be here under the rules of the European Union. Others are refugees and asylum seekers. In both cases their situations are different from those of the people from countries of the former British Empire who now have a well-established presence in this country.
- The process of constitutional devolution has underlined the fact that the 'white British' themselves do not constitute a simple entity. To the relatively new issues that attracted the attention of authors in the 1990s we now have to add longer-standing questions, such as those of the sectarian divide in Northern Ireland or bi-lingualism in Wales.
- The language of the argument has changed. In the 1970s and 1980s both those who were against racism and those who had some sympathy for it normally discussed the issue in terms of race and colour. Racism has not gone away. However, in public discourse at least, it is now more likely to take the form of suspicion of the impact of other cultures on that of this country and, in particular, the form of hostility to Islam.

I cannot claim to be an expert on all those aspects of the issue. I have some impressions of how work on cultural diversity is going, but have not conducted a piece of systematic, evaluative research. Like many, I am still getting to grips with the developing cultural diversity of the UK. I am an Englishman whose work in early years has all been in England (in fact, nearly all in Yorkshire and Humberside). Thus, while I am interested in what is happening elsewhere in the UK and say something about it here, I cannot speak on it from direct experience. It is on the fourth of the factors outlined above that I will concentrate.

You may be surprised, even disappointed, that the first part of this book is not about work with children. The focus is on broader social and political questions. This is because I am convinced that we cannot help children live in a world of cultural diversity until we have begun to manage that ourselves. What is more, we cannot do that until we have a reasonably clear notion of our own cultural identity (including the fact that our cultural identity may not be very clear cut).

The first three chapters deal with the general context:

- Chapter 1 asks you to consider your own cultural identity and to use that reflection to think about just what is meant when we speak of someone's culture.
- Chapter 2 addresses the issue of multiculturalism and its alleged failure, suggesting different ways in which policy on this matter can be understood.
- Chapter 3 introduces the idea of inter-cultural competence and argues that the changing situation in which we find ourselves makes it necessary to develop skills in responding to cultural differences rather than just to acquire information about the cultures we expect to meet.

The middle section of the book deals with aspects of early years practice:

- Chapter 4 describes some of the background to practice, including both curriculum guidance and discussions in staff groups and with parents.
- Chapter 5 addresses aspects of daily practice.
- Chapter 6 is concerned with the inclusion of children who are not white British.

The last two main chapters deal with two particular types of situation:

- Chapter 7 speaks about the relevance of the issue to settings in areas that are overwhelmingly white British.
- Chapter 8 speaks about the particular situation of the setting where the majority of staff and users are *not* white British.

There is also a brief Conclusion and there are two appendices, one of which gives advice on finding resources for work on cultural diversity.

Throughout the book there is a number of activities to help you think through the issues under discussion. All of them can be used by groups of practitioners or students during in-house training or other events. Most of them can also be used for individual reflection, and for that reason should be useful for childminders as well as those working in day care.

A note on terminology

It is a central proposition of this book that people do not usually belong to 'cultures' with fixed and essentially unchanging boundaries. To the extent that something like this ever happened, modern communications and economic inter-dependence are undermining such situations. Thus to a large extent I have chosen to speak of 'cultural background' or used similar phrases. However, sometimes – for the sake of brevity – it is useful to speak of a particular 'culture'. I hope that the reader will not see in this a deviation from the basic point being made.

In the 1960s there was a fierce debate about the propriety of the term 'race relations'. It was argued that to use the term at all was to concede that there were quite separate 'races' which had to be in some kind of relationship with each other. Others argued that there was, after all, an issue and that 'race relations' was a convenient shorthand term that could be used to refer to it. In the 1990s a way out of the dilemma was sought in referring to 'ethnicity' rather than 'race'. That term appeared to embrace both physical and cultural characteristics. Some objected to it for that very reason, arguing that the problem of racism had to be confronted head-on and that the term 'ethnicity' blurred the issue. Talk of culture, they claimed, fudged the issue even further. After all, we have had some race riots over the last few decades. No one has ever spoken of 'culture riots'. The issue was particularly critical for people whose parents came from different ethnic backgrounds. Some of those people argue that the struggle against racism requires that they identify themselves unambiguously as black (as Barrack Obama has done in the United States). Others argue that they should take pride in their 'mixed heritage' and see in it a sign of hope for the future. I have no way to offer out of the problem of the best language to employ. In some contexts I have spoken of people who are 'not white British' because the topic in hand has been the response of the majority population to people some see as not belonging to it. Similarly, I have sometimes spoken of 'black and Asian people' where it seemed more relevant to use that language than to employ a term that also covers white minorities. I have also used the conventional term 'black and minority ethnic' although I appreciate that to emphasise the minority status of a group can be a way of reinforcing their separation. All the language available to us on this issue has disadvantages. To speak bluntly of people who are different in appearance is to risk reinforcing the notion that these differences are and should be of great significance. To avoid speaking of them is to risk dodging the issue of the crucial place of racism in modern British society. Some day it may be possible to speak of cultural diversity without encountering these difficulties.

1

What Is Your Culture?

> **This chapter:**
>
> > Outlines the nature and importance of cultures
>
> > Uses a fictional example to demonstrate that people do not belong in an uncomplicated way to cultures that have clear and unchanging boundaries
>
> > Invites you to consider your own cultural identity as a way of underlining some of the key issues
>
> > Discusses, in particular, the question of 'Englishness' as a form of cultural identity

I was sitting in on a staff meeting at a fairly large nursery, listening to a discussion about the steps they would take to improve the setting following a recent review they had conducted. One of the decisions was to purchase more 'cultural playthings'. I knew what they meant, of course. They were talking about playthings that came from, or at least reflected, cultures other than the white British one to which all of us present belonged. However, the implication that the climbing frame, the copy of *We're Going on a Bear Hunt*, the toy farmyard and the runaround toy in the form of Noddy's little car had no cultural connotations at all was rather odd.

Behind the phrase 'cultural playthings' there lay an unspoken assumption: 'We are normal and some other people have cultures'. Cultures might, of course, be very colourful and interesting – worth more than a quick look. The way they are described might, in other words, sound very positive. It remains the case that they can be seen as exotic, abnormal, something unusual that it requires a particular effort to understand.

The word 'culture' has a number of meanings. On the one hand, it refers to higher forms of refined sensibility and their products in the forms of art, music, literature and comparable activities. On the other hand, it is now used frequently to refer to the rules and habits that bind a particular society together. More recently, there has been greater interest in the academic world in cultural products – popular fiction, fashion, the mass media and so on – that may not aspire to the status of great art but are also important as reflections and developers of values.

The idea of culture as the set of practices that keep a society together and allow its members to find meaning in their lives was first articulated in the studies conducted by social anthropologists from the late-19th century onwards. Much of this research was undertaken among remote peoples whose ways of life were very different from those of Europe. It may have become a term we apply to ourselves as well as to peoples whose lives are significantly different from ours, but for some people the idea that the word 'culture' refers to the exotic remains. To have a culture is to be different, and what those who have a culture are different from is 'us'.

The complications of cultural identity

Life is a bit more complicated than that. Take the (fictional) case of a particular individual.

Mary is a woman in her thirties working as an early years practitioner in a Sure Start Children's Centre in the north east of England. She is married, with two young children. She and her husband are practising Roman Catholics. Already busy, she still finds time for her hobby of painting pictures.

So far, the story sounds fairly simple. Let me now add that Mary and her husband are both Hakka-speaking ethnic Chinese from Mauritius who came to the UK soon after their marriage.

What has been added is not just another bit of information. Mary does not have a Hakka/Chinese culture in the way that she might have, say, a nice fitted kitchen. It is not a simple possession. Perhaps she brings to the care of her own children values and practices she learned growing up in Mauritius. Perhaps her paintings are influenced by Chinese brush painting. However, it gets more complicated than that. Her religion (Roman Catholicism) was introduced to the Far East in relatively recent times and was seen for centuries in England, where she now lives, as an alien and threatening religion (much as Islam is seen by many people today). How does she see her religion fitting in with her Hakka culture or her British nationality? Her understanding of her faith may have been influenced by other parts of her life. Aspects of her background may have brought her to see her professional work with children in a slightly different light from that of her colleagues. Her work in the Sure Start Centre may have brought her into contact with a wider range of beliefs and attitudes and experiences in ways that have led her to re-think aspects of her faith.

Mary is neither just another early years practitioner more or less like any other, nor is she merely a representative of Hakka culture. She is someone living her life and trying to make sense of it with a variety of tools drawn from a variety of cultural influences – Hakka society, the north east of England, her church and her professional training among them. She has in some ways a culture of her own. It is not so much that she has a particular culture as that everything she does is shaped by a complex interaction of cultural perspectives drawn from all the aspects of her life so far.

The best of the early social anthropologists would have had little difficulty in recognizing this. People such as Franz Boas (1858–1942) described particular cultures as accurately as they could, but recognized that cultures were products of history and changed with changes of circumstance, including interaction between different societies. It was not so much that people were governed by a culture to which they belonged as that they had to develop cultural norms in order to interact effectively with those around them. Cultures might be conservative because the very purpose of their existence was to make social interaction as predictable as possible, but social anthropologists recognized that they always have the capacity to change.

The importance of the cultural dimension of our lives can be difficult to acknowledge. For example, the study of child development was until recently usually based on what happened in middle-class Anglo-Saxon communities. Assumptions that were made about what is natural and biologically determined were, in fact, derived from observing the culture of such societies in action. However, it is clear that the young child's response to the 'strange' situation of the child development laboratory where she is left by her mother or encounters unfamiliar figures is going to depend significantly on the extent to which care in her everyday social circle belongs primarily to a maternal figure and how often she encounters unfamiliar people. The need for security is built into her. What security means to her in practice will depend on the culture in which she is being raised. In other words, a child's responses may be based on biological need, but they can only be expressed through culture (Cole, 1998, especially pp. 22–6; Super & Harkness, 1998; Robinson & Jones Diaz, 2001).

In spite of this, there is still a strong tendency to see what happens in middle-class Anglo-Saxon society as natural and other forms of behaviour as oddities that have to be explained by understanding other cultures. Similarly, when dealing as an early years practitioner with families from a different cultural background, it can be very easy to see their culture as a special explanatory factor of a kind that does not come into play if children are white British.

The case of Mary demonstrates something of the complexity of cultural identity. Her situation demands of her that she reconciles various ways of being in the world that have come to her from her ethnicity, her religion, her profession, her roles as a wife and mother, her whole personal and family history. It is not that she is an individual in the sense that she was born with a fully developed personality or has simply invented the type of person she wants to be. All the 'scripts' she uses (consciously or unconsciously) to form her identity were largely written before she came along. On the other hand, the 'scripts' are many and in using them she is also modifying them. In this respect her situation is the same as that of all of us today.

Identifying your own culture

If you were asked to identify your own culture, you might find this task easy or difficult. You might be inclined to deny that you had a particular culture. Alternatively, you might identify yourself quite readily with a nationality, ethnicity or some other grouping. People whose lives involve periods in different countries may have alternative identities. Uwins (2008, p.43) speaks of one early years practitioner who 'considers herself to be black British when she resides in Britain and black African when she is in Nigeria'. Some people have the opposite reaction, speaking proudly of their original cultural or national identity while in Britain, but becoming aware of how British they are when visiting the homeland of their ancestors. The cultural identity that someone develops will be an adaptation to circumstance – perhaps quite unconscious in the case of someone who stays in more or less the same society all her life, much more self-conscious in the case of someone who chooses to live elsewhere or is for one reason or another an exile from her place of origin.

The two activities that follow are intended to get you thinking about your own cultural identity.

 Exercise

What aspects of your life help to determine your identity? In answering this question you can take into account:

- your family roles (partner, daughter, son, parent)
- your family's history
- your profession
- your social class

- your nationality
- the part of the country in which you live
- your affiliation to a religion (if you have one)
- your ethnic identity
- your interests, your taste in music, reading and so on
- anything else that is important to you.

How far has thinking about those things made it possible for you to identify your culture?

You can do this as an individual exercise or get all the members of a group to do it and then share what they have written down.

Quite possibly, answering all those questions has still left you uncertain of what to say about your cultural identity. Part of the reason for this may be that you are uncertain of what to say about some of the elements listed above. Take the case of nationality. You may be a British citizen, but wish to identify yourself as black British or Welsh or in some other way. Are you then saying that your culture is British, but that you belong to some specific sub-section of a wider British culture?

If you can identify your nationality without any question, do you feel comfortable with everything that seems to be implied by that? For example, I would say that I am English and that this is a key element in my identity. However,

- I do not drink tea very often
- I am not a member of the Church of England whose participation in church services is, nevertheless, restricted to weddings and funerals
- I am not interested in cricket
- I speak more than one language
- I rarely use an umbrella.

In other words, there are several ways in which I do not match the stereotype of what many people in other countries, and even other Englishmen, would think of as typically English. (In other respects, of course, I fit the stereotype more neatly.)

Have another stab at discerning your cultural identity by tackling the next exercise.

Exercise

Imagine that there has been a major disaster. The economy and public services are in serious disarray. It has been decided that, in order to cope with the situation, the majority of those fit to travel will have to be evacuated to other countries that have agreed to take them as refugees. This exercise is being organized by the United Nations.

You and your immediate family are to be evacuated to another country. Because of the gravity of the situation, you have no say on the matter of your destination. The emergency will last for some time, so you must expect your stay to be long-term, perhaps permanent.

Write down:

- five things you would want to take with you. These can be of practical or sentimental value. You should be able to fit all five plus some changes of clothing into a small suitcase.
- five things you would want to continue doing once you arrive; examples might include wearing British-style clothing or working in the same occupation.
- five things you would be willing to do in order to fit in with the society you are about to join; examples might include learning a local language, studying a citizenship course and so on.

You can do this as an individual exercise or ask members of a group to write down individual responses and then share them. Some people might be reluctant to share some of their answers with the whole group. For example, the objects someone wishes to take might include one whose significance is so personal that she is reluctant to discuss it in the whole group. That is fine. The object of the exercise is to help each participant focus on what she or he finds important. Sharing that information is optional.

Do not worry too much about the feasibility of the scenario. The point is to get people thinking about what is important to them and what this indicates about their identities.

I have not identified the country to which you are being sent. If someone in your group comes from or is reasonably knowledgeable about a particular country, you might decide to select that as your country of refuge and ask that person questions which might influence some of your responses.

Doing this exercise might help people to see the situation of asylum-seekers in a new light. If so, that is all to the good. However, the key purpose is to help people think about what is important to their own identities.

If you have undertaken the exercise on your own, ask yourself how far the objects you have chosen to take reflect your cultural identity. They may seem to be about your personal life or tastes, but still reflect your cultural background. Taking a wedding ring or some other token of a significant relationship will itself say something about how relationships are seen by people of your cultural background. It may just happen to be the case that you like marmite or thick–cut marmalade, but many people would see these as typical of a peculiarly English taste in food. You can also ask yourself how far your answers to the second and third question help you name those aspects of your identity that are so important to you that you would be unwilling to abandon them, however flexible you wished to be in your new circumstances. If you have run it as a group exercise, encourage participants to share as much as they are happy to share about their answers and look at some of the common features and those where there are differences.

Has this exercise taken you much further forward in defining your own culture?

The particular case of Englishness

There is always a tendency to think that the way we do things is normal and that deviations from that pattern are oddities requiring explanation. This is a key factor in the way in which cultures other than white British may be seen. There is, however, an additional complication in the case of the English. For a long time – and still to a great extent today – the terms 'British' and 'English' were seen (by the English at least) as interchangeable.

Scottish, Welsh, Irish or other forms of national identity were seen as mere regional variations, no more significant than being from Yorkshire, Devon or Kent. It is still possible for a serious report to speak of something being true of the United Kingdom when it is true only of England. Clark & Waller (2007, p.5) describe an example.

This situation has been altered by the process of handing over aspects of government to new assemblies in Scotland, Wales and Northern Ireland and the pressures that led to that constitutional change. People in other parts of the United Kingdom are now much less likely than the English to identify themselves as British. The saints' days of St Patrick, St Andrew and St David are celebrated in a way that St George's Day is not. The decline in the military and political power of the United Kingdom and the recognition of much that was wrong with the establishment and administration of the British Empire have undermined the ability of people to feel pride in the British identity. At the same time there remains a further uncertainty about pride in being English.

This situation has led to the publication in recent years of a range of books that approach the English identity in different ways. Some are content to list and praise the more attractive places in the country. A few pamphleteers take an assertively nationalist stance. Bragg (2006) celebrates the progressive strand in English history and sees this as the basis for a different form of patriotism. Miles (2005) traces the ethnic mix that has led to the English nation. Paxman (1999) observes his fellow countrymen with the sardonic detachment of a journalist. Fox (2004) is also humorous, but also brings to the subject her skills as a social anthropologist. Ackroyd (2002) uses history, literature and other arts to describe the nature of England in ways that may surprise many. Jones (1998) moves even further from the conventional, seeing England not as the 'Protestant nation' many would have described in the past, but as having its real foundations in the Catholic Middle Ages. The vast differences of approach and understanding among these authors illustrate the uncertainty as to what it means to be English.

The complication of national identity is brought out by the fact that many black and Asian people living in England are happy to fly the English flag during the World Cup or other international sports competitions, but would shun the Union flag, which the far right has taught them to see as a symbol of racism (Bagguly & Hussain, 2005). At the same time, many white English people are suspicious of English nationalism and prefer to speak of Britishness. There have also been cases of those in authority trying to prevent the flying of the English flag on the grounds that it might offend black people.

You may have your own views on Englishness. Whether or not you are English yourself, try the following exercise as a way into defining what you think English culture might be.

 Exercise

The following statements are taken from a discussion among people from a small town in the middle of the country about the way they see their cultural identity and national heritage.

How many of these statements would you be prepared to describe as typically English? Can you construct some kind of picture of English culture from them?

- Our patron saint is St George and you often see representations of him on public buildings etc. but I don't think he means very much to most people. He is not an important symbol.
- The flag is very important. It is a symbol around which everyone can rally. I think it has become more important in that sense in recent years.
- Conquering Everest was a big step for us. It made us feel we had literally 'made it to the top'.
- What really distinguishes us from other countries and their people is our common sense.
- There may be examples of intolerance, but basically we are a very tolerant society. We make people welcome as long as they meet us halfway. I think that is the value that distinguishes us from many other nations.
- We are very practical and pragmatic.
- When people talk about 'cultural heritage' you think about grand buildings etc. but other things are just as significant. Lavatory jokes, for example. People might say they disapprove of them, but they always raise a laugh.
- It is in doing the ordinary, simple things that you feel our common heritage – like decorating the tree at Christmas.
- Our old churches are part of what makes us feel part of a nation. People might not go to church very often, but they have strong feelings about the great cathedrals.

(Continued)

(Continued)

- If you really want to know what it means to belong to our nation, you have to go to the countryside. The cities are big, anonymous places and with so many international retail outlets you could be anywhere in the world a lot of the time. It is the country that represents what is best about our society. We have to defend it.

You can undertake this as an individual exercise or in a group. The composition of a group will have an obvious impact on the degree of consensus it is possible to reach and on what that consensus will be. A group of English people might come up with different responses from a more mixed group.

If you undertake this exercise as the facilitator of a group, wait until the discussion is over before revealing that the 'town in the middle of the country' is Sabadell. If that name is unfamiliar, it is because the discussion did not take place in England at all, but in Catalonia, a region of Spain, which has its own language and where the regional government has a considerable amount of devolved power. To the extent that many of the statements sounded true of England, or at least as though they were the sort of thing that English people might say about themselves, this exercise shows up how problematic the idea of a unique national identity can be. I have cheated, of course. Catalonia is in Western Europe and has many features in common with England as with other West European countries. I have also suppressed some of the things that were said when this conversation took place because they would have given the game away. The exercise does, however, raise questions about claims to the uniqueness of any given national culture.

Summary

In all our dealings with other people we rely on habits, conventions and rules that we may help to modify but which came from outside us. We can (with some effort) change the cultural context in which we operate. We cannot hope to operate outside any cultural context at all.

However, this is about culture as a means of understanding the world and making effective relationships. It does not mean that any of us belongs to quite specific cultures with closed boundaries and unchanging natures. All cultures are subject to the historical process of change. All of us operate in a number of cultural spheres determined by our nationality, preferred language, religious faith or secular values, profession or a number of other things to which we belong and which give us ways of deciding how to live our lives and to seek significance for ourselves.

Any approach in an early years setting or elsewhere to people whose cultural background is significantly different from our own depends on our understanding of this fact. It is in this light that we can consider the broad question of multiculturalism or the specific questions that arise from daily practice.

Further reading

You may want to look at some of the books mentioned in the chapter. Siraj-Blatchford (2000) *Supporting Identity, Diversity and Language in the Early Years* is a particularly good book on this topic. Fox (2004) *Watching the English* offers a light read on the question of the English character, but is underpinned by some very clear thinking.

I have deliberately avoided saying a great deal about social anthropology, but that academic discipline lies behind much of what has been said here. Hendry (2008) *An Introduction to Social Anthropology* is a readable text for those who already know something about the subject as well as for newcomers.

The topic of the cultural dimension of child development is covered in Smidt (2006) *The Developing Child in the 21st Century*.

2

Multiculturalism
and its Alleged Failure

This chapter:

> Describes the way that multiculturalism, far from being a matter of universal agreement, is the subject of sometimes bitter dispute

> Outlines the variety of arguments made against promoting cultural diversity and some of the ways in which these can be countered

> Suggests some principles on which it may be possible to agree

---

At the start of this book I spoke of the ways in which marking and celebrating cultural diversity are now established aspects of the way that early years settings operate.

The view that this is essential to good practice may be more or less agreed within the profession. In the world outside things are a little different. There the view is often expressed that the commitment to multiculturalism has been a serious mistake. The tone of argument (especially on the Internet as opposed to other media) is frequently angry and aggressive – curiously reminiscent of the sneering denunciations of intellectuals and their 'harmful cosmopolitanism' that were often heard in the Soviet Union.

Part of what is happening is that the debate about ethnicity has changed. In the 1950s and 1960s there were many prepared to talk in overtly racial terms about the danger posed by the presence of relatively large numbers of people whose origin lay outside the UK as a result of post-war immigration. Gradually, this explicitly-racist language is being dropped. There have been several reasons for this:

- Growing familiarity with people with different skin colours or other physical characteristics or at least with the fact that they are around has made differences in physical appearance less startling.
- The science of genetics has destroyed the theory that there are some specific races more advanced than others.
- Few people wish to be seen to share the views of Nazi Germany where belief in the significance of racial distinctions led to mass murder.
- The legislation in 1968 and later on racial discrimination has made those who hold specifically racist views cautious about expressing them, and this has had a developing impact on the tenor of public debate.

Those who have remained suspicious of people who are not white British have been led to drop explicit opposition to what one Conservative MP speaking in 1964 called a 'chocolate coloured, Afro-Asian mixed society' (cited in Foot, 1965, p.129). Instead, those who remained unhappy with the changing nature of the population began to assert that people with different skin colour need not pose any problem as long as they adopted significantly different behaviour, supporting for example the English rather than the West Indian, Pakistani or Indian cricket teams. The issue began to be discussed in terms of the ethnic or cultural identities of minorities rather than of race as such.

It would be easy to over-simplify this situation. It is obviously true that a straightforward racism based on older ideas about skin colour or other physical characteristics can be disguised by alleged concerns about culture. 'Muslims' often becomes a code word for Asians, one that helps people evade some of the consequences of the law on race discrimination. The fact remains there has been a significant change in the way in which public debate is conducted.

Division of opinion, however, remains. While many in government and the professions have said that cultural diversity is something to celebrate, others have taken a different stance. Even relatively friendly critics note that multiculturalism lacks a 'coherent philosophical statement of its central principles' (Parekh, 2000). Musgrave describes it as absurd (www. multiculturalbunk.com, last accessed 6/7/09); Schmidt (1997) goes even further, describing it as a menace.

It is difficult to judge the state of popular opinion. A poll conducted by MORI for the BBC in August 2005 (i.e. just after the London bombings) found that 62 per cent of their sample believed that multiculturalism made Britain 'a better place in which to live' and only 2 per cent were prepared to admit that they were 'very racially prejudiced'. The BBC chose to report this on their website under the headline 'UK majority back multiculturalism'. Other responses recorded during the poll raise questions about this conclusion:

58 per cent thought that 'people who come to live in Britain should adopt the values and traditions of British culture' and 38 per cent of non-Muslims thought that women should be forced not to wear any headscarf. This suggests that at least some of those questioned had only a hazy idea of what multiculturalism meant when they agreed that it made Britain a better place and that the reservations of the minority were forceful ones. Moreover, few people would be prepared to describe themselves as preju-diced against anything. To do so would be to admit what is usually seen as a moral fault. Rather than showing multiculturalism triumphant, the poll would seem to illustrate deep ambivalence about it (http://news. bbc.co.uk/1/hi/uk/4137990.stm, last accessed 17/7/09).

Thus the commitment of early years practitioners to the celebration of cul-tural diversity cannot be an uncontroversial or merely professional matter. It operates in a context where such commitments are the subject of fero-cious polemic and a degree of public disquiet. We cannot ignore this and carry on regardless. Practitioners need to determine more clearly where each stands personally on the issues involved. This entails examining the arguments against multiculturalism.

 Exercise

The first two schools based on the Islamic faith but receiving state funding (one in Brent in London, the other in Birmingham) were set up in 1998 on the basis of a legislative change dating back five years. There had, of course, been faith schools linked to various Christian denominations and funded by the state for some time. There has been controversy as to whether Islam, Hinduism and other faiths should be allowed to establish their own grant-aided schools. Many who oppose this development are also hostile to the existing Christian schools. Some believe that the establishment of more faith schools is bound to lead to widening the gap between communities, and they point to the example of Northern Ireland as a country where they claim that segregation of schools is connected to tension between communities and the violent conflict that has resulted in the recent past.

What do you think?

This can be an individual reflection or the basis of a group discussion

Among questions you can take into account are the following:

- If the existence of separate Catholic schools is a major cause of violence in Northern Ireland in the recent past, why has it not led to similar violence in England in the same period?
- If religious differences are a major cause of conflict, why have some of the worst conflicts of recent years been between peoples who share religious faiths? (The War of Independence fought by Bangladesh against Pakistan was one between Sunni Muslims. The genocide in Ruanda was committed by one group who were mainly Roman Catholics against fellow Catholics in another ethnic group).
- Those seeking to establish more Muslim schools argue that these will provide a necessary base for them to find a place in British society with confidence (see, for example, Sarwar, 2004, p.7). This certainly happened to many children from working-class families of immigrant origin who attended Catholic state-aided schools in the 1950s and 1960s. Do you see any merit in this line of argument?

The case against multiculturalism

The word 'multiculturalism' covers a number of different ideas and practices. It is necessary to unpick these in order to evaluate practice based upon it.

It is not always clear whether those opposed to multiculturalism are voicing hostility to either

- the sheer fact that there are now large numbers of people living in the UK whose cultural roots are at least to some extent elsewhere,

  or

- specific policies and practices that celebrate and promote the cultural diversity that results from their presence.

To some extent that ambiguity may be deliberate. It is likely to make your audience less uncomfortable if you say that politicians or professional experts have got something wrong than if you say something that implies hostility to a large segment of the population.

Whether people object to the simple fact that we have large numbers of people living here whose origins lie in other cultures or to some of the policies devised to respond to that fact, there are several different arguments made against multiculturalism.

The argument that there are too many people of foreign origin here for social coherence to survive

There are some who believe that there are too many people who have come to this country in the recent past and that the problems of accommodating them (materially and socially) are themselves the cause of friction.

It is, of course, true that unplanned migration can lead to problems. It did so when people moved in large numbers from other, usually rural, parts of the country into the growing urban centres of Manchester, Leeds and other cities during the Industrial Revolution. It can do so now whenever large numbers turn up, often unexpectedly, in a particular location. The answer our ancestors found in the 19th century was to re-design the physical layout and administration of cities rather than to try sending people back to rural areas that could not sustain them. They may not have applied that answer with as much efficiency and humanity as could have been wished, but they did achieve a great deal. Something like that needs to happen again.

If might be said that things are different now precisely because it is people from other cultures who are coming and that makes life more difficult. However, the contrast such an opinion suggests between our experience and that of the 19th century can be seriously over-stated. The Irish may have been white, but their culture was as alien to many Englishmen in the 19th century as those of black and other minorities today. In fact, many people in the early 19th century thought that social cohesion would be at risk if too many people moved *between different English parishes* in search of a better life.

Moreover, it is simply untrue that larger numbers of people from an outside culture are harder to accommodate than very small numbers. Hostility to black and Asian people (or even to some Europeans, such as Poles, Maltese and Cypriots) was often violent and overt in the period after the Second World War, precisely because the numbers of such people were small and the opportunities for interaction and familiarization were consequently rare. Familiarity does not always succeed in undermining hostility, but it can help. When the *Daily Mail* bravely took up the case of the family of Stephen Lawrence, the young black man murdered on a London street, many were surprised. It did not fit neatly with that paper's perceived stance on ethnic minorities. No doubt the editor, Paul Dacre, was impressed by the justice of the family's cause. He may have been led to pay it close attention in the first place because Stephen's father, a professional plasterer, had previously done a good job on re-plastering his house (Davies, 2008, p.73).

The argument that multiculturalism can be used as an excuse for unjust attacks on aspects of historical white British culture

Many of the complaints about multiculturalism are based on particular steps taken in its name. Some of these complaints are amply justified, but that is a case for carefully considering what respect for other cultures might mean in practice rather than abandoning the whole principle.

The Anglican Archbishop of York (himself originally from Uganda) expressed bewilderment in the week before his enthronement that respect for other cultures seems in some people's minds to entail abandoning or deriding an English sense of identity (report in *The Times* 22/11/05). He has repeated those sentiments since on several occasions. He is, of course, right to say that people cannot develop a proper and informed respect for other cultures without a positive, if critical, appreciation of their own. (This was a major line of argument in the first chapter of this book.)

There are times when it seems that the wish to avoid offending the adherents of other religions is being abused by some as a way of covertly attacking Christianity. A few years ago one local authority refused to allow Father Christmas to operate in one of their shopping centres on the grounds that this would offend non-Christians. When journalists took the trouble to ask local religious leaders if they had any objection, the Muslims, Sikhs and others all stated clearly that they did not see why anyone should object. The only criticism came from an Evangelical Christian Pastor. He pointed out (correctly, if a little pedantically) that Father Christmas may have started life as a Christian figure, Saint Nicholas, but is now presented in ways that owe more to Shamanistic religion and the advertising of a particular soft drink than to Christianity. He felt that making Father Christmas a central feature of the celebration detracted from the Christian message and was objectionable for that reason.

Incidents such as this show that people in authority can get things wrong. They raise questions about the *ways* in which people try to respond to multiculturalism rather than their overall *objectives*.

The argument that assimilation to the host culture is possible only if new arrivals completely abandon their original culture

Culture is integral to interaction and cooperation between people. Life would be impossible if we had to negotiate every contact with another person in the absence of any agreed principles and procedures. More than that, people feel at ease with each other because of shared feelings about symbols, places, pieces of music. Social anthropologists study how such systems work and they have helped us to become more conscious of them.

Given the importance of shared principles and symbols, some people ask whether multiculturalism can ever work. Do we not need a single culture in this country or any other country? Is it not the case that increasing crime, the disintegration of the traditional family and other symptoms of what some have described as a 'broken society' have arisen because a whole variety of cultures are jostling for position? Is it, perhaps, inevitable that the attempt to respect all cultures has undermined the respect for the culture of the nation, which – like all cultures – often operates in an almost unconscious way? Could multiculturalism even have undermined the notion that *any* culture or set of values has validity, or at least more validity, than any other? It is all very well – it might be said – for intellectuals, who spend their time chattering about these issues, to rejoice in a world they describe as 'post-modernist', but can our society operate without a single culture having the upper hand? If it cannot, then surely multiculturalism must be abandoned.

It is well known that European society has benefited from ideas imported during the Middle Ages from the Islamic world (including ideas whose origins lay in ancient Greece or in India). The impact of technical devices coming from China towards the end of the Middle Ages was far greater than has been widely recognized so far. Nearer to home, it is evident that work with young children in the UK has benefited from the ideas of foreigners, such as Fröbel and Steiner, Montessori and Malaguzzi and a host of less well-known figures responsible for developments in policy and practice in Spain, Scandinavia and New Zealand.

Those who argue against cultural confusion do not have to deny the value of such influences. They do not want a complete isolation of our culture, simply much greater restriction on the way influences operate. If societies, particularly those that are more exotic, maintain their traditional cultures firmly, British tourists can enjoy visiting them. Commerce can be conducted without the participants needing to have too much to do with each other outside business negotiations. Ideas can be taken from other cultures through books or other sources of information without more personal interaction between people from different cultures. (Osama bin Laden, that arch enemy of multiculturalism, was happy to use the knowledge of structural engineering he had gained from the West to plan the destruction of the twin towers).

The strength of this argument is underlined by the failure of Gordon Brown's attempt at a re-definition of 'Britishness' to generate any resonance among his fellow citizens. His tentative definition of what it means to be British is based on a set of ethical principles for which widespread acceptance could probably be secured in many countries (d'Ancona & Brown, 2009). What it lacks is any of the sense of shared feeling and history that lies at the base of loyalty to a nation or any other social grouping. John Major, when he was Prime Minister, invoked a picture of old maids bicycling to church down country lanes to describe what it meant to him to be British (this was in a speech delivered in April 1993, cited by Paxman, 1999, p.142). Major was somewhere nearer to any real sense of a national culture, even if he was being sentimental in a way that was pretty feeble and failed to reflect the feelings and experience of many white British people, let alone others, living in this country.

While recognizing the strength of the idea that social coherence must depend on attachment to a single culture, it is important to recognize its weakness. Except in communities that are exceptionally separated from others – communities that have been kept isolated by physical geography, low levels of economic development or extreme suspicion of the outside world – the normal situation throughout history has been one of cultural interaction. It is true that the relationship has often entailed a ruling elite from one culture having domination over ordinary people from another, or of armed conflict between communities with different cultures. However, only a few people have claimed that the success of their own culture depended on the complete avoidance of contact with them or even on the extermination of another culture.

The idea that states could work only if they were based upon single nations with single cultures is comparatively recent. To some extent, this started in the 16th and 17th centuries when societies were faced with a choice between Catholic and Protestant Christianity and felt that any one society could operate effectively only on the basis of a clear decision for either option. However, the key moment came at the end of the 18th century with the French Revolution.

When France abandoned monarchy and executed the king, a new basis for loyalty to the state had to be found. An attempt was made to launch a new religion, the worship of the Goddess of Reason, but that was a pretty dismal failure. The authentic new God was the Republic itself, 'one and indivisible'. Indivisibility meant, among other things, a single language. As early as 1492 the Bishop of Avila in Spain had asserted that 'language is the perfect instrument of empire', (Greenblatt, 1990, pp.16–7). By the time of the First World War, Breton, Occitan and Basque, which were widely spoken in France a couple of decades earlier, were dying languages just about surviving in remote rural areas. Meanwhile in the UK Cornish had already disappeared as a living language by the 18th century and Manx suffered a similar fate in the 19th century. Loyalty was now expected to the dominant English language and culture. Children in Ireland who came to school with traditional Gaelic names were given anglicised versions of them. (This policy is given savagely satirical treatment in Flann O'Brien's novel *The Poor Mouth* (1973), in which every boy with a Gaelic name is told firmly on his first arrival in school that his name is now 'Jams O'Donnell'.) Welsh children were severely punished for using their own language among themselves in the playground. In Italy, which became a single state in the second half of the 19th century, the dialect of Tuscany became a new national language and languages such as Sardic and Sicilian were ruthlessly discouraged.

However, the insistence on a single language and culture has always faced challenges. In the 20th century many looked for a sense of significance and belonging in cultures that were more local and intimate. Energy was put into securing a better status within regions for local languages such as Romansch, Basque, Catalan, Galician, Aranes and Welsh. Efforts were even made to revive languages, such as Burgundian and Cornish, which had died.

It is worth noting that even when a single monolingual culture came close to full domination, the ruling class itself often lived in a kind of multicultural world. One example is that in Britain a knowledge of Greek and Latin and the culture of the Classical world played a significant role in the education of those who governed church and state until halfway through the last century. Another is that French was widely used in the 18th and 19th centuries among the ruling elites in Russia and parts of Germany.

The US, which was concerned to integrate the immigrants it received from other countries, has also managed to live to a large extent with multiculturalism. The USA has an ugly record of racism, but it is also a country where people can think of themselves as Italian Americans, Greek Americans, Jewish Americans and, increasingly, as African or Native Americans without necessarily seeing any conflict between the two aspects of their cultural identities.

Clearly, if a society is to function, some cultural coherence is essential. Without a strong measure of shared identity, values and habits, people will find it difficult to get along. On the other hand, uniformity is often rejected, especially when it is imposed by a dominant culture. People look for more local loyalties at the same time that they seek the efficient functioning of a wider society. Those loyalties are often ones they have inherited already from their family histories and cultural backgrounds. This is just one of the factors making for change within cultures.

The problem is to determine where uniformity and where diversity are helpful rather than oppressive or divisive. There are no easy answers to that question. Certainly those who seek a solution to the dilemma in the establishment of a monocultural society are trying to buck the way things have normally gone in history and drifting into the oppression of others.

 Exercise

Describe the behaviour you would consider essential if someone were to become a member of staff at your setting (in any capacity).

Are all the forms of behaviour you have identified ethical norms that you think would be valid anywhere in the world?

Are there any which are more specifically reflective of British values? If so, why? Does this alter your designation of them as 'essential'?

Again this can be a personal reflection or used for a group discussion.

The argument that technology is driving us towards a single world culture

There is a counter-argument to what I have just said. It is said by some that, although cultural diversity and mixing have been common in the past, this is being eroded at an increasing pace by technology. Improvements in transport and the means of storing and communicating information are bringing about closer contacts between different communities and moving people all over the world towards a single culture. This started some time ago with improvements in shipping and the invention of printing. The pace is now quickening. There is no way of avoiding this because everyone wants the superior standard of living and the greater sense of power the new technologies have brought. We are moving towards a uniform, single culture and the best thing we can do for our children is to help them live in it. Multiculturalism is just a hopeless attempt to hold up an unstoppable historical process.

In the 1950s and 1960s this process, then often labelled 'modernization', was described and lauded by a number of academics, especially in the US. A key text is that by Lerner (1958). People like him not only expected all societies to gradually become modern, but in doing so to become more American even in trivial details, such as styles of clothing. For a while it seemed that there was an alternative possibility in Soviet Communism. When that fell some believed we had reached a kind of end to history (Fukuyama, 1992). All that now remained was the continuing process of modernization or, as it was increasingly called, 'globalization' (Steger, 2003).

In this context any attempt by less powerful, often smaller, communities to retain their distinct culture is at best harmless sentimentality, at worst an obstacle to progress. Any action by governments or public services to encourage such conservatism and obscurantism is perverse and doomed to failure. We are all becoming Americans or (if that way of putting it causes offence) becoming part of modern culture and our best hope of happiness depends on going along with that process.

Whether or not that is the case, the question remains whether organizational coherence demands cultural uniformity. Diversity seems important in helping people find a place where they feel comfortable in the wider society. The focus in the debate is often on people whose upbringing has been in the cultural contexts of Africa and Asia. Some argue that continuing adherence to those other cultures is mere conservatism. However, the urge towards diversity can also be seen in the invention of new cultures, such as the various 'youth cultures' (with their accompanying forms of music and dress) in the period since the Second World War.

I would add that uniformity could itself become conservative and a block against development. We may need some measure of cultural mixing to open our eyes to new possibilities. Reading about other cultures seems unlikely to generate new ideas in the same way that direct contact will do. It is easy to dismiss another culture as worthless or backward if you have not had to engage with those who come from it.

Particular policies and professional practices that seek to celebrate cultural diversity may be mistaken. The need to reconcile diversity and coherence in a world of massive technological change remains.

The argument that multiculturalism has meant, in effect, the appeasement of radical Islamism

Some of the opponents of multiculturalism might agree that in many ways diversity is essential to the good life. Their argument is not with diversity as such, but with the ways in which they believe the commitment to multiculturalism has weakened the defence of democracy and intellectual openness in the face of a specific threat from Islam.

The antagonism between the West and Islam has a long history, but one that is more complex than is sometimes recognized (Halliday, 2003; Southern, 1962; Walker, 2005). In the Middle Ages, the West came into conflict with Islam in the Iberian peninsular and in the Middle East. In Spain and Portugal, Christian kings gradually pushed back the boundaries of Islam, completing the process with the fall of Granada in 1492. This military triumph led to the abandonment of respect for Islam (and with it toleration of the Jews) that had often characterized earlier Iberian history. In the Middle East the attempt by invaders from the West, the Crusaders, to secure the area where Christ had lived and died failed. That failure led to an appreciation of how difficult it would be to defeat Islam by military might alone. Some turned to attacking it intellectually. However, that, in turn, meant an effort to understand it, which had been singularly lacking previously.

The invasions of the Ottoman Turks, first of the Middle East, then of the Balkans, generated a new fear of Islam. When the assault in Europe was turned back in 1683 after the failed Turkish siege of Vienna, a new and much more positive view of Islam began slowly to emerge – at least among the intellectual leaders of society in Western Europe. (Fear of Turkey remains a potent factor in parts of Eastern Europe and helps explain hostility to Turkey's application for membership of the European Union.) Islam was seen by some in the 18th century as a simpler and purer form of religion. The study of Islamic literature began. (The collection of stories often known in the West as *Arabian Nights* was published for the first time in translation into a European language in Paris in 1704.) Interest extended to other aspects of Islamic culture. Mozart's *Rondo à la Turque* was one of the first attempts by a European to get to grips with the special character of the music of the Islamic world.

As the threat from Islam receded even further, interest in the Muslim world began to focus on the exotic. In painting and in literature the Islamic world was seen through the perspectives of the Romantic movement as a place of forbidden, sensual pleasure. This began to infect even serious scholarly attempts to understand the other culture (Said, 1978). At the same time, Britain and France were consolidating their conquest of much of the Islamic world. The different parts of the Indian sub-continent, the Middle East, North Africa and much of black Africa, including those parts where Islam was the dominant religion, became outright colonies or subordinate states headed by local monarchies but effectively under Western control. While this was happening, Russia conquered and absorbed much of Muslim Asia, and the Netherlands had colonies in parts of the Far East where Islam was the majority religion.

Inevitably, a fight back against imperialism began in the Islamic world as it did in all colonialised countries. Matters reached a head after the end of the First World War when the Islamic Ottoman Empire was dismantled and Britain and France consolidated their power in the Middle East. A new complication arose after the Second World War when the state of Israel was created in what had been a predominantly Muslim region without any effective opposition from Britain, the principal imperial power in the area. The reaction against the imperialist powers sometimes took a secularist form, sometimes drew inspiration explicitly from Islam. Many sought to create a single Muslim movement across the world, one that could confront the West and secure a new economic, political and ideological independence.

Because Islam had this universalist ambition it was seen by advocates of modernization as a major enemy in the way that more local cultures were not. In 1993, long before the emergence of Al Qaeda, Huntington spoke of a 'clash of civilizations' in an article he later (1996) enlarged into a full-scale book. He argued that global markets might make for peaceful cooperation and the end of Communism might mean the end to one kind of conflict, but there was still potential for struggle between different 'civilizations'. The greatest danger lay in tension between the Islamic world and the West. Less dramatically, a recent history of Turkey describes that country in the very title of the book as existing 'between the West and Islam' (Rubiol, 2004). The picture is being very clearly drawn that Islam and the West are incompatible. The events of September 11th 2001 in America, of July 7th 2005 in London and a number of other instances added to the notion of Islam as the enemy of 'our way of life', one that was physically as well as intellectually threatening.

In this context multiculturalism was often interpreted as appeasement of militant Islam. In the view of former government minister Norman Lamont book burning, fatwas (formal statements of opinion on matters of Islamic law) and multiculturalism were all of a piece (*Daily Telegraph*, 8th May 2002). The far right began to speak less of immigrants or ethnic minorities and more often of the 'wicked religion' of Islam. On the other hand, many also saw multiculturalism as a threat to women because it inhibited, in the case of Muslim families, the kind of official intervention that would be expected to follow from the ill-treatment of girls or women in white families.

Behind all this lies a view of Islam as garbled as many of the portrayals of it in previous history. What is primarily wrong with much of what is said is the attempt by people outside the religion to define the essence of Islam by selective reference to certain ideas or actions. People who accept a religious faith (or a comprehensive secular belief system, such as Marxism) are bound to believe that their particular interpretation of that belief system is the most authentic. People who speak about a religion from outside are in no position to define what it is 'really' about. They can point to things that appear to characterize it in its current manifestations, but it is always important to recognize the potential of any belief system to change and develop in response to new situations. Some of the things that are said to be essential to Islam are anything but that.

- It is not true that some of the ways that women are treated in some Muslim cultures are an essential feature of the religion. In many cases they are local customs that did not die following the conversion of those communities. For example, many of the features of the Pushtun code of conduct in Afghanistan flatly contradict what is said in the Qur'an about the rights of women to own and manage property or seek divorce. Daoud Owen, one of the 10,000 white converts to Islam in this country, has suggested that people like him will have a crucial role to play in separating what is required in the founding documents of Islam from those features that merely reflect local cultures in those countries where Islam is the dominant religion (Ansari, 2004, p.16).
- It is not true that Islam has always been anti-Semitic. The early days of Islam were marked by tensions and conflicts with other religious groupings, including Jews. However, Mohamed insisted (according to the tradition recorded by al-Bukhari) that Jews were human beings who merited respect. Throughout the Middle Ages, Jews often had positions of power and influence in Islamic societies. Muslim countries provided a refuge for Jews escaping persecution in the West. The anti-Semitism that is often heard now from some Muslim teachers follows from the

establishment by force of the state of Israel in what had been Arab territory. The older tradition has been severely damaged by events in the Middle East, but it has not been extinguished. In May 2003 when terrorists bombed Jewish restaurants and clubs in Casablanca, large numbers of Moroccans marched through the streets chanting 'Muslims and Jews together!' (it was the terrorism rather than that show of solidarity that was highlighted in the Western press).

- It is not true that Islam believes in 'Holy War'. Christianity has a word for 'Holy War' and that word is 'crusade', the name given to a military intervention in other people's territory at the behest of leaders of the church. (The word itself replaced the more cumbersome phrase 'taking the cross' only towards the end of the period of active crusading. It entered the English language as a common term when first used by historians in the 18th century.) Now, of course, the word 'crusade' has lost most of its religious connotations and is used in the West to describe any serious, self-sacrificing effort made on behalf of a good cause. The Arabic word 'jihad' originally meant precisely such an effort. The term was used to refer to armed conflict with non-Muslim societies quite early in the history of Islam, but the systematic attempt to make military jihad a central feature of Islam started only in the 18th century and was a response to Western imperialism (Allen, 2006). It is now a significant strand in Muslim theology, but for those outside the faith to claim that it is the basis of Islam is as much ill-informed nonsense as it would be for a Muslim to assert that all Christians are subject to the Pope.

- What is often lost in the talk of a clash of civilizations is the debate within Islam about how those who are followers of that faith can live in a multicultural society where the dominant belief system is not their own. One answer is that they cannot. It is sometimes pointed out that the bombings of 9/11, 7/7 and on Bali killed Muslims as well as non-Muslims. Those who draw attention to this apparently hope that this observation might give Al Qaeda pause. Omaar (2006), himself a Muslim, claims that the targets of the bomb attacks in London included Edgeware Road precisely because it represented a relationship between Islam and the West, being at the heart of one of the city's largest Muslim districts. What happened was a deliberate attack on the idea that Muslims and others could live together.

For those who hold to this Muslim version of the clash of civilizations the West is characterized by *jahiliyya* (literally 'ignorance'), the term originally used within Islam to refer to pre-Islamic society. The description of non-Islamic lands as *dar al-harb* (the home of war) also has a long history in Islam, although it does not appear in the Qur'an.

Modern Muslims trying to work out what it means to live and work in societies that are not Islamic have had recourse to other descriptive terms that can be used in such situations – d*ar-al'ahd* (the place where agreement on specific issues is possible), *dar al-amn* (the place where Muslims are allowed to live in peace even if the dominant ethos is not Islamic) and – most positively of all – *dar al-ahl al-kitab* (literally the 'land of the people of the book', i.e. the world of the three major monotheistic religions). They argue that it is possible to negotiate a way of living in the West and to find security there since no Western country has a law forbidding the practice of Islam, even though all those countries have laws permitting practices (such as the drinking of alcohol) forbidden in that faith. Another way of describing the West is as *dar ad-da* (or to use a comparable Christian term, 'a mission field'). The view here is that Muslims must not be content with keeping to themselves, but must try to help their neighbours see the truth of Islam by persuasion.

There are, in other words, many instances of Muslims trying to re-think what it means to live in a multicultural society, especially in the context of globalization where no society can hope to remain in isolation. Ramadan (1999, p.143) declares that in this context it makes little sense to refer to the world of Islam and other worlds. The whole world is now the context in which Muslims and others operate.

 ## Exercise

Note down the ideas or images that the word 'Islam' conjures up for you.

How far is your list one you think would be similar to that produced by someone who is a Muslim (if you are not) or by a non-Muslim (if you are)?

Even if things are on the list, are they likely to mean the same thing to someone who is Muslim or to someone who is not? (What, for example, is the significance of the headscarf, if that is one of the things that has been named?)

You can do this as an individual exercise, but it might be more productive if it is conducted as a group exercise, particularly if the participants include some people who are and some who are not Muslim. If you plan to conduct a group exercise in a mixed group of that kind, are you confident that everyone will feel free to speak, even if there is some embarrassment?

The argument that multiculturalism implies rigidity of cultures

Many object to multiculturalism on the grounds that it assumes that people belong to cultures by birth and that those cultures must remain unchanging. Malik (2008) argues that what he calls the 'politics of difference' undermines liberty and enforces conformity precisely because it seeks to preserve cultures in their existing state (pp.166–89). Sen (2006) is happy with a society that includes a variety of cultural options, but condemns 'pluralistic monoculturalism' in which several cultures may co-exist, but each individual is doomed to remain in the culture into which he or she was born. Halliday (2003) sees the willingness of some liberals to accept whatever happens within a minority community as an understandable reaction against the facile sense of superiority of the imperial age; however, he argues that it poses dangers to everyone, including Muslim communities themselves (p.130)

This point is well made, but again it is a criticism of some of the particular policies that have followed from the principle of multiculturalism rather than the principle itself. Sen is right to describe this as 'pluralistic monoculturalism' rather than as 'multiculturalism'.

If cultures are strategies for dealing with the world, they will alter as the world changes. There is a tendency to see this as degeneration, but just as easily it can mean change for the good. A couple of hundred years ago (a relatively short time in historical terms) in this country we used to hang children for what would now be regarded as petty crimes. Many of the children who did not become criminals were sent into factories, up chimneys or down mines to work in very dangerous circumstances. You could argue that these things were intrinsic to English culture at the time. Certainly that is how some people argued when efforts were made to ban such practices in the mid-19th Century. Is it a matter of regret, a step or two towards a broken society, that we abandoned those parts of our culture? You would have a hard time trying to find many people who would defend that position now. Why should minority communities or individual members of those communities not seek to refine and re-define their own cultural identities? After all, as several of them say, their real cultural identity is no longer one of the society from which they or their ancestors came, but one that seeks to make sense of their position in Britain (Gilroy, 1993; Najmudii, 2007; Gordon, 2007; Sardar, 2008). This has the potential to be a rich rather than a confused identity.

Summary

The disputes between those who want to see a continuing celebration of cultural diversity and those who believe that this kind of multiculturalism has failed are sometimes about overall objectives, sometimes about particular attempts to work towards those objectives. Thus people like Halliday (2003) and Sen (2006) are sympathetic to the objectives of those who argue for multiculturalism, but believe that some of them have gone about things the wrong way. In general, they are obviously right.

A number of things should be clear:

- There is no way we can go back to a situation of greater cultural isolation. For better or worse the genie is out of the bottle. History and technology in their different ways have brought all of us out of that situation into one where some form of multiculturalism is inevitable.
- Respect for other cultures entails an appreciation that those who belong to them are trying through them to understand and get by in the world and that the effort to do this should command our attention and understanding. It does not mean that we cannot criticize them or that any differences are trivial and unimportant, a matter for private choice. It shows more respect for another person's religious faith to say that, after consideration, there are aspects of it you cannot accept than to say that it does not matter all that much what that person believes.
- Cultures are not static entities. They are products of history. They change and will go on changing, although it is also possible to see continuities, so that the past may have explanatory value for the way the members of a particular culture behave now.
- Change within a culture will be a response to change in circumstance, but it must come largely from the reflections of those who belong to a culture. It cannot be imposed successfully by outside agents. To doubt whether the USA can create democracy in another country by force of arms is not to argue that the members of that society are in some way congenitally incapable of democracy.

(Continued)

(Continued)

- No one is a member of a single culture and nothing else. We all operate in a variety of contexts and have to make sense of their inter-connections.
- To describe someone as belonging to a particular culture is, therefore, to offer a limited and vague piece of information. Someone asked the way to a particular building might respond 'It is over there somewhere' while pointing. This is much less helpful than giving detailed directions, a precise map reference or full postal address, but it is not meaningless and might be of some assistance. Similarly, if I say that someone is a Brazilian or a Sikh, this does not tell you anything very precise about her personality, her abilities, even her appearance. It does, however, give you somewhere to start looking to find out what kind of person she is.

The difficulties that have often arisen from multicultural initiatives usually have their origin in a failure to recognize much of this. The next chapter looks at some of the ways this issue has been tackled elsewhere, while the rest of the book applies that more specifically to early years settings.

Further reading

Many of the texts that have been cited here can be used for further reading on the controversy about multiculturalism.

Rageh Omaar's (2006) book *Only Half of Me* is one of several readable accounts of their experience of living in this country by people who are not white British. Another is Janmohamed's (2009) *Love in a Headscarf.*

Vron Ward's book *Who Cares About Britishness?* (2007) presents an account of encounters with several people who are not white British, but live here or have had significant contact with this country.

3

The Idea of Intercultural Competence

This chapter describes:

> Some significant differences in terminology between the UK and other European countries in the debate on cultural diversity

> The concept of inter-cultural competence

> The related concept of 'cultural shock'

There are fundamental problems with the concept of 'multiculturalism' as it is employed in the UK and in other English-speaking countries.

- The word-ending 'ism' suggests that multiculturalism is an ideology, a social or political programme, a set of beliefs entailing clear-cut objectives and means. At the same time it is clear that the concept is considerably less developed than this would imply. As a result, ill-considered actions taken in the name of multiculturalism can lead to sweeping rejection of the entire idea.
- The use of the prefix 'multi' conjures up a picture of a variety of separate cultures whose relationship to each other (in practice or in the value ascribed to them) is ill-determined.

The previous chapter attempted to bring some clarity to the picture by identifying the different issues that critics of multiculturalism have attempted to address and spelling out the fact that those critics often have very different, even contradictory perspectives. The confusion about the concept is underlined by the fact that Canada is cited in polemics on the Internet as either an example of multiculturalism working triumphantly or as proof that it leads to disaster.

Note

Canada has a higher per capita immigration rate than any other country in the world. In addition, it has seen a long-running campaign for the rights of the substantial French-speaking minority (mainly living in Quebec). As early as 1964 a leading Senator called for an explicit commitment to multiculturalism. This stance was adopted as official policy in 1971. In 1988 royal assent was given to the Multiculturalism Act (which, among other things, laid the framework for distribution of federal funds to ethnic groups to help them preserve their particular cultures). The commitment to multiculturalism is now embodied in Section 27 of the Canadian Charter of Rights and Freedom. The extent of Canada's commitment makes assessment of what it has achieved particularly relevant. It is especially interesting that most of the initiatives behind this policy were taken by centre right rather than centre left politicians – a stark contrast with the situation in the UK. (http://en.wikipedia.org/wiki/Multiculturalism# Origins_in_Canada/, last accessed 15/08/09)

In this chapter I want to examine the issue further by describing related ideas from other countries, which are likely to be unfamiliar in this country but which seem to me to throw some useful light on the issue.

The view from Spain

I start by considering the broad approach taken to cultural diversity and, in particular, its relevance to education and social policy, by commentators in Spain. There are significant differences between Spain and the United Kingdom, but there are also similarities that make ideas from that country useful. Like the UK, it is one where greater political autonomy is being achieved by smaller nations within it after a long period where those identities were given little recognition. It is also a country that has in common with the UK (and with much of Western Europe) the loss of most of its former colonial empire and a recent history of immigration, especially from poorer countries in the southern hemisphere. This makes responses to multiculturalism there relevant to us, although a full appreciation of the ideas outlined below would require a more detailed explanation of the Spanish context than is possible here.

Moñivas Lázaro (1998) points out that the issue of contact and cooperation between people from different cultures is usually indicated in English-speaking countries by the word 'multiculturalism'. He contrasts this with practice in his own and other European countries, suggesting that it is better to use the term *multiculturidad* to describe the situation of contact. (In Spanish the word ending *'idad'* suggests a fact or set of circumstances rather than a set of ideas). The solution to the problems to which *multiculturidad* can give rise he sees as being *interculturidad,* a word that might be translated as 'interculturality' or better by some phrase such as 'intercultural activity'. Again, the formation of the word suggests a situation or activity rather than an ideology or programme. In his words, it is about the 'dynamic interaction' between cultures.

Writing in the same issue of Spain's leading journal on social policy Gallego González (1998) also speaks of her preference for the European term *interculturidad* because it entails exchange, reciprocity and interaction. She underlines the fact that this means that cultures change when in cooperative contact with each other and sees this as a positive process making for progress. She believes this precludes 'cultural relativism', that is to say, the belief that every culture is to be considered valid for those belong to it. Although such an idea may appear to put cultures on an equal footing, its consequence is, she argues, to leave those belonging to minority cultures trapped in what are effectively ghettoes. The process of intercultural interaction, of contact between people from different cultural backgrounds and a readiness to learn from each other, is the real foundation for equality. Her article goes on to describe some of the work on intercultural communication in which she has been involved in her own country and the impact this has had.

These two authors write from a social policy perspective, although they also refer to developments in the educational system, especially in the south of Spain. Lluch (2009) writes as an educationist whose specific objective is to identify ways in which the school system can help to create a plural society with a collective identity, one that moves beyond the mere fact of diversity to create a new cohesion. His concerns are shared by other Spanish educationists, such as Pérez (2000).

As a Valencian whose language of preference is Catalan rather than Spanish, Lluch is also acutely aware of the error of speaking of the 'host community', as though it was a single cultural entity, in its dealings with immigrant communities or much longer established minorities, such as Spain's gypsies. There are parallels here with the implications of the commitment the Welsh Assembly Government has made to bi-lingualism in its education system and consequences for the way that relations with people from other cultures are perceived. Lluch's basic proposition is that diversity is an intrinsic characteristic of social existence, not an oddity or a problem, but something quite natural. He is also anxious to locate the debate in the context of globalization and the cultural hegemony of America that some see as an intrinsic part of that process. Similar points on globalization and the need for a new concept of citizenship that takes into account both local culture and the global situation are made by the Brazilian social scientist Gimeno Sacristán (2000). Although Llluch sees a number of difficulties, including the gulf that exists at present between the notional commitment to cultural diversity in his own country and what happens in practice, his outlook is essentially optimistic, precisely because he sees multicultural existence as normal. Examining ways in which the education of children can reflect cultural diversity adequately is in his perspective less a matter of tackling problems than of seizing an excellent opportunity to review and re-make the culture or cultures to which we belong.

I have spoken here about Spain, but it should be noted that similar language is used in other parts of Europe. In Germany or Italy the subject matter of this book would be described as 'intercultural pedagogy' rather than multiculturalism (Auernheimer, 2007; Portera, 2006).

The brief summary offered above and to a certain extent what the authors themselves have to say is at a level of fairly generalized propositions. It will, perhaps, be evident that these ideas informed what was said about multiculturalism in this country in the previous chapter. There is a need to move beyond this theoretical clarification of the issue to more specific ideas for practice. The second part of this book deals with practice specifically in early years settings, but this is best seen in the context of some broader ideas on ways in which intercultural communication and cooperation can happen.

 Exercise

In any situation in which a number of cultures are present or represented there has to be some level of contact between them.

What kind of relationship do you think you might establish with people from another cultural background in any of the following situations?

- Living on the same street.
- Buying goods in a shop.
- Working together as colleagues.
- Joining in a religious or secular celebration.
- Delivering or receiving a professional service (such as medical care) that is likely to entail the user being asked for personal information.
- Close friendship or sexual partnership.

Which of those relationships would *have to be* a matter of intercultural communication and cooperation because of the nature of the activity itself? Why?

Which of them might cause you some uncertainty or anxiety? In what ways do past experiences in your life affect your responses, or are you guessing at what might happen in a situation you have not experienced for yourself?

This exercise can be a matter of personal reflection or of group discussion. If it is undertaken in a group discussion, it is important that ground rules are set that allow for critical questioning of attitudes expressed and avoid the kind of condemnation of them that can lead to defensiveness.

Intercultural competence

One approach to the question of communication and cooperation is based on the notion of 'intercultural competence' (also known as 'cross-cultural competence' or '3C'). This idea has been developed in a range of professional settings.

One of those professional settings is that of the armed forces in the US. This might seem at first unlikely. However, soldiers often find themselves operating in foreign countries where they may be in armed conflict with people from a radically different cultural background, or be asked to keep or enforce the peace between different communities, or where their government has armed forces because of cooperation with the government of the country concerned. Even in the first instance, soldiers will not be engaged in active fighting all the time and need to learn quickly how to understand the mindset of people whose perspectives may be significantly different from theirs.

 Note

The complications of cross-cultural contact were illustrated by an incident early in the American occupation of Baghdad. Having learned in other circumstances that playing heavy metal music very, very loudly was a way of disorienting crowds, they tried the same tactic again, only to find themselves surrounded by large numbers of enthusiastic young Iraqis who had been heavy metal fans for some time.

The experience of the US armed forces around the world has led to a number of attempts to quantify the extent to which their personnel have acquired cross-cultural competence. Those techniques seem to me worth attention whatever the views one might take on the military interventions in which the US has engaged across the world. Some of these techniques have grand titles such as the Inter-Cultural Development Inventory or the Cultural Intelligence Scale (Abbe, Gulick & Herman, 2007). These are useful attempts to describe more precisely the characteristics of someone capable of adjusting quickly to new cultural circumstances. One particular tool, the

Inter-Cultural Adaptation Potential Scale, appears to be especially useful in *predicting* the ability of an individual to adapt in the course of inter-cultural dialogue, doing so more effectively than general intelligence or education can do (Matsumoto, et al., 2007).

Many people have reservations about this kind of work. The fact that the concept has been developed by the American military makes some people cautious from the start. Others assert that the entire effort should be held in suspicion because it implies that people's outlook and understanding are bound by the particular cultures from which they come. This may be true of some of the work in this field, but most of those who have conducted such research are happy to recognize the complexity of cultural identity. The focus of the relevant personality tests is on the individual facing the need to adapt rather than on the cultures that have to be understood. It is indicative, for example, that the title of Matsumoto et al.'s scale includes the word 'potential'. The real difficulty lies probably in just this focus on the 'adaptation potential' of the individual, however carefully measured. It could be argued the dynamics of the situation provide a more central factor than personality attributes. The key issue is probably that of whether someone's cultural background encourages flexibility and openness.

Another context in which the development of intercultural competence has been developed is that of foreign language studies. Anyone who has ever attempted to learn another language will have realized quickly that when something is translated from one language to another there is rarely a word-for-word equivalence. Ideas are expressed in very different ways (especially in relation to verbs and tense). As someone's competence in a foreign language increases, that person becomes more aware of subtle differences in ways of approaching issues that different languages appear to entail. (This is not, of course, to say that people are bound by their linguistic inheritance to think in certain ways. If that were the case, the human race would never have got beyond basic signals about practical hunter-gatherer issues similar to those of all pack animals.)

As the field of foreign language teaching has begun to move, in response to demands by employers, from grammar and literature to a stronger emphasis on communication skills, more attention has been paid to the whole process of engaging with someone who speaks another language – on expectations about behaviour during conversation, on the ways these expectations vary between cultures and on the need to acquire sensitivity to this as well as knowledge of language in talking with people. In this country a key figure has been Professor Byram of the University of Durham (Byram, 2008). He follows the approach taken by those who have attempted to define cross-cultural competence operationally in emphasizing more than knowledge *about* other cultures. However, he has some reservations about the extent to which it is possible to quantify or judge by formal tests the ability of someone to interact competently with people with different cultural backgrounds. He speaks of:

- attitudes, including curiosity and what literary critics call the 'willing suspension of disbelief' (when trying to appreciate a poem or other piece of literature based on religious or other ideas one does not share)
- knowledge about other cultures
- skills of interpretation of communications in the light of that knowledge
- skills of discovery – the ability to acquire new knowledge, not just in the study, but in the course of interaction
- critical self-awareness.

The fourth of those issues is, of course, of critical importance. You can work at gaining knowledge about a culture with whose adherents you know you will have to deal. However, no one can know about every culture there is – or every language.

 Note

I have had a couple of friends, each of whom was reasonably fluent in some two dozen languages. That was pretty impressive. However, I am told by a colleague who works for the local authority in Barnsley that almost 90 different languages are now spoken in the homes of children attending schools there. This is in spite of the fact that a higher proportion of the population of Barnsley was born there than is true of any other local authority area in England. If one can encounter users of up to 90 languages in an area such as Barnsley, the numbers are likely to be even greater for major cities with higher percentages of black and minority ethnic people. Speaking two-dozen languages would be just a start.

The idea that you can deal with problems of cross-cultural contact by knowing all about the other cultures stumbles against the fact that there may already be more cultures than any one person can gain a comprehensive knowledge of and the fact that there can be new encounters at any time.

 Note

I recently had contact with an early years setting whose staff took some pride in the work they had done to understand the Pakistani background of the large number of children from such families they had attending. One day they were asked to take the child of a recently arrived refugee family from Burma. Because the child was South Asian, they assumed his family was Muslim and some initial

(Continued)

(Continued)

awkwardness resulted. Statistically speaking, a person from Burma is likely to have a Buddhist background. In fact, this particular family were members of the Karen ethnic minority in Burma and, in common with some 30–40 per cent of that community, were Christian. The practitioners then went into an unnecessary moment of panic because they did not know anything about Burmese culture. They had in quick succession made two unwarranted assumptions: first, that they would understand the culture of that family because they were used to dealing with Asians, and second, that they were incapable of understanding it because it was not one they had previously encountered.

This kind of experience is becoming an increasingly familiar one. Many parts of the UK that have had little previous experience of immigration have recently found themselves with large and sudden influxes of families from other parts of the European Union, especially Eastern Europe and Portugal. Other places have found themselves hosting asylum seekers and refugees from African countries with little history of emigration to the UK.

Where this happens what is demanded is not an impossibly encyclopaedic knowledge of other cultures, but the skills to respond to new situations. Statements of fact about black and minority ethnic communities made in books and other publications intended to help professionals in public services easily become out of date. They can then handicap people in understanding the users they encounter. Byram's emphasis on flexibility is vital. He himself has made useful contributions to understanding the perspectives of people from other cultures finding themselves in this country (de Korne et al., 2007).

 Exercise

Imagine yourself in a situation where you are called upon to make a new arrival welcome. An example would be a new member of staff in a work setting, but any example will do.

What would you normally do to make the person welcome? Be as specific as you can about the type of action that you would take. How formal a mode of address would you employ? Would you make any physical contact with the person (such as a handshake)? What information would you need to offer or request?

Can you think of situations where what you would normally do might not match what the other person considers normal because of her cultural background?

> If you are facilitating a group discussion along these lines and one or more members of the group are from a different culture from that of the majority in the group, bear in mind that their initial responses might reflect what is normal in the group's majority culture rather than their own inclinations. They may need support in bringing out these differences.

Byram calls upon people to engage in self-examination in the process of developing cross-cultural competence and this has been echoed by Risager (2000) and other academics in Denmark in the specific context of education. This is a valuable contribution, but it is one made by people engaged in the particular fields of foreign language teaching and preparing students to teach foreign languages at secondary level. The work of Cohen-Emerique (1999) offers a route into understanding one's own intercultural competence that may be of wider relevance and more directly useful to early years practitioners.

Margalit Cohen-Emerique and the concept of 'cultural shock'

Since the early 1990s Cohen-Emerique, an academic psychologist, has been developing a framework for understanding intercultural communication. She is part of a wider group of people (including Carmel Camilleri and Sonia Fayman) concerned with this issue and, in particular, with the activity of public servants dealing with migrant workers in Europe. She speaks of three stages:

- Understanding what she calls 'cultural shock'.
- Understanding the cultural system of the other person from within.
- Effective interaction.

It is on the first stage that I will concentrate here since it provides a useful introduction to what is said about work in early years settings in the chapters that follow.

Her focus is on the shocks that can sometimes be caused by the way someone from a different cultural background behaves in situations where personal interaction is required. She outlines seven spheres in which significant differences may occur:

1. Attitudes people have to their own and other people's bodies.
2. Understanding of space and time.
3. Family structure.
4. Rules of social interaction.

5. Ways in which requests for or offers of assistance can be made.
6. Religion or other belief systems.
7. Cultural change.
(Cohen-Emerque, 1999)

Of those seven spheres it is the third and sixth that may seem most familiar. It is known that family structures vary significantly. These differences are not always well understood, but people are aware they exist. Similarly, the fact that people from other countries often belong to religious traditions that are quite different from those of the UK is a familiar one, whatever the level of understanding. There can be surprise that arises from finding more similarities in attitudes to children or marital partners or a broader agreement on matters of basic ethics than some might anticipate. However, it is the differences that are most likely to strike people initially. There is also a difference between knowing about something and encountering it in reality. It can come as a shock for a white person to engage for the first time in conversation with a woman who is veiled except for her eyes.

 Exercise

Soon after the MP Jack Straw had made a public statement about feeling uncomfortable when Muslim women came to his constituency surgery wearing headscarfs, especially in the form in which most of the face is covered, I overheard a conversation in Sheffield city centre. Two young white men were inviting passers-by to sign a petition against what Straw had said. A young white woman politely refused to sign it, explaining that she regarded the headscarf as a sign and instrument of male domination. I know Muslim women who would have regarded her relatively skimpy dress as a sign and instrument of her own sexual availability and, therefore, domination by men.

Would you agree with either of these points of view (or neither)?

What difference does it make to your understanding of the issue that you are a man or a woman?

If you wear a hijab yourself or have done in the past, what meaning does it have for you? If you do not, what meanings do you think it could have for women who wear it? What does the form of clothing you wear tell people about yourself and, therefore, your cultural background? How much does the clothing other people wear determine the ways you respond to them? Are there circumstances in which you would consider drastic alterations to your normal form of clothing to facilitate communication with others? Have you ever done this in practice? How did it feel?

This exercise can be conducted as a personal reflection or group exercise. Again, if a group engaged in this discussion involves some people who are and some who are not Muslim, particular care in the management needs to be taken by the facilitator.

The shock that can be caused by the headscarf when it takes the form of the niqab, covering most of the face, is partly because many of us who are European depend on facial expression to negotiate the business of conversation. There is some difference of emphasis here between the European reliance on visual images and the suspicion of such images and greater reliance on words in Muslim culture. It is important to recognize that there is a difference (and, perhaps, the potential for a shared perspective) here. The insistence of some Europeans that the headscarf (especially in the most complete form of the burka) 'dehumanizes' the wearer entails a failure to recognize an essential feature of the situation – differences between Europe and the Muslim world on the significance of the visual presentation of oneself.

One of the current changes in European society is that young people who have grown up with the mobile phone appear to give equal weight to dialogue by phone or text as they do to face-to-face conversation (something people of my age find difficult to grasp). It may be that new conventions on conversation are developing that will render obsolete the common European insistence on face-to-face encounter. It is still, however, strong at present.

The shock some people feel when encountering the wearer of a hijab is also partly based on the fact that most white British people have no clear commitment to a particular religion or set of ethical principles or – if they do have such a commitment – are used to dealing with people for whom this is not true. The hijab might be required by someone's interpretation of Islam, but it is also relevant to the first and fourth of the elements outlined above. The ways in which people present themselves in public or the extent to which eye contact or physical proximity are allowed are rules that each of us absorbs from our own culture almost without recognizing it.

Both the initial shock of appreciating that something you have taken for granted is unacceptable elsewhere and the difficulty in adjusting behaviour to fit new circumstances are common.

Note

An Englishman used to travel in Arab countries would probably feel no surprise or discomfort if a male North African friend takes his hand while engaged in conversation. It would feel quite normal because of his familiarity with local custom. On the other hand, the same Englishman would find the same gesture from another English man to be unusual and significant and would be anxious to establish its significance. It would not be possible to take the gesture casually.

It is possible to understand and adapt to differences about such matters, but the first time you meet such a situation can be extremely disquieting. If you are brave enough, you can try the experiment of offending against some rule of social behaviour in a group where you normally feel comfortable. For example, if it is customary to use first names, switch to more formal types of address (Miss Smith, for example). Not only will this disquiet your companions – the probability is that you will feel awkward, embarrassed, or even – at worst – slightly nauseous. Yet the deviation from standard behaviour is slight and it would be difficult to assert that the behaviour adopted is intrinsically wrong.

Failure to recognize what is normal for another can lead to serious misunderstandings. Hendry (2008, p.52) describes the way in which it is customary for new arrivals in a neighbourhood in Japan to introduce themselves to the neighbours. People who come from some Western countries may wait for the neighbours to introduce themselves. Thus, if a Western (especially American) family comes to live in a Japanese neighbourhood, no contact at all may happen and each side may believe the others are being unfriendly.

To recognize what is normal in another culture entails more than acquiring pieces of information. You need to develop some idea of how the other person feels about the issue. For example, you may know that some people have dietary requirements because of their cultural background. This is not the same as knowing how it feels to them to be confronted with food that is forbidden. The following exercise may help you.

Exercise

Imagine yourself invited to a buffet meal where the following items are on the menu. Make a real effort to imagine your reactions or how it would feel to eat any of the following, perhaps for the first time:

- Barbecued dog's leg
- Griddled rattlesnake
- Sun-dried beetles
- Boiled or deep-fried earthworms
- Snails cooked in their shells with garlic and butter
- Frogs' legs
- Sheep's eyeballs
- Bulls' testicles

This exercise can be undertaken as a personal reflection or a group discussion.

Even if you are not vegetarian and are happy to consume other forms of meat, you may find the list a bit stomach-churning. The point is that all of these items, if cooked properly, are perfectly harmless and nutritious. I have eaten most, though not all, of them myself.

What were your responses? What do you think the reasons for those responses were? Can you get over them or are they too intrinsic to the way you feel? Have you ever learned to eat something that you first found disgusting?

If you are not Muslim or Jewish, has this taught you anything about the way that adherents of those religions feel about pork, rabbit, seafood and so on?

Cohen-Emerique's second element can be particularly relevant here, since again it is unspoken rules that are likely to govern behaviour and people may break other people's rules without intending to do so.

 Note

In Italy it is normal to arrive a little later for a meal than the time specified on the invitation. In Germany this would be considered seriously impolite. In Iran and Indonesia it is polite for a guest to refuse the first or even several offers of a drink before accepting. In many European countries, this would be taken at face value, perhaps even be considered an ill-mannered thing to do. In many Arab countries children will greet the adult guests of their parents, anticipating the traditional gift of sweets or cakes. This may extend to children approaching Western tourists in the street and asking for sweets. English people, with their sensitivities about paedophilia and related sex tourism, may find this behaviour disquieting.

Cohen-Emerique's fifth element – differences relating to the ways in which offers of or requests for assistance can be made – is, of course, of particular relevance to anyone in public service, including early years practitioners. If one person helps another, this can be seen as an example of kindness and concern. There is, however, also the possibility that the action will underline the power relationship between the two people. The person offering help may be demonstrating her position of greater power, status or wealth in doing so. The person receiving help may be able to demand it because of the nature of the relationship, and this can be an exercise of power over the helper. This can be true of both personal relationships and relationships created on the basis of professional or other formal roles. The assumptions the other person brings to a relationship in which assistance is offered can create a sense of shock and injustice. What Westerners think of as bribery of a public official may be seen in some societies as turning the encounter into a more equal one of mutual exchange.

Cohen-Emerique's final element is that of differences relating to attitudes to change. It is often said that the West differs from other societies in being open to change, while the others are more committed to tradition. As in many stereotypes, there is some truth in this, but even greater misunderstanding. Those who are most conservative in some respects have often shown ingenuity in their use of modern media to get their traditionalist message across. Fundamentalist leaders of various religious creeds have been skilled in the use of television. Moreover, the issue is not simply one of established belief systems. Many people recently arrived in this country will have come from situations where their settled pattern of life was severely disrupted by natural disaster, economic catastrophe, war or political oppression. Having had to cope with extreme change, they may have adopted a variety of strategies to cope and their feelings about change will vary according to what has seemed to work for them. Even someone who has come here freely, anticipating new opportunities, may find the changed social situation affecting their attitudes to change itself.

The shock of contact with another culture can create panic or hostility. It can also create an opportunity to re-think one's own understanding of the world. Cohen-Emerique's analysis of the different types of shock provides a tool for standing back and working out what is happening. This in turn should help us to re-think our own cultural identity in a way that is positive and dynamic (Camilleri & Cohen-Emerique, 1989).

The way that things go depends considerably on the ability of both sides to transcend the sense of shock and the feeling of being under attack that sometimes follows. The readiness of the early years professional to move towards this new understanding is crucial. Thus Laot (2006), commenting on

Cohen-Emerique's work, argues that what is required in the development of intercultural competence is not the adoption of 'a number of ready-made recipes' (p.8) but sensitivity and understanding, an understanding that does not start with knowledge about the other, but a readiness to look at oneself. 'If the other person is different, I am different for the other person.' The point is that you must analyse yourself from the perspective of culture and identity before you can understand and get to know the 'other' (p.3).

Summary

Chapter 1 attempted to demonstrate something of the complexity of the idea of cultural identity. Chapter 2 described some of the types of criticism that have been made of the idea of celebrating cultural diversity and suggested the need for clearer thinking on objectives and the ways we might secure them. This chapter has gone mainly outside the UK and has certainly stayed outside debate within the early years profession for ideas on how to approach the issue. I believe this is a necessary preliminary, that acquiring the tools to understand our own feelings and responses is much more important than acquiring a lot of information about other cultures. The rest of the book deals more directly with day-to-day practice in early years settings, but is still based on that basic principle.

Exercise

This exercise is one that can only be tackled as a group exercise, preferably in a fairly large group of one to two dozen participants. It also requires sufficient space so that discussions can go on between two sub-groups without overhearing what the other is saying. Although it is possible to tackle it with a single facilitator, it is much better to have two.

Prepare for the exercise by having two information sheets, each describing a particular society and its culture. The two societies should be ones that contrast in many ways and should be entirely fictional. (The reason for basing the exercise on fictional societies

(Continued)

(Continued)

is that this makes it possible to test and develop intercultural competencies while avoiding the complication of some participants knowing much more about a given culture than others.) It is, however, useful to give invented names to the two societies, something that gives them a more realistic 'feel'.

Each information sheet should deal with only one of the two cultures. However, they should be written in a way that reflects the fact that the two cultures are contrasting and different. Perhaps

- one is easy going and informal, while the other has a more rigid code of etiquette
- one has a wide number of religious beliefs, while a majority of people in the other are still active followers of a particular religious tradition
- one values story telling, music and dance, while the other places more emphasis on the production of pictures, pottery and other art objects.

You can go on adding to these characteristics. You can also devise codified gestures for the two societies, perhaps different ways of greeting a stranger met for the first time.

Divide the whole group into two sub-groups, each of which will identify with one of those societies. Allow at least half an hour for the members of each to familiarize themselves with the features of the societies to which they will pretend to belong.

Each 'society' then sends a delegation to the other. There has to be a point to these encounters. Perhaps the two societies wish to avoid a possible conflict over territory that lies between their two lands. Perhaps one is engaged in primary production (of food or raw materials), while the other has more skills in the production of finished goods. Allow 30 minutes for this negotiation.

The two delegations return to their own 'societies' to report on progress on the issue under negotiation and how they have found the other society.

If there are two facilitators, each stays with one of the groups. If there is only one, that person will have to move between the two.

At the end of the session, the two groups report on how they each felt about the other. The facilitators try to draw out some general lessons.

If people do well at absorbing the culture of 'their' society, there may be tensions and misunderstandings between the two groups. The reasons for this can be explored.

If they do less well, there may be more specific references in the negotiating sessions to the differences ('In our culture we …'). The facilitator can point out that the determination of behaviour by cultural influences is normally not fully conscious or articulated in this sort of way.

If you are not confident about producing your own materials for this exercise, you can purchase ready-made kits from a company called Simulation Training Systems. They have two versions – Rafa' Rafa' and BaFaa BaFa'. The first is simpler than the second and is intended for younger people. The second is aimed at an older group and addresses the issue of gender relations in the two cultures. This is often a key topic in cultural difference, but may be more difficult to bring out in a group consisting entirely of women (as is often the case with early years practitioners).

Further reading

Books that offer an overview of the subject covered in this chapter include:

Gundara (2000) *Interculturalism, Education and Inclusion*. London: Sage.

Moodian, M.A. (2008) *Contemporary Leadership and Intercultural Competence*. London: Sage.

4

The Background to Daily Practice: Curriculum Guidance, Discussion with Interested Parties and Twinning with Settings Abroad

> **This chapter deals with what might be described as the background to daily work in the field of cultural diversity. In particular it speaks about:**
>
> > The official guidance on the issue of cultural diversity in early years settings in the four major parts of the UK
>
> > Discussion of the issue of cultural diversity with staff
>
> > Discussion of the issue with parents
>
> > Twinning arrangements with settings abroad

The official guidance

It is possible to see curriculum guidance and other material coming from government as nothing more than a set of rules to be followed. An intelligent response to government policy, as it is embodied in official documents, demands a more critical response than that, even if the official policy is seen as matching the needs of children. As it happens, the Foundation Stage guidance that came into force in England in 2008 has been the subject of considerable controversy. Some of the opposition comes from fears of what head teachers and education officials would make of it as much as it does from the guidance itself. Others have seen the text as flawed. Their criticisms have to be taken on board and, if practitioners agree with them, they have to modify the practical application of the guidance or seek amendment. Commitment to children should prevent people from taking the line that the law is the law and we just have to get on with it.

This section does not go into great detail about the guidance that applies in the various parts of the United Kingdom. In all cases a considerable effort has been made by official bodies to familiarize practitioners with the guidance and the thinking that lies behind it. In this respect there has been an advance on earlier policy initiatives of this kind, including the previous Foundation Stage guidance for England. The documents and websites available make any detailed summary of what is said on cultural diversity unnecessary here. Instead I want to raise a number of questions.

The 1989 Children Act consolidated previous legislation by requiring that due attention should be paid to the religious, racial, cultural or linguistic background of a child in early years or other settings. In practice, as was said in the Preface to this book, that requirement was often interpreted more widely. The statutory framework for the early years Foundation Stage in England fully confirmed the shift that had taken place since 1989 by giving providers of early years services responsibility in law for ensuring positive attitudes to diversity and difference in their settings. This is 'not only so that every child is included and not disadvantaged, but also so that they learn from the earliest age to value diversity in others and grow up making a positive contribution to society' (DCSF, 2008a, 1.14). The objective must be that by the end of the Foundation Stage children should have 'a developing respect for their own cultures and beliefs and those of other people' and understand that 'they can expect others to treat their needs, views, cultures and beliefs with respect' (DCFS, 2008a, 2.8)

The statutory requirements in relation to cultural diversity relate to the objectives it is hoped to achieve by the time any given child reaches the end of the Foundation Stage. (In some cases this could mean close to the child's sixth birthday.) They assume the kind of self-awareness and sensitivity to the feelings and perspectives of others that will begin to emerge fully only at that stage. Such sensitivity depends to a significant extent on well-developed language skills and what psychologists call 'the child's theory of mind' (Astington, 1994), that is to say, the ability to understand that everyone sees things from an individual perspective. Most of the (non-statutory) practice guidance dealing specifically with cultural diversity is concerned with articulated understanding and, therefore, is focused on children aged 40–60 months. This is particularly true of what is said in relation to 'Personal, social & emotional development' and 'Knowledge & understanding of the World'. There is advice in relation to 'Creative development' about reflecting the diversity of cultures in work with children aged 22–36 months (for example, in what is said about 'Music & dance' on p.111). It is only in relation to 'Communication, language & literacy' that there is any reference to the need to reflect diversity in the material used in the setting for all ages (DCSF, 2008b, p.40).

It could be asked how adequate this is. Certainly, the English curriculum documents allow for greater sensitivity to cultural diversity than the most explicit references to the subject might suggest. They speak of each child being 'unique' and of the need to foster 'positive relationships'. These principles link with the five outcomes of a good childhood outlined in *Every Child Matters* (DfES, 2003). However, the principles can be effective only if the cultural dimension of each child's life situation is recognized and valued. In spite of the underpinning principles in *Every Child Matters* and the curriculum guidance, the difficulty remains that a mechanical application of what is said to be expected at any given age could lead to a less comprehensive appreciation of the cultural dimension than the basic principles suggest, and this is among the difficulties some have seen with the Foundation Stage.

All the constituent parts of the United Kingdom have minorities of black or Asian people. However, the celebration of cultural diversity entails more than a response to their particular heritages. Every country within the union has a longer-standing distinct cultural identity.

Like all the countries that make up the United Kingdom, Northern Ireland has a small part of its population whose origins are in Africa, Asia or the Caribbean. It also has a number of immigrants from other parts of Europe, including, of course, England. The most salient issue in relation to cultural diversity is that of bringing people together across the sectarian divide between Protestant unionists and Catholic nationalists. Nevertheless, the assaults that took place against a number of Romanian families in South Belfast in the early summer of 2009 demonstrate graphically that sectarian conflict is not the only problem in inter-community relations. The two government departments concerned with early years – the Department of Education and the Department of Health & Social Services – are both committed to the promotion of greater understanding and cooperation.

The curriculum guidance first issued in 1997 by the Northern Ireland Council for the Curriculum, Examinations and Assessment is still in force. Although it makes reference to inclusion, the greatest emphasis in the original document was on special educational needs. Perhaps in 1997 the issue of sectarian conflict was too sensitive for consensus on how to handle it at pre-school level. A review took place in 2006, partly to take into account the requirements of a new political settlement where the two communities were expected to live together peacefully. (It also strikes out in a different general direction from that of England by giving less attention to outcomes and more to the opportunities to be created for pre-school children and older learners.) However, the guidance itself may have had less impact than some of the particular local projects, of the sort described by Vevers (2006) that address the same issue.

The question of cultural diversity is addressed rather more directly in Scotland's *Curriculum Framework for Children 3 to 5* (Scottish Consultative Council on the Curriculum, 1999). The guidance is, however, not very detailed or explicit. This reflects the overall nature of the document, which has been praised by some because of the way it leaves the practitioner free to determine how the broad framework will be implemented. Much of the text consists of case studies – 'Examples from practice'. These invite the reader to draw her own conclusions. One of them (p.12) deals with a situation where cultural diversity has a particular relevance. In 2002 work began on a new *Curriculum for Excellence* covering education for children and young people aged 3–18 years of age. The publication of a draft curriculum in 2004 was followed by a number of pilot studies. Full implementation was scheduled to take place over the period 2009–2011. One of the eight designated curriculum areas is 'Religious & moral education'. The guidance includes a section on world religions. However, what is said is fairly general. As with earlier curriculum guidance in Scotland, there is more emphasis on respecting the professional judgement of teachers than was evident in English curriculum documents in the period that Tony Blair was prime minister.

By way of contrast the curriculum guidance for children aged 3–7 years in Wales is much more detailed than that of Northern Ireland or Scotland and comes in a series of bi-lingual booklets issued in January 2008 by the Department for Children, Education, Lifelong Learning and Skills. Although it is detailed, it has been seen by many as better than the English EYFS guidance because it lends itself less easily to being translated into a highly prescriptive curriculum and because of the way that it modifies the boundary line between pre-school and school education. It was also developed and introduced with particular care.

Two of the distinguishing features of the Welsh documentation are especially relevant to the issue of cultural diversity.

One is that one of the areas of learning – 'Personal & social development, well-being and cultural diversity' – makes reference to the issue in its very title. In addition, the commitment to fostering respect for other cultures runs throughout the document collection in a much clearer way than it does in similar guidance from other parts of the UK. This is reflected in the photographic illustrations and in what is said in several of the booklets about music. It is also notable that the documentation also raises very clearly the issue of 'differing ... views and beliefs' as a key aspect of cultural diversity (DCELLS, 2008a, p.16).

The other distinguishing feature is that Welsh Language Development is an additional area of learning. This reflects the Welsh Assembly Government's commitment to Welsh and particularly to promotion of its use by children and young people. The available statistics suggest that this move has been very successful so far. The booklet in the Foundation Phase Curriculum Guidance series on Welsh language development defends this commitment in a way that reflects the views of Lluch outlined in Chapter 3 of this book. 'In a world that is fast becoming a global village, having a particular identity, such as being Welsh, can be exciting and enriching' (DCELLS, 2008b, p.5).

It is still rather early to make judgements on how well the Welsh have integrated the dual commitment to cultural diversity in general and the promotion of specifically Welsh language and culture in particular. There does not appear to be any published research specifically on this topic so far. In Catalonia in Spain the 'normalization' of the Catalan language has led to difficulties with many migrants from Spanish-speaking countries. They had assumed that their knowledge of Spanish would mean they would have no difficulty in a region of Spain, and they are often resentful when this turns out not to be the case. It remains to be seen whether Wales will tackle this kind of difficulty more effectively.

There is also the issue of how far the commitment to bi-lingualism has been put into effect in English-speaking settings and what the consequences have been. For many settings (perhaps especially for English-speaking childminders working on their own and having little or no knowledge of the Welsh language) this will be a challenging area and there is a clear risk that they will place it quietly to one side. There is still too little evidence of how that potential difficulty is being tackled in practice.

There is a variety of cultural backgrounds across the United Kingdom and these are reflected to some extent in the way that the devolved regimes have tackled curriculum guidance. Of course, none of the constituent nations is entirely homogeneous. The situation in England has its own specifics. In that country local loyalties are often key to people's sense of personal identity. Some white communities that have arrived since England first established itself as a country have been completely assimilated. The leading example is that of the Huguenots (16th-century Protestant refugees from

Catholic France) who have effectively disappeared into the local populations in London and Yorkshire. (There are many people in Yorkshire with surnames that are clearly of French origin, but which are now pronounced in a completely English way.) Other communities – such as the Gypsies, Irish and Jews – have often retained much of their own cultures, as have the people who came from various parts of Europe in the immediate aftermath of the Second World War. However, for the most part cultural diversity within England is not seen as an issue except in relation to people whose origins lie outside Europe. This is not the case elsewhere in the UK.

 Exercise

Identify the passages that deal explicitly with cultural diversity in the official curriculum guidance for your part of the UK.

Do these passages:

- Make clear your statutory responsibilities?
- Give you useful ideas on what you can do in practice?
- Deal with any difficulties you have experienced?

You might want to compare the curriculum guidance for your part of the United Kingdom with that of another.

Alternatively, you could compare it with the guidance from another country altogether. Te Whárriki, the curriculum guidance for New Zealand, is an obvious example, since it is written in English and its commitment to cultural diversity has been widely praised. If you do undertake work on the curriculum guidance of a country outside the United Kingdom, try to avoid the mistake of thinking that lessons from them can be applied mechanically. Early years services abroad may have impressive features. However, they will be a product of the local culture and social expectations. They cannot be used as models without taking such cultural differences into account. They may draw our attention to principles that are relatively neglected here. They certainly demonstrate that things can be different. They do not provide simple recipes to be applied without further thought.

There has been considerable interest in the ways that curriculum guidance for the early years has been formulated in all the four major parts of the

United Kingdom. There has also been some evaluation of the effectiveness of guidance. However, there has been no published research to date that has focused specifically on the question of cultural diversity. We have little information on the ways in which the application of the guidance is impacting on the ability of children to grow up confidently in a multicultural society. We do have some knowledge about particular local projects (see, for example, the discussion in Connolly & Huskin, 2006), but we have no general picture yet of the effectiveness of the guidance in this respect. The confident assertions to be found on many pages on the Internet that multiculturalism in education has all been a waste of time or worse can be dismissed as ill-informed prejudice. On the other hand, there is little research evidence to point to the benefits. To proceed on the basis of faith is a reasonable initial step. There is now a need to go further and evaluate things more carefully.

There are other official documents that relate to cultural diversity, especially in England. The key examples can be summarized as follows.

In 2005 the Department for International Development, the Department for Education and Skills and the Qualifications and Curriculum Authority produced non-statutory guidance on *Developing the Global Dimension in the School Curriculum.* This asserted the need for children and young people to understand global issues and relate the various areas of the curriculum to them. It applied that principle to early years education as well as later phases. Using the six areas of learning from the earlier (2001) English Foundation Stage, it offers brief descriptions of a number of different activities that might be undertaken and highlights a particular activity in a school in Poole in Dorset (DfID, DfES & QCA, 2005, pp.6–7). The document was intended to be used in early years settings receiving the nursery grant, but the fact that the word 'school' was used in the title may have led to its being ignored in nurseries and pre-schools. This is a pity. It does a useful service in demonstrating that the global dimension in education is not just for students sufficiently mature to be able to grasp complex political and economic issues. The basis for understanding the global context in which we now live has to be established much earlier than the teenage years. The document also has a number of good ideas for activities developed in association with a number of schools and voluntary bodies. There is a comparable document that was produced for schools and other educational institutions in Wales (Welsh Assembly Government, 2006).

In more recent times the Labour government sought to balance appreciation of diversity with the need to develop community coherence. Unlike those who reject multiculturalism, the Labour Party sees these two as different sides of the same coin. Coherence is to be achieved through mutual understanding rather than the imposition of a single outlook. Under the 2006 Education & Inspections Act maintained schools in England have had a statutory duty since September 2007 to promote community coherence. Guidance on achieving this was issued by the Department for Children, Schools and Families (DCSF) in 2007. The duty is one that falls only on maintained schools, but the guidance is of relevance to other bodies working with children. One does not have to endorse every detail of the Labour government's stance on this issue (summarised in a speech given by Ruth Kelly in August 2006 on the occasion of the launching of the Commission on Integration and Cohesion) to see it as a positive development in the understanding of what the celebration of cultural diversity can mean and how it can prevent rather than encourage social breakdown. (For Ruth Kelley's speech see http://news.bbc.co.uk/1/hi/uk_politics/5280230.stm, last accessed 17/7/09.)

Finally, mention should also be made of the United Nations Convention on the Rights of the Child (1989). It is a matter of debate how far this has in practice directed the approaches of government in the UK. However, it has been an important reference point for many engaged in pressing for improvements in early years services as in other aspects of work with children and young people.

Discussion in the staff group on the issue of cultural diversity

Like all other aspects of daily practice, work around cultural diversity requires that attention be paid to it in planning meetings and in-house training sessions. There may be an advantage in giving to one member of staff a particular responsibility for the development of work in this sphere. There is always the risk that such a person will be left to handle the issue on her own. The active involvement of all staff is essential. Full discussion is key to the realization of that involvement.

Managers organizing such discussions should bear a number of things in mind:

- It can be useful to remind staff of official requirements, but the object of the exercise will be radically undermined if this is the only reason given for addressing the issue. To say 'We have to keep the inspectors happy' may stifle opposition to spending time on the subject in the first instance. In the longer run, it suggests that the manager has reservations about the commitment. It places the responsibility for taking on this work with an outside body and undermines its acceptance as a responsibility of the setting itself.

- It is important for the person leading a session to anticipate objections or reservations that may emerge and have some idea of what might be said in response.
- The discussion group (whether it is a regular staff meeting or a training session) must be a safe place for people to voice any reservations or difficulties they have. Practitioners may need to be reassured that there is nothing wrong with starting from a position of ignorance about any given community or expressing any lack of confidence that results from this. In most cases it is a mistake to respond to statements that are clearly prejudiced with the sort of condemnatory comment that throws the person back into resentful silence. Questions such as 'Why do you think that?' or 'How do you know that?' can lead people into a critical re-evaluation of their own position. The exception is where the statement is potentially hurtful to someone else who is present whose interests may require defence. (Drawing attention to their hurt can be another way of forcing the person making the prejudiced comment to reconsider the implications of what was said.)
- The manager must provide appropriate support to any member of staff who has a particular responsibility in the setting for work in this field or who is known to be facing a particular situation that is relevant. This need not mean agreeing with everything she says on the topic. Sometimes people who have been given particular responsibilities can assume positions that are over-assertive and antagonize others. It should mean taking steps to secure the understanding and general support of her colleagues.
- The manager must not rely on pure discussion. Ideas can be fleshed out with exercises (such as some of those in this book) or by illustrations of positive experiences related to cultural diversity told by visiting speakers or in DVDs and so on.
- Relevant equipment has an important part to play, but beware of discussion that shifts from talk of relationships to talk about equipment that can be purchased. This can be an evasion. It is fine to have a wok in the home corner, but how is reference to this used in exchanges between practitioners and children?
- The person leading a discussion should try to close it with some statement of shared views on the subject. Any unresolved issues to which participants will need to return in the near future should be recorded.

In some settings the issue of cultural diversity may feel difficult on occasion. Ignoring it will not make the problem go away. It is important in its own right. Just as importantly, problems that practitioners have with this area of work may be symptomatic of other difficulties. They may be struggling with understanding young children's developing sense of identity, working in full cooperation with parents or other aspects of practice.

 Exercise

Examine your setting's policy on equal opportunities and in particular the part of it that deals with anti-racism and cultural diversity.

What is the origin of that document? Did it come from outside the setting itself – for example, from your Local Authority, from the National HQ of a nursery chain to which you belong or from an agency that drafts policies for settings? If it comes purely from within the setting, was it written by the Manager or through a process of discussion with all the staff? Was it there when you arrived or has it been written or revised since you arrived? How do these questions of origin influence your attitude and commitment to it?

How often is explicit reference made to it in staff meetings?

Could it be improved in any way? Does it reflect the setting's current situation? (For example, have you experienced the recent arrival of a large number of children from a cultural background you had not previously encountered?) Does it reflect all the issues you see as relevant?

If you think it could be improved, what will you do about it?

Discussion of the issue with parents

There is now widespread recognition of the need to work in close cooperation with parents. Despite this recognition, it is still something that can be problematic. It is a common experience that some parents will expect a more formalized kind of education than settings offer, especially if their children are close to the age when they will start school. That is one area where differences in outlook can lead to misunderstanding and even tension between practitioners and parents. Cultural diversity is another. The setting may rely on activities around various religious festivals as a way of celebrating cultural diversity. This may not fit with the expectations of parents who have their own strong religious views or, for that matter, hostile attitudes to all religions.

 Case study

Happy Days Nursery is a private nursery situated in a largely white British area of moderately priced owner-occupied housing. Nearby there is a neighbourhood with mainly older housing, also owner-occupied but with an increasing number of families of Asian origin, several of whom own shops catering particularly for their own communities.

The nursery has taken relatively few children who were not white British, but practitioners there have always done their best to make welcome any such children whose parents sought places. They would say that they attempt to reflect the multicultural nature of our society in their practice. The celebration of Divali has always been popular with both children and parents.

In September three families of Pakistani origin from the neighbourhood close by sent their children to the setting. They explained that they wanted to give their children the opportunity to learn English properly before they started at school. Only a few weeks after this the parents came as a group to see the manager. They expressed concern, even anger, at what their children had told them about plans to celebrate Divali, saying that as Muslims they could not accept this.

How should the Manager respond?

Should the setting have done something at an earlier stage to deal with this issue?

The celebration of festivals raises particular issues, which are dealt with later. They provide just one of many potential flashpoints if some parents are unhappy with the setting's approach to cultural diversity.

Parents need to be fully informed about the setting's commitment to intercultural work. This entails discussion with them. Arranging such discussion may not be easy. During initial contacts, especially, there is a lot of information about the child that has to be exchanged. Broader issues about the way the setting operates can be pushed to one side. Even in the best-run settings the periods in which children are delivered and collected tend to be a little hectic – not the ideal context for the exchange of non-urgent information.

However, if the first time a parent raises the issue of the setting's policy on multiculturalism is when a problem has arisen, mutual understanding and cooperation are going to be all the more difficult. Discussion of the setting's values at the earliest stage and at intervals thereafter can place any particular issue in its broader context. Parents may not always agree with practice in a setting. At least if they understand the rationale for it, they are less likely to be shocked by what happens and may be more ready to discuss a problem they perceive.

It is real dialogue that is required. Settings cannot let themselves off the hook by passing across a set of written policies (including one on cultural diversity or equal opportunities) and then blaming the parents if they have not read them. It is only in exchange of views that the implications of a policy are likely to emerge. It is, moreover, dialogue that is required and not a one-way explanation of policy. The objections of parents to some line of action the setting undertakes in this field will not necessarily be based on racism or religious obscurantism. They may spot mistakes the setting is making – failing to be serious about the religious dimension of a cultural activity, falling into stereotypical (if apparently benign) thinking about a particular culture or just getting something fairly simple wrong.

 Note

One setting I know was asked by a puzzled Chinese parent why they were advertising an alcoholic drink. The brightly coloured banner in Chinese script that the setting had acquired from somewhere and put up as part of its Chinese New Year celebration was, in fact, urging people to purchase a particular brand of whisky produced in Taiwan.

The crucial role of discussion goes beyond talk about the setting's policies and what they imply. Many settings, especially those that have specific Sure Start status, are becoming involved in a number of activities with parents, including activities designed to foster parenting skills. Such groups can be used as a means of helping parents understand the implications of living in a multicultural society. This is an aspect of the subject in which the National Academy of Parenting Practitioners has taken a close interest recently. Work on cultural diversity may well be as much a matter of helping some parents learn about the majority culture in which they live as about helping white British parents achieve a better understanding of the new communities. Exchange within the context of a group where all the members are parents rather than some being providers and some users of a service can do a great deal to foster mutual understanding. The skills required to facilitate exchanges of that sort are different in some respects from the skills involved in other types of parent advisory work. However, it should be possible to find people able to undertake this kind of initiative in your area.

Twinning with settings abroad

There are a few – relatively few – instances at the moment of settings in this country establishing twinning arrangements with settings in other countries (for an example, see Kirby, 2006). However, this can provide some useful background to work on cultural diversity. Settings can swap information with each other on the work they are doing. It may be possible to arrange exchanges of staff or, if the foreign setting is not too far away, exchange visits for families.

This kind of relationship can give a new and important dimension to understanding another culture. In particular, your setting may be able to learn new ideas from the practice in another country. It is already the case that many settings in this country have benefited from direct or indirect contact with work undertaken in Reggio Emilia in Italy. The same might happen elsewhere. For example, early years settings in China make much more extensive use of music in their everyday routines and have a different approach to teaching quite young children specific skills in drawing and painting. Contact with a Chinese setting might provoke challenging ideas on what could happen in a British setting.

Although such contacts can be an important source of new ideas, it is always important to remember that a setting in another country will have a different cultural background. Their forms of practice cannot be simply taken on in the way that it might be possible, for example, to use a piece of engineering design from another country. The key advantage of carefully considered contact with work in a setting in another country should be that it demonstrates that things can be done differently. It should help us reflect critically on our own practice rather than simply providing an alternative to what we have been doing. (A similar point is made by Cooper, et al. (1995, p.131) in their book comparing child protection systems in England and France.)

Twinning arrangements may be established in a number of different ways. Sometimes practitioners on holiday have made contact with settings in the areas they have visited. Foreign embassies may be prepared to help set up arrangements. International professional bodies, such as ECCERA (the European Early Childhood Education Research Association) may also be able to assist.

Summary

The topics that have been discussed in this chapter – study of the curriculum and other official guidance, discussions with the adults concerned with the children attending the setting – provide the essential background to daily practice. It is to aspects of that practice that the next chapter turns.

Further reading

It is useful to go back to the curriculum guidance for your type of setting and re-read it with a particular focus on the ways in which it deals (or fails to deal) with the issue of cultural diversity.

5

Daily Practice with the Children: Resources, Sources of Support, Festivals and Dealing with Prejudice

This chapter deals with a variety of topics related to daily practice:

> Material resources

> The support of people from outside the setting

> The celebration of festivals

> Responding to evidence of prejudice among the children

> Safeguarding children from other cultural backgrounds

Material resources

Equipment and material provide the most immediately visible indication of a setting's commitment to the celebration of cultural diversity. You can see at a glance signs in foreign languages, pictures, musical instruments, dressing-up clothes, cooking implements and various other resources that reflect life outside white British culture. The absence of such tangible evidence would certainly be worrying. Its presence does not prove that all is well. The interested outsider (a parent, an inspector, a development worker from the Local Authority or a voluntary agency such as the Pre-school Learning Alliance, or PLA) will want to know how the material is being used.

In one particular case there is a lot of guidance available on the use of equipment. Persona dolls were developed primarily to help practitioners address equal opportunity issues with small children and they have proved particularly successful in doing so. This is because of the extensive and sensitive guidance that has been issued in books and films on the issue (see, for example, Brown, 2001). There has been less advice on many of the other types of material in use in early years settings.

It is not always necessary to articulate the learning potential a picture or other material resource embodies. Pictures and books that illustrate other social contexts, for example people whose appearance is different or who live in a different landscape, can have an impact on children without the practitioner necessarily drawing the child's attention to it. However, effective practice in this sphere cannot rely on that kind of impact alone.

Brief guidelines on the use of material resources

- Ensure that you understand the significance and context of any material resources that you purchase. The kinds of organization that are most likely to be able to supply them will also be one of the best sources for advice on their use. Such organizations include Development Education Centres, Local Authority bodies set up to promote the educational interests of children from black and minority ethnic communities, and also shops and resource centres established by black and Asian communities, or by educational projects. (There are more details on bodies of this kind in Appendix I.)
- Purchase items that have a track record of providing children with both fun and learning opportunities. Again, the agencies mentioned above will be a good source of advice as well as a source for the resources themselves. One of the examples of a resource that has proved successful in many settings is that of material for traditional block printing (such as those from India or West Africa). Another is that of musical instruments associated with non-Western cultures.
- The reading of maps does not come naturally to people. Many adults find it difficult. Children aged 3–5 are likely to start with what might be called a 'narrative' approach to maps, moving across the page from one point to another in the way that someone might travel rather than looking at the whole picture. (The maps produced in Europe towards the end of the 15th century were examples of such 'stories', depicting as accurately as possible what happened as a ship moved from point to point along a coastline. It was only much later with the work of pioneers, such as Mercator, that a new approach to maps, standing back as it were, began to develop.) Young children will not move from 'story' maps to the kind on offer in an atlas without help and guidance. One way of assisting them is to use very large maps so that they can physically find

their way around them and see more easily how near or far away are some of the places to whose cultural backgrounds they have had some introduction. Such activity has a part to play in the move from enactive to iconic modes of learning, that is to say the move from learning by physical contact to learning through picturing (Bruner, 1963).

- Recorded music from other societies can be a useful resource for dance and creative movement. So-called 'world music' is slightly less fashionable than it was a few years ago, but is still available on CD in large record shops. A company called Putumayo has produced a series of CDs of music from around the world specifically for use with young children.

- Understanding the context is more important than the authenticity of artefacts. Tic-tac drums and other traditional percussion instruments from Africa can be made fairly easily by anyone. Children can learn something about traditional Aboriginal art from Australia using the standard painting material in a setting. Masai bead work can be undertaken without using traditional materials. (The Masai themselves have been making use of imported beads rather than the traditional dried seeds for some time.) Similarly, if children dance to non-Western music, it is not essential that they learn the movements that are associated with such music in its places of origin; just enjoying movement to the music can provide a good experience.

- Be careful not to give the children a picture of other societies that is based entirely on traditional life and, in particular, traditional crafts. It is worth remembering that the Apartheid regime in South Africa often gave positive encouragement to traditional crafts, but applied strict censorship to writing or art products that suggested black people could be part of a modern society. The children need to appreciate that people in Africa, Asia and Latin America often live in cities, work in factories or offices, use cars and other modern forms of transport. Craft activities and the use of traditional forms of clothing for dressing-up activities are fun and can provide a useful introduction to different lifestyles. You should complement these with pictures and story-books that illustrate people with different cultural backgrounds living in modern settings.

- Try to make connections with everyday life, especially food and cooking, which are always a source of fascination for young children. Many of them will already have encountered types of food from outside Europe (and possibly implements, such as chopsticks) in restaurants they have visited with their families. Woks are becoming more commonplace in white British households. Even if cooking and eating implements are out of their ordinary experience, the enjoyment of food will provide a connection. Similarly, a good way of introducing children to the fact that there are different alphabets around the world is to spell out their own names in one or more of them. I am not, of course, suggesting that you do this in order to teach them any of those alphabets. Introducing them to the idea that words can be written in many different ways is a useful exercise, and doing so by means of spelling out their own names is a way of making a connection with their lives.

- There is already a number of children's story-books that reflect cultures other than white British, and are widely enjoyed. The number available is growing all the time. These can be a good way of getting children to think about people from other cultural backgrounds, but work best if the quality of the story-telling and illustration is high. There are some recommendations in Appendix I, but this is far from being an exhaustive list.

- Non-fiction books can also be useful, although it is more difficult to find ones that are designed for pre-school children. The books published by Frances Lincoln, dealing mainly with African topics and illustrated by photographs, are intended for primary school rather than pre-school children. However, they can be used at circle time with some careful planning.

- As with all material resources, it is important to monitor and review those that reflect the diversity of cultural backgrounds. Look out for the need to renew equipment that is out-worn and consider which resources are or are not well used. Try to work out why some are not well used. Is it because they are less accessible or look shabby or have not been explained to the children – or are they just not as useful as some others?

 Exercise

Conduct an audit of the material resources at your setting (or a setting with which you are familiar if you are not employed at one at present).

Relate each piece of equipment to what you see as its cultural background. Do this with all pieces of equipment, including those whose cultural background is deemed to be white British, or relate to a more specific background (English, Welsh, Scottish or Irish, or regions within any of the nations in the United Kingdom).

Construct a table indicating how many pieces of equipment appear to derive from each of the cultural backgrounds you have identified.

Have you had difficulty in ascribing a cultural background to anything?

(Continued)

(Continued)

Do the percentages of pieces of equipment in use reflect the cultural mix of the local area? If they do not, why has a cultural background that is over-represented been chosen for this treatment? (There could be some perfectly good reasons for doing so, but they should be articulated.)

The extent to which any given cultural background is represented by the number of resources is just one basis for judging your setting's ability to reflect cultural diversity. Are some resources more frequently used or much better used than others? Why is this so? Are there good reasons for it, or does the extent of use reflect the habits of the staff group?

The support of people from outside the setting

The increasing cultural diversity of the United Kingdom is in some respects a relatively new phenomenon. In earlier periods of history there were considerable differences of language and culture between the various parts of the country, but most people only came into contact with others from their own local communities. It is the increase in migration in the period since the Second World War that has made us (and other European countries) a multi-cultural society in a new sense of the term. Because the situation is new, it is only now being reflected in professional education and the daily experience of practitioners. We often need help from outside with this area of activity in a way that is less true of some other aspects of the work.

There are at least four types of people whose assistance might be sought:

- parents
- other non-professionals in the area
- professional development and support workers
- people with specialist expertise in art or craft activities.

The Vetting and Barring Scheme (VBS) in England, run by the Independent Safeguarding Authority under the terms of the Safeguarding Vulnerable Groups Act, was introduced in 2009 and at the time of writing is planned to be fully up and running by the end of 2010. It makes new requirements of people working with children and vulnerable adults, including volunteers. There are very similar schemes in the other parts of the United Kingdom. It has yet to be seen whether this will create complications that discourage settings from seeking the kind of outside help I describe below, especially in the case of people from the local community who do not undertake work in schools and early years settings as a major part of their paid work. Concerns about this were expressed by a number of children's authors in the early summer of 2009. I do not share their view that it is insulting to suggest that they should be subject to checks. Nor do I see vetting as something that might encourage an unhealthy distrust between children and adults. In the absence of any reason to think otherwise, children will tend to trust those adults to whom they are entrusted by their parents or other carers. They will not be aware that that trust is based sometimes on formal vetting schemes. However, the authors were right to question whether the VBS might be used over-extensively in a way that could inhibit activities of the sort discussed here. However strictly the VBS is applied, those who come into a setting to demonstrate aspects of the life of particular communities should always be working alongside staff from the setting rather than left on their own with the children. This is as much for pedagogical reasons as it is for purposes of safeguarding.

Parents

Parents whose own cultural background is not that of the majority of practitioners or user families at the setting may be willing to come in to explain or demonstrate some aspect of their own cultural backgrounds. They might be nervous about their ability to do this properly. However, it is not teaching skills that are asked of them but rather the ability to explain aspects of their ordinary lives or perhaps special occasions in their lives (such as birthdays, weddings or major festivals). It should also be possible to reassure them about performing in front of the children. Offer them the same kind of practical advice (about simplicity of language, use of repetition, involving the children through singing or chanting, checking their understanding and so on) that might be given to a relatively new and inexperienced member of staff.

One way of underlining the diversity of cultures is to ask two parents from different backgrounds to come in to explain what happened to them when they got married or celebrated the arrival of a new child in the family. They may be able to bring in to the setting the various special items associated with these celebrations. The contrast might be between, say, a white British woman who had had a traditional church wedding and a Sikh woman who had been married (here or in India) according to the traditions of that community. If the session is to go well, it is important that the two people agree to address similar issues and plan the organization (including timing) of the session with one of the practitioners. The joint presentation might highlight special dress, the use of flowers, the significance of a place of worship in the ceremony and food. (Since the food served at wedding receptions is often standard food within a community but served on a slightly grander scale, the two people may have to be reminded to address this issue specifically. The children are often as interested in the kind of food served at the wedding 'party' as they are in the special clothing worn by the bride and groom.) At least some of the children are likely to have attended weddings recently and can be encouraged to chip in with further contrasts.

Another way of involving parents (both those who are white British and those who are not) is to ask them in a session organized for the parents themselves about the kinds of play they enjoyed as children. Some of the best experiences I have had in running pre-registration courses for prospective childminders from particular black or minority ethnic communities have occurred when I have asked that question. The conversation has usually become so animated as to defeat the interpreter, but the pleasure of the participants has been obvious. Setting up such an exchange among parents connected with your setting may give you brand new ideas on the sort of games in which to involve all the children and at the same time help everyone involved appreciate how many common elements there are in the play of children all over the world.

The advantages of asking parents to explain features of their cultures are that:

- they are likely to give a more realistic picture
- since their children attend the setting, other children may be more able to understand that they are talking about something that happens routinely in their area rather than something exotic
- they may be more than happy to make a contribution for nothing, although they may have expenses that should be met, and it is always a nice idea to present a gift of some kind afterwards.

Among the issues that arise are the following:

- It is essential that the planning of the sessions in which parents participate is part of the overall curriculum planning. The setting must be clear why parents have been invited to participate in this way and what they hope to gain from any session. These ideas must be shared with the parents and possibly modified in the light of their comments.
- Parents may lack confidence about dealing with the situation in the setting and need support before and during the session (and discussion once it is over) in order to give as much as they have to give.
- In some cases, particularly if cooking is involved, health and safety issues can arise. A parent working in the kitchen at home is alert to the risks that the preparation of hot food entails and already has an established relationship with her own child and a routine about the

preparation of meals. This can make it less easy for her to anticipate the potential risks when a larger group of children and an unfamiliar environment are involved.

- Her own child(ren) may feel pride in a parent's performance but may also feel uncertain about this blending of the two environments of home and setting, which may be quite separate in their minds. Attention should be paid to their feelings.

Non-professionals

In areas where there are community organizations, places of worship or shops and restaurants reflecting various cultures, there may be opportunities to invite people working there to contribute to sessions.

The principal advantage of this kind of arrangement is that it can draw the attention of children to aspects of their area of which they had not given much thought previously.

Many of the issues that arise are similar to those that can arise when parents are asked to contribute. Once again, careful preparation of the session, support while it is going on and some discussion with the person afterwards are essential.

Professional development and support workers

Professionals engaged in support work and coming from Local Authority Early Years Services or agencies such as the Pre-School Learning Alliance, the National Day Nurseries Association, the National Childminding Association, the local Development Education Centre or specialist support agencies can make a valuable contribution to helping a setting review its work on cultural diversity. In some cases they may be able to provide some demonstration work. Sometimes interventions from such people may be invited because of adverse comments made during inspections by Ofsted or the equivalent bodies in other parts of the UK. Critical comments about a setting's performance in relation to cultural diversity by inspectors can often provoke a very defensive reaction, but the setting needs to move on from there. The contribution of support staff should help a setting make much more of what might at first seem like a setback.

Specialist service providers

In the large cities especially it is often possible to secure (usually for a fee) the services of musicians, story tellers, people with skills in various craft activities or others with similar forms of specialist knowledge and expertise to provide learning experiences for the children, introducing them to particular aspects of cultures that may be different from their own. There may be opportunities to identify funding from sources other than the ones early years settings frequently use. For example, Chalta (2005) describes a project of this kind that was funded by the Arts Council:

The expertise and the experience that visiting musicians, storytellers and other artists often have of working with children (although not necessarily pre-school children) mean that they can bring something very valuable to the sessions in which they participate. If the most is to be obtained from the use of such services, there is a number of things that are crucial:

- The session should be planned as an integral part of the curriculum and objectives clearly defined. The timing of the event within the day and within the term or other longer period of time should be calculated with a view to both practical issues and learning objectives.
- The setting must be clear about the ways in which it has made contact with the artist involved. If the person comes via an agency, is that agency familiar with the needs of an early years setting? What checks have they done on the people they have recruited? Are these restricted to assessment of their expertise in their particular craft or art, or have they been properly assessed for their suitability to work with young children? This is not just a question related to safeguarding. There may also be issues about the ability of the person to communicate with very young children.
- Even if the visitor is someone the setting knows is experienced in working with groups of young children, it is essential that the session should be planned with that person. It may be tempting in the middle of a busy day to settle back and leave everything to the visitor for an hour, but this is not the way to get the best out of it. How will the event be fully integrated into the rest of the setting's curriculum planning? What planning has been done for follow-up with the children once the visitor has left?
- The visitor may be quite unfamiliar with the setting or even the locality in which it is based. It is essential that the setting supplies information about itself (including directions on how to find the place, as well as a general description of the kind of setting it is).
- You will need to check whether the session will require any material resources. If so, will these have to be provided by the setting or will the visiting person bring everything that is needed?
- You should consider whether there any health and safety issues that arise in connection with the particular activity. How will they be resolved in discussion with the visitor before the session takes place?

- There should be an evaluation of the session and you should be clear beforehand who is going to undertake this work and offer feedback to the visitor.

What has been said here has been said with the particular contribution of artists representing other cultures in mind. It should be evident that good planning in this respect is really no different from planning for the visit of any specialist. It does not make much difference to the kind of preparations and follow-up that are needed, whether the visiting musician (for example) is going to play Gilbert & Sullivan on the piano or traditional Sudanese music on the oud. However, the risk that the visit will be seen as simply a bit of entertainment is, if anything, probably greater when the artist comes from a cultural background that is not British and must be resisted all the more strongly.

 Exercise

The word 'resources' should cover more than the equipment and other material resources that are available to your setting.

What are the other types of resource available to your setting in its work on cultural diversity?

You should consider the following:

- What are the cultural backgrounds of the staff (including any non-professional staff, such as the cook, the cleaner, the secretary)?
- What are the cultural backgrounds of the families using the services at the setting?
- How many different cultures have some kind of presence in the catchment area for the setting? Are those groups with cultural backgrounds that are not those of the majority new or well established?
- What are the opportunities for children's play in the catchment area? How far do those opportunities reflect the majority culture only? Is the playground in the local park well used by children from all the communities in the area? If it is not, do you have any explanation to offer as to why this is the case? What could be done to address the issue? (Is there, for example, a mechanism for

(Continued)

(Continued)

regular communication between the Local Authority department responsible for the park and a community organization representing the interests of local residents that could provide a forum for discussing this question?)

- Are the civic leaders in the local area (councillors, headteachers and so on) from more than one cultural background?
- Do the shops, restaurants and other commercial operations in the catchment area reflect a variety of cultural backgrounds?
- What places of worship are there? Do they represent a range of cultural backgrounds?
- What community organizations exist? Are they multicultural or do they, in effect, each serve particular communities?
- Are there any local festivals or other events (such as fund-raising summer fairs, amateur dramatic productions)? How far do these involve people whose cultural backgrounds are not those of the local majority?

Having identified these elements in the catchment area for your setting, ask:

- Has the setting already involved them in any of its activity?
- If it has not done so, or has made approaches that have failed, are there new ways that could be found to involve them?
- What considerations should you bear in mind when planning to approach them about cooperation and involvement?

Festivals

The celebration of various festivals has been one of the most common ways in which settings attempt to reflect and celebrate diversity since this practice was endorsed in the Swann Report in 1985. The very fact that it is a common device makes it worthwhile to consider the reasons for it.

 Exercise

Summarise the practice of your setting in relation to festivals.

You may undertake this exercise on your own, thinking about your own setting. On the other hand, it would be useful to do it as part of a staff discussion in a day care setting. The members of a network or less formalized group of childminders could also discuss the matters raised here and examine how much in common their practice had in this respect.

Which festivals are celebrated?

What are the reasons for the selection of these particular festivals? There could be a number of reasons, including one or more of the following:

- Festivals are celebrated that reflect the cultural backgrounds of the children in the setting. They are the ones the children cele-brate at home. Celebration of those festivals in the setting pro-vides a form of recognition of the varied home backgrounds of the children.
- Festivals are celebrated to enhance the self-esteem of chil-dren. The point here is similar to the one made above, but it could also cover festivals that are not traditional and may not be celebrated at home. An obvious example is Kwanzaa, a festival invented in the mid-1960s to celebrate African American culture, which has been taken up by some set-tings in the UK that have Afro-Caribbean children attending (Mercer, 2000).
- Rather than reflecting the cultural backgrounds of children in the setting, festivals may be celebrated as a way of intro-ducing children to cultural backgrounds that are unfamiliar to them.
- Sometimes the decision to celebrate a particular festival might be undertaken as a way of counteracting negative stereo-typing in the mass media. For example, a setting might choose to celebrate Christmas partly by activities that reflect traditions from the Maronite Church (in Lebanon) or the Coptic Church (in Egypt) as a way of encouraging a more positive view of the Arab world. Any local examples of anti-semitism might provide part of the rationale for the celebra-tion of a major Jewish festival.
- Festivals might be selected for celebration because they sound like fun. This is a good reason in its own right and might pro-vide the initial impulse, but it is always important to take other factors into consideration in the planning. Otherwise the cele-bration can be merely a form of tourism.

(Continued)

(Continued)

- Quite frequently festivals seem to be selected for celebration because it is relatively easy for settings to secure advice and relevant artefacts. This is probably the weakest reason. It is worth asking why some festivals – particularly Divali and Chinese New Year – are widely celebrated, while other festivals are celebrated less often. Given that there are large numbers of Sikhs in some of our cities, a setting might choose to celebrate Vaisakhi, the Harvest Festival of the Sikhs (a festival also celebrated by Hindus and Buddhists, although it is in the Sikh faith that it has particular resonance). If such a decision were to be made, it would not take too much work to track down information and ideas on the Internet or by contacting a local Sikh community.

Once you have reflected on the reasons why certain festivals are regularly selected for celebration, ask yourself (or put to a group discussion):

- Were there any surprises in what you have discovered?
- How coherent does your thinking on this issue appear in the light of this critical examination?
- What will you do next?

There may be good reasons for celebrating in the setting a festival that none of the children are likely to celebrate at home. I have suggested some of those above. It remains the case that it is always best to try to start from something with which the children are familiar. If a festival that is not part of their background is to be celebrated, connections need to be found between one or more aspects of the festival and things that are part of their usual experience.

There are many places where you can find information about festivals or practical ideas for their celebration in early years settings. For that reason such recipes do not figure here. However, there is a number of issues to consider once there has been a decision to celebrate a particular festival, whatever the rationale behind that decision.

- Most festivals have a religious origin. To celebrate one of them is to raise issues of belief. This can be difficult for white British people who are not practising Christians to understand, since in the United Kingdom the major festivals have become detached in the minds of many from their faith origins. This is most obviously true of Whitsun, which has become little more than the major bank holiday. Easter is celebrated with symbols of mainly pagan origin, such as Easter eggs, flowers and pictures of rabbits rather than images from the Gospel story. Christmas has to a large extent become a celebration of childhood and family life rather than a celebration of the Christian doctrine of the Incarnation. The difficulty many practitioners may have in grasping the religious dimensions of the festivals they wish to celebrate means this issue must be confronted in staff meetings planning such projects. One example is that Christian parents may object to what the staff have seen as the harmless fun of celebrating Hallowe'en. It is also important to appreciate that adherents of a particular faith will attach considerable significance to this aspect of the celebration and to be sensitive to their feelings. Settings sometimes display artefacts connected with religious celebrations or religious texts written in calligraphies other than the Western alphabet, not appreciating that such displays outside an explicitly faith context can be offensive to adherents of that religion. Apart from this kind of sensitivity, it is also important to recognize the ability of quite young children (at least once they have achieved basic oral skills) to understand that people have different beliefs about God and similar topics. They can become very impatient with adults who fudge such issues – and they are right to do so. The authors of the Welsh curriculum guidance seem to have been more willing to confront this fact than those who wrote the curriculum guidance for other parts of the UK.

- There may be good reasons for celebrating festivals from a variety of traditions. It is also worth giving consideration to the possibility of celebrating two or three festivals from a single tradition over the course of a year. This will create further opportunities for children to develop an appreciation of another society or culture. For example, the Chinese New Year is celebrated in many settings, but it is less common to find them following this up by celebration of the Dragon Boat festival in the summer or the mid-autumn festival (although in Chinese culture this last festival is particularly associated with children).

- If there is a settled routine of celebrating certain festivals, it may be worth livening this up by introducing elements from other cultures. Hogmanay celebrations can be given a new twist by adopting some of the features of Ganjitsu, the Japanese New Year festival (again, one that has a particular association with children). Celebration of Easter can be enhanced by creating 'Easter baskets' of the kind traditional in Poland. A contribution to Christmas celebrations can be made by the construction of a *Mghara* (a representation of the nativity scene traditional among Middle Eastern Christians).

- Some of the ceremonies or other activities associated with various festivals involve lighted candles, swords, sticks, fireworks, open water or the preparation of special food in frying pans on oven hobs. All of these things will raise health and safety issues. Fear of the consequences may lead some to back away from these aspects of the festival. This is an unnecessary response. Proper risk assessment should enable a setting to determine what is possible. Those who are used to celebrating the festival in their homes or places of worship will be familiar with some of the issues and their assistance may be particularly valuable in this respect.
- There is a tendency to see the celebration of festivals as something that happens indoors. However, most of them are celebrated outside in the lands in which they have their origin. Processions and dances in particular make more sense outdoors. It is important not to forget the potential use of the outdoor area of a setting in planning the activities that will be associated with the festival.
- Festivals are fun, but a lot of the point is missed if they provide a form of entertainment that falls outside the 'real' learning that takes place in the setting. The planning for a festival should take into account all the potential areas of the curriculum to which it might be relevant.

Settings can, of course, devise their own festivals to celebrate the particular cultural mix they represent. Undertaking such events can raised new issues.

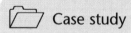 Case study

Street Corner Children's Centre is a relatively new community nursery in an inner-city area. It has been successful in attracting children from a wide variety of backgrounds. However, most of the members of staff (including the manager) are white British, with one practitioner from Mexico and another who is an Afro-Caribbean woman born in the UK. The management committee is also overwhelmingly white, with just one member of Asian origin (a man who is prominent in the local Bangladeshi community).

The staff group would like to be more representative of the area and would also like this to be true of the management committee. They decide on several steps they hope will achieve this. One is to involve more parents more directly in day-to-day activity at the Centre.

> The idea is proposed at a staff meeting, asking parents from the different backgrounds in the area to prepare food typical of their communities for a party celebrating the first anniversary of the setting. At first this idea is simply welcomed, but then one or two people at the staff meeting start asking questions. If the food is served buffet style, how will they prevent children eating things that contradict the dietary requirements made by their parents? What will be the consequences if this does happen? Supposing one of the food items evokes a negative response from some who try it? What about food safety requirements?
>
> What kinds of plan are needed to make this event a success?

Perhaps the most important thing to remember in planning festivals is that, precisely because they are a kind of party, it is easy to see them as somehow separate from the 'real world'. They are often the most obvious indication of a setting's wish to celebrate cultural diversity. They are also the form of activity that lends itself most readily to becoming a kind of tourism. Thinking about why the festival activity is being undertaken is always going to be more important than finding out how to do it. The best sources of guidance on the celebration of particular festivals will always reflect that fact.

Responding to evidence of prejudice among the children

The research evidence is clear. Children as young as three are frequently aware of the fact that people come from culturally different communities (Aboud, 1988). Our responses to times when children indicate that awareness, even say things that suggest prejudice and discriminatory attitudes, are frequently muddled.

Some of this goes back to the 18th-century philosopher John Locke. He spoke of children as being like recently arrived immigrants on planet earth. They need to have our world explained to them. He was trying to get away from the idea that new-born children are in the grip of Satan and need rescuing from the sins to which they are naturally inclined, a rescue that often involved harsh treatment. Insofar as Locke's views led to more humane treatment of children, this was a step in the right direction. However, it also led to the belief that the mind of a young child is a blank sheet of paper on which adults are free to write. It left aside any notion that children themselves are struggling to understand the world around them. One consequence of this is that racial or cultural stereotyping by children is often seen as the result of some kind of infection by an outside agent rather than as an attempt on their part to understand what they encounter.

Racism as a doctrine is something of comparatively recent origin. A form of racism (specifically anti-semitic) developed in Spain in the later Middle Ages. However, the main articulation of racism as an idea came later. When the first European explorers encountered foreign civilizations that were in advance of their own in some respects, they had few problems recognizing this in spite of the fact that (in their own eyes) they had the only true religious faith. There were sometimes questions raised as to whether the people who lived in societies that were less materially advanced were also descendants of Adam and Eve (although the majority view among academics and church leaders was that they clearly were). By and large, the European explorers did not assume that people of different appearance were congenitally different, let alone inferior. This included a readiness on their part to appreciate aspects of social organization as well as superior technology.

 Note

An example of this readiness to appreciate the positive aspects of other cultures is supplied by the 16th century Portuguese sailor Galeote Pereira, who on one occasion was accused of various crimes by two leading figures in the part of China he was visiting. In spite of the fact that they were powerful and influential, while he was in an extremely vulnerable position and had little knowledge of the local language, the court found in his favour. He asked pointedly whether an Asian would have received justice of this kind in any European court (Spence, 1998, pp. 22–3).

The doctrine of racism arose from seriously mistaken attempts to understand the variety of human beings in ways that were scientific and not bound by the traditional Christian notion that all humans are descended from a single couple. That doctrine is comparatively new, but prejudice against outsiders and a tendency to stereotypical thinking about them is a long-established aspect of human life. It is the defective form of two perfectly natural processes:

• In our attempts to understand the world around us, we all have recourse to generalizations that we have inherited or which are based on personal experience. There is nothing essentially wrong with that. We cannot interpret each new situation from scratch. The problem comes when we insist that the generalizations with which we started *must* be true and true in all cases. That is where generalizations become prejudiced stereotypes.

- We are all hesitant in unfamiliar situations. That is a wise precaution bred into us by the process of evolution. The problem comes when such caution is transformed into continuing distance from or hostility to the outsider whatever happens in the meanwhile. That is where uncertainty about how to deal with a new situation turns into active discrimination.

Young children will often make mistaken judgements when they attempt to understand the world around them. Rules and routines are important to them, so they will often construct a general rule on the basis of what they have learned so far. When they make the mistake of over-regularizing verbs (saying, for example, 'I runned' rather than 'I ran'), they are unlikely to provoke a strong response, only a gentle attempt to correct them. When they assume that a darker coloured skin is a sign of dirt, the response of adults may not be as calm. The assumption should not be made that they have said what they have said because they have been taught racist attitudes. They may have been. On the other hand, they may simply be attempting to make sense of an unfamiliar skin colour from the information they have to hand. When the people of some American societies began to encounter European explorers for the first time in the 16th century, they often assumed at first that these strangers really had nice brown skins like normal people and that their white complexions were the consequence of dust, make-up or disease. The uninformed white child's initial assumption that a darker skin may be a sign of dirt could be just as innocent. Yet it can be difficult for us to appreciate this because the racist connection made between skin colour and dirt is a long-established one. We can respond to what we know about society in general rather than to the individual child. Similarly, when children object to some method of preparing or eating food, it is likely to be because they have been taught the 'proper' way of doing so, rather than that they have been taught specifically that other ways are wrong. If they are suspicious of people whose appearance (including clothing) is unfamiliar, this may be natural caution rather than something caused by prejudicial attitudes that they have been taught.

This does not mean that statements which appear to be stereotypical or prejudiced do not matter, that children will just grow out of them. Their gradually improving understanding of the world may do something to help them drop initial assumptions. The child's developing appreciation of the fact that different individuals see things from different perspectives mean that the 8-year-old child may well be more strongly defended against stereotyping than a 4-year-old. The fact remains that their natural tendency to over-generalization and to caution in the face of the unfamiliar make them vulnerable to the development of prejudicial beliefs. We cannot rely on the child's natural, cognitive progression. After all, we correct mistakes in grammar. We should correct mistakes about people from other cultural backgrounds in a similar manner.

This will be done all the more easily and effectively if it is seen as a matter of helping the child to shape her understanding rather than stamping out evil. Yet, practitioners are often thrown off balance by apparently discriminatory statements by small children – unhelpfully over-anxious to stop the child thinking that way, worried that they may be setting themselves up for conflict with the child's parents (often the putative source of the prejudice expressed), perhaps worried in some cases that the child is expressing a reservation about another culture that the practitioner herself shares.

It is essential that the response to such expressions of prejudice should be calm and calculated. Any indications of anger or concern (in facial expression as well as the words used) will tend to send the child into unhelpful retreat. The practitioner should:

- try to discover more about the ideas and assumptions that lie behind the child's statement; the child is likely to find it difficult to articulate those assumptions, so that their precise nature may be difficult to identify; it is, nevertheless, important to try to get beyond the surface meaning of what is said
- correct any mistaken assumptions, appealing wherever possible to things that lie within the child's experience to do so
- provide comfort and support to any child that may have been hurt by what has been said (because it was directed at her community or for any other reason)
- consider the options that are available for presenting an alternative perspective to the whole group.

Sometimes, of course, it is not incidents in the setting but news from the world outside that is a source of difficulty. Children see news broadcasts on the television and, even if these do not offer explicitly negative messages about other societies, they may do so by default. Wars, riots, famine, disease and flood can suggest a picture of people living in other countries as irredeemably violent or as pitiful victims. Some of this may be due to the prejudices of journalists. There is a more deep-seated problem in that man-made and natural disasters generate more striking images than the negotiation of a peace settlement or steady, economic development. We need to consider the impact of this on children – not forgetting the fact that sometimes the disaster in the news is closer to them than we may have realized.

 Case study

Toy Town Pre-school meets every morning and afternoon, Monday to Thursday inclusive, in the local church hall. Most of the children are white British, but the Thursday morning group includes the child of an Algerian mature student at the local university, a child with a Spanish mother and British father, and also a Jewish child who has some close relatives in Israel.

On Wednesday the television news broadcasts were dominated by stories about a bomb attack in Israel in which a number of school children were killed. While the children are gathered together for drinks and biscuits, in the middle of the session one child asks the staff whether 'the Arabs' might bomb them. Some of the children appear distressed when this is asked, although one little boy – in playful rather than aggressive mood – starts fantasizing out loud about 'getting the bombers'.

How should the staff react?

What might they have done at an earlier stage to make it easier to deal with this situation when it arose?

Things might also be said that could indicate a seriously stereotyped view of another society, but without any expression of hostility.

 Case study

High Hill After-School Club operates in an inner-city area. It takes children from a wide range of cultural backgrounds. This includes a couple of Somali children, although there are no

(Continued)

(Continued)

other children at present whose families have their origin in black Africa. The club prides itself on the quality of its work on cultural diversity and has been praised for this in a recent inspection report.

A certain amount of work has been done in the last few weeks about Africa and the club has attempted to give a realistic, yet at the same time optimistic, picture of the continent. In particular, there has been some focus on South Africa's achievements in the period since the ending of Apartheid.

A session is organized outside with opportunities for imaginative play. Some of the boys announce that they are Africans and that they are going off to the jungle to hunt lions.

How should the staff react?

One of the issues that merits consideration here is that the apparently stereotypical view of Africa displayed may be more indicative of the attraction for some children of the idea of a hunter-gatherer existence. It is exciting and adventurous. Whether it is realistic may not be relevant in their eyes.

When this case study has been used with groups on training exercises, I have sometimes been surprised at the variety of issues that emerge. Some people have been more worried by the boys' interest in hunting and killing animals than they have been by the image of Africa that is implied. Some have even been concerned that the children know so little about lions that they imagine they live in the jungle rather than on open grasslands. These might be real issues, but if they dominate the discussion, then probably more central difficulties are being evaded.

To summmarize: stereotypical thinking needs to be challenged as much as any directly discriminatory remark, but this should be seen in the context of supporting the children's knowledge and understanding of the world and of their social, emotional and personal development rather than in terms of opposition to an ugly political creed, which need not be the source of the children's images of other communities.

A note on safeguarding

One of the unintended consequences of increased awareness of the need to respect other cultures is that professionals have sometimes been unhelpfully inhibited when dealing with a child protection issue in the case of a family whose cultural background is one with which they are not familiar. This is not sensitivity. It is failure to take the needs of such children seriously. Evidence that could indicate that a child is being abused requires response whatever the cultural background of the child.

Of course, evaluation of that evidence must depend on sensitivity to cultural issues. The practitioners in a setting have an advantage that is not usually available to the social worker visiting a family for the first time as the result of a referral. Practitioners know, or should know, the family with which they are dealing. That knowledge should include an awareness of aspects of the child's culture and of the particular circumstances of the child's family that could provide possible explanations other than abuse for behaviour that may have given rise to concern. That does not mean that the setting should undertake a complete investigation itself. It does mean that there is information that needs to be taken into account when referral to child protection services is being considered. It also means that there is information that should be conveyed to those services if the evidence is there to justify a referral and that close cooperation with any investigating agency will be important to a successful outcome. The general advice on responding to evidence of possible abuse of a child in the setting is the same as it would be for a white British child. There may be particular aspects of the family background that should be taken into account when evaluating the significance of any evidence and considering the steps that may have to be taken. The duty to safeguard remains.

 Summary

This chapter has touched on several issues that arise in day-to-day practice with children rather than offering recipes for activities focused on cultural diversity. This is because there is already a number of resources that do that job very efficiently. The focus has been primarily on presenting the multicultural nature of our world to all the children, a majority of whom will be white British in most settings. The next chapter considers the issue of inclusion of children who are not white British.

Further reading 📖

Among the publications offering advice on practical activities related to global education and cultural diversity are:

Brightwell, J. & Fidgin, N. (2005) *To Begin at the Beginning*. Development Education in Dorset (DEED)

and

Garvey, V. Giffin, H. & Unwin, R. (2007) *Developing Global Learners: Supporting the global dimension in early years foundation stage settings*. Development Education Centre for South Yorkshire (DECSY)

The best source of advice on celebrating a number of festivals is to be found in the two-DVD pack *A Child's Eye View of Festivals* issued by Child's Eye Media. Among the advantages are the engaging visual presentation, the manner in which the festivals are seen through the eyes of young children from the communities with which the festivals are connected, the illustrations of the role that parents can play and the back-up material written by Linda Mort and Angela Gould.

6

The Inclusion of Children from Minority Communities

> **This chapter describes:**
>
> > The welcome offered to a new family from a cultural background that is not the majority one in the setting
>
> > The situation of bi-lingual children
>
> > The use of interpreters in conversations with parents
>
> > Some of the issues that arise from differences in child-rearing in different societies
>
> > The way the children in a setting can contribute to inclusion

The concept of inclusion found its way into early years discourse in the context of policy on children with special educational needs. More recently the meaning of the term has been widened. It is now taken to refer additionally to the inclusion of children from black and minority ethnic communities and of children at risk of being, in effect, excluded from full participation in the life of their setting for any reason. This wider concept is now incorporated in official documents, for example in the Statutory Framework for the new Early Years Foundation Stage in England (DCSF, 2008a, 1.14). That children from different cultural backgrounds should be made welcome and fully included has become part of the professional consensus.

Welcoming a new family

The experience of welcoming a new family from a non-white British background may be a familiar one to practitioners at a setting. Or it may be happening to them for the first time. In either case it needs considered action. The welcome offered to *any* new family requires such thought, but there are likely to be some additional issues if the family comes from a cultural background other than that of the majority of people running or using the setting. Some people might see this as posing a problem. It can, on the contrary, have the advantage of testing the effectiveness of existing admission procedures that have become a mere routine.

 Exercise

Remember an occasion when you joined a new social group or organization. Perhaps you have had the experience of being on your own in a foreign country. It might be something as simple as going to a new school or starting a new job.

What made it easier for you to settle in to your new environment?

What made it more difficult?

What would have made it easier than it was?

What does this reflection tell you about the needs of families coming to a setting for the first time, especially if they are from a cultural background that is not white British?

If this exercise is conducted among a group of students or practitioners, allow time for each member of the group to reflect on her own experience before opening up the discussion to the whole group.

There are some general principles to bear in mind when dealing with the arrival of a family from a background that is not familiar to you:

- *Don't panic.* There may be stumbling blocks to building up a relationship with this new family. However, it is important to bear in mind that the parents want to bring the child to your setting. This shows they are coming to you with goodwill and a readiness to believe you can help their child. That is a good starting point.
- *Don't make assumptions.* Stories are still told of settings where the staff take it for granted that a black or Asian parent who has arrived for the first time will not be fully competent in English. This may be so. It may

not be. Take the trouble to find out. If there do appear to be difficulties that are due to the parent's limited knowledge of English (and not to some other cause, such as the parent's anxiety about approaching what she may see as officialdom), discuss with the parent how these problems can be jointly overcome.

- *Do not assume that differences in outlook are due to ethnicity.* For example, research among the parents in Australia several years ago appeared to uncover significant differences between families of British and families of Italian origin. However, when the researchers compared only people from the two communities who shared similar socio-economic circumstances, the degree of difference was significantly reduced. In other words, factors such as economic well-being played at least as great a part as 'culture' (Cashmore & Goodnow, 1986).

- *If you cannot make assumptions, then you must ask.* Be prepared to admit your own ignorance about any aspect of the country or cultural background from which the family comes. The fact that you are a professional does not mean you have to know everything. You should recognize, however, that the fact that the two of you may not understand each other's cultural background well is at least as much *your* difficulty and weakness as it is theirs. Demonstrate your willingness to learn. Do not be inhibited about asking certain questions. In many parts of this country the tensions in the past between different Christian denominations have left people hesitant to ask questions about religious faith. The subject is seen as 'too personal'. This sort of thing can get in the way of seeking information that is really needed. If something in the behaviour of the parents surprises you, explain your failure to understand and ask them to say more about it.

 Case study

Bridle Lane Pre-school is based in one of the suburbs of a major city. It has rarely had children who are not of white British origin.

It has recently taken a child whose parents come from one of the countries that joined the European Union in 2004. The father has a highly skilled job in industry. The mother speaks some English, but is far from fluent and is trying to improve her knowledge of the language. (She let slip on one occasion that she knows some German and Russian as well as her native language.) In spite of the differences in competence in spoken

(Continued)

(Continued)

English, it is the mother rather than the father who makes all the arrangements for the child's participation in the pre-school. She sometimes has difficulty in explaining things. For example, the practitioners are puzzled by the fact that the child appears to be called either Mirek or Vladimir and both names are used. Similarly, the pre-school have difficulty explaining things to her. She seems completely bemused in one conversation when the subject of playdough comes up and the staff members do not know whether this is because the material is unfamiliar to her or for some other reason.

The child appears to be reasonably well settled in the pre-school, but is not very forthcoming yet. The practitioners are worried that he could remain isolated in the group.

What strategies are open to the staff?

Note: *The answer to the puzzle about the child's name is that 'Mirek' is an informal version of the name Vladimir, one that is in common use in many Slavonic languages. An issue to discuss with the mother here would be which version of his name would the child find it more comfortable for the practitioners to use.*

- *It is routine to ask for the name of a child.* The structure of names can vary between cultures. It is not necessarily the case that the first name in the sequence will be the name the child is called at home. It may be the family name or denote religious or ethnic affiliation. Take into account the fact that there can be variations on personal names (like Jack, or Johnny for John, in English) as in the case study above. If the child's name feels like one that white British staff will find it difficult to pronounce, get them to persist in conquering it. A child's name is important to her identity. She may be amused if their efforts are not entirely successful. She will be puzzled if they do not even try. It is depressing that so many people with names of Indian, African or Celtic origin feel it necessary to adopt 'anglicised' versions of their names to make life easier for white British people. It suggests that they anticipate that people will be too disinterested to attempt to conquer the pronunciation of an unfamiliar name.
- *Seek advice from an expert.* If you are about to begin work with a family coming from a particular cultural background, an expert on that background

may be able to help and advise you. Assuming that you can find one (and this may be problematic), you cannot hand over responsibility to that person. The expert will not be there all the time. You have to find ways of coping with your own contact with the family.

One good indication that parents are happy with their relationship with the setting is the quality of the relationships they make with each other. This is evidence that is easy to miss. Heyden, de Gioia & Hadley (2003), in a report on 'non-English speaking' families' use of three early years settings in Australia, found that less than 4 per cent of those parents spoke of friendships they had established through their use of the services at the centres. This suggests something worrying about the extent to which they felt at home there or failed to do so. It might also be connected with the relatively low number of such families seeking advice from staff in the settings. It would be interesting to see similar research in the UK.

Bi-lingualism

The word 'bi-lingualism' in the heading to this section of the chapter implies that it is only two languages that are involved and may further be taken as suggesting that one of those will be the original language of the child's family and the other English. There are many societies in the world where several languages are spoken and there is nothing unusual about someone, even someone poorly educated, speaking two or three languages. A child may come from such a background and then confront the need to learn English as well. In many instances the issue will be multi-lingualism rather than bi-lingualism. However, here the focus is on the fact that a child may speak at least one language other than English (or other than Welsh, Gaelic or Irish in a setting conducted in one of the longer established minority languages). I hope the reader will understand that the term is being used in that context.

Languages vary in their grammar and syntax. You cannot simply substitute English for Welsh or Urdu (for example) on a word-by-word basis. Similarly, the sounds that are typical of languages vary. There are different rhythms and cadences to sentences. Some languages are 'tonal'; that is to say, the musical pitch of any given sound determines the meaning of the word in which it occurs. Many languages have sounds that are unique to themselves. There is ample research evidence that children pick up the sounds of the language that surrounds them early on and, once these patterns are established, have difficulty in adopting the typical sounds of another language. Hence someone might be reasonably fluent in a language, but still speak with an 'accent'; that is to say, in a way that makes evident that the language they are speaking is a foreign one to them.

As a result, anxieties have often been expressed about the difficulties of children being raised in a bi-lingual environment. Questions can be raised about the impact this will have on the child's development of communication, language and literacy skills. Parents whose own first language is not English are sometimes advised to speak English exclusively at home so as to allow their children to develop fluency in it. Such advice is based on an assumption that children can be confused by exposure to different languages – an assumption that the research evidence does not justify.

There is no real evidence of young children becoming less articulate as a result of living in bi-lingual environments. Children raised to speak more than one language often cope well (Turner, 1997, pp.139–40). One of the developments that may occur is that they come to associate the different languages they speak with different contexts. English will be the language of the early years setting. Another language may be associated with home. This can lead to a child having difficulty in discussing things associated with one context in another (Tassoni, 2003). However, this should be a familiar issue. It can occur even when different languages are not involved. How many white British children, when asked by their parents what they did in school that day, reply 'Nothing' because they do not know how to describe their experiences in ways their parents will easily understand?

The overwhelming evidence from research is that quite young children can manage bi-lingualism (Datta, 2000). In fact, there is evidence that it can be positively beneficial, helping children develop a greater awareness of language in ways that support their cognitive development (Carroll & O'Connor, 2009; Cosh, 2002). It is bi-lingualism that is questioned and inadequately supported that can become a problem. Children coming from families where one language is normally spoken may have difficulties with another language spoken in the setting because they have not been allowed to develop their capacity in their family language properly.

Early years practitioners may for a variety of reasons have or acquire the ability to speak more than one language, but there are very many languages that might be encountered. Thus, in a particular instance it may be helpful if a practitioner is fluent or has even a limited competence in the language spoken by a child at home. However, no setting is going to have a staff group that can speak all the languages that might be relevant some day. The real need is for skills in supporting children as they learn how to communicate verbally and for these to go with understanding of how the use of another language can enhance the child's understanding of

English (or whichever language is routinely used in the setting). Among the steps that should be taken are:

- Paying particularly close attention to facial expression, body language and tone of voice as indications of the general meaning of what is being said.
- Demonstrating an interest in and high valuation of the child's original language by saying this explicitly and by learning a few phrases (such as greetings) in that language.
- Correcting mistakes in English sensitively, for example by confirming that the child is right in what she says but repeating it in a more correct form.
- Underpinning your verbal communication with the child by facial expression and gesture.
- Describing what you are doing in simple English (for example, 'I am putting the book back on the shelf').
- Reinforcing the learning of new words by other senses wherever possible (for example, using taste and smell as well as sight to identify a particular fruit).
- Giving children time to respond to what you have to say (since a pause may indicate the struggle the child has to formulate a thought in English rather than any kind of hesitation about the response as such).
- Making use of repetition, rhyme and other devices to familiarize the child with key elements in English.
- Making use of open-ended questions.
- Dealing promptly and firmly with any negative comments from other children or adults about limitations to the child's knowledge of English.

Much of this, of course, is essentially what you would do with any child at the early stages of language acquisition and reflects ideas coming from the American Highscope approach about supporting the child's developing skills in communication. However, all of these things become even more important in the case of the child whose family language is not English, and a couple of the guidelines just offered are more specifically about the situation of the bi-lingual child.

Using an interpreter

It is important for their own survival and well-being that people new to this country learn to speak English as quickly as possible. The fact that the Government reduced the funding available to support the learning of English as an additional language in 2007 has done nothing to facilitate community cohesion. If people living here whose first language is not

English should be encouraged to learn and use it, there will still be some circumstances where you will need an interpreter to communicate effectively with a parent. This may happen either at the point of initial contact or at some later stage because of a particular incident or situation or just as part of the process of maintaining the relationship. Almost certainly the parent will have some knowledge of English in order to have found her way to the setting at all, but it may be insufficient for some of the discussion that needs to take place.

Finding an interpreter is often difficult. If you live in an area where there are large numbers of people whose first languages are other than English, you may find that your Local Authority maintains either a small translation and interpretation team or has a database with details of people able to provide translation or interpretation services. There will usually be a fee to pay for their services and this may limit how often you can use them. You may also find that the service covers only the most widely-spoken languages in the area (often Urdu, Hindi, Bengali, Tamil, Arabic, Cantonese or Somali). If your need is for interpretation in another language, one less-widely spoken in your area, the official service may be unable to help you. However, you should not assume that this is the case. They may have contact with someone competent in interpretation who speaks a language that is not widely used in the UK. Those in Sheffield who were involved in receiving and working with children who had come from the war in Kosovo were amazed and grateful to receive an offer of help from an early years practitioner of Albanian origin living a short distance from the centre where the children were initially received. You do not get that kind of luck every time, but it can happen. Even if the Local Authority is unable to help, it is important that it is assisted to recognize that there is an issue. For example, in various parts of the UK the number of speakers of various West African languages or of the East European variant of the Roma language has grown significantly in the last few years. Unsuccessful requests for help with interpretation may prompt the Local Authority to recognize that this is an issue. This will be important even if it does not solve the immediate difficulty facing the setting.

In the absence of someone experienced in interpretation you may have to rely on someone from the family of the person with whom you need to discuss things or with someone else from their community. This can turn out to be the least bad choice available to you. Nevertheless, you should think carefully about accepting suggestions that such people provide a service. To do the job well an interpreter needs professionalism and objectivity as well as language skills. Someone who is related to the user of your service may censor what you say or what is said in response because the questions raised are sensitive. An obvious example would be a child protection situation, but sensitivities can arise in less dramatic circumstances. It may be particularly difficult for a relative who is younger than the person with whom you are discussing something to interpret fully and accurately. Someone who comes from the relevant community organization and is not a professional interpreter may also be tempted to modify some of what is said to protect the reputation of that community or because of culturally determined ideas of what it is proper to discuss with outsiders.

 Note

A childcare inspector once met with a group of women who were thinking of setting up a playgroup in their community centre. The members of the organizing group were newly arrived in the UK and none of them was yet fully competent in English. A male member of the community centre's management committee agreed to interpret. At one point when a question from the childcare inspector had been translated, a lively and prolonged debate took place in which initial disagreement seemed to end in compromise as far as she could make out from the body language and the tone of their voices. Once the discussion was over, the interpreter turned to the childcare inspector and said with a smile, 'Yes, that is OK'. Without speaking a word of their language she knew that, while that might be an adequate summary of the *outcome* of the debate that had just taken place, she had lost any real sense of what was happening. She guessed that the interpreter was reluctant to be frank about what had just taken place. It took her a lot of work to discover the issues that had led to initial concern. It was important for her to do so. It was a significant indicator of their understanding of the conditions of registration.

If you are able to secure the services of an interpreter (whether a professional or someone who is simply close to the user), there are several things to bear in mind:

- You must plan what needs (from your point of view) to be covered in the discussion and to be prepared to respond to issues raised by the parent. If this is the initial contact with the parent, you will probably have a schedule of matters to cover laid down in your admissions policy or elsewhere. Remember that some issues may need particular discussion because of the cultural differences.
- Make every effort to meet with the interpreter beforehand and go through the matters to be discussed. You may have to discuss the ways in which terms commonly used by practitioners are to be translated. Many parents, including ones who are white British, will not understand phrases such as 'Early Years Foundation Stage' and need to have them explained. There are less obvious forms of jargon. For example, in English the word 'professional' can mean (1) that work is undertaken

for payment, (2) that you need to be formally qualified to undertake it, (3) that the person undertaking the work is highly skilled, or (4) that the person has a commitment to certain ethical principles that go beyond what might be stated in a contract between provider and user. It may be reasonably obvious to another English-speaker which of those meanings is relevant to use of the word on a given occasion. It is important to ask the interpreter to explain how the term will be translated from English and to explain the connotations of the word that will be used in the other language. Another apparently non-jargon word that might cause difficulty is 'intelligence'. People in Anglo-Saxon countries tend to use it to refer to the kind of cognitive skills that are measured by IQ tests. However, someone from one of the countries of the Far East might find it puzzling if it were said that a child was misbehaving because her high level of intelligence led her to being bored with what the rest of the group was doing. The idea that a child who was socially inept could be described as 'intelligent' would not make sense. To some extent there is a similar equation of intelligence and social behaviour in the West. A French child who is being naughty will be advised to be wise (*'sage'* in her own language). In parts of this country an ill-mannered person may be described as 'ignorant'. The work of Howard Gardner (2001) has accustomed us to the idea that there are different types of intelligence. The implications of this for interpretation can still be missed and misunderstandings arise as a result.

- Check that the service user is happy to accept the contribution of the interpreter before the meeting is set up and at the beginning of it. There could be problems that might not have occurred to you. For example, if the parent has come from a country that is currently or has been recently engaged in a civil war, she might be reluctant to accept assistance from someone who comes from what she sees as 'the other side'. It will make life difficult if the parent is unhappy with the interpreter and you have to abandon the arrangement. It might make life even more difficult if you persist with an arrangement when there are clearly issues between the persons involved that you do not understand.

- Allow plenty of time. Interpretation slows down the normal pace of any discussion considerably. You have to wait for your words to be interpreted and the interpreter to listen to the other person. This is complicated by the fact that practice in relation to pauses during a conversation varies between different cultural backgrounds. Frequent pauses are part of the pattern of conversation in many cultures (in parts of the Far East, for example) and are not necessarily a sign of awkwardness or embarrassment. On the other hand, there are some cultures (in parts of the Arab world, for example) where pauses are seen as indicating a problem and may be filled rapidly in a way that interrupts the flow of interpretation. Allow at least twice as long as you might do for a conversation in English with a parent, preferably three times as long.

- Be formal and explicit. People who come from the same cultural background pick up signals from each other beyond the explicit messages that are being conveyed. This may not work in a meeting between people with different cultural backgrounds. You may pride yourself on being approachable and informal with parents. The same level of informality may work much less well when you are using an interpreter.

- You also need to bear in mind that what counts as formality or politeness varies significantly between cultures. The English when making a request tend to be excessively apologetic about it. 'Excuse me. I'm sorry, but I wonder – if it is not too much trouble – if you could possibly tell me the way to the railway station?' That is a bit of a caricature, of course, but perhaps you will recognize what I mean. Such ways of speaking can be puzzling to people who are unfamiliar with English culture. Similarly, their way of asking for directions to somewhere may sound blunt or even rude to an English person. In other cultures politeness may be expressed by body language, by versions of the word for 'you' that express deference or by way in which the speaker refers to herself. Many languages spoken on the Indian sub-continent employ the syllable 'ji' to emphasize that the speaker wishes to demonstrate respect. The manner in which politeness is expressed is another issue that can be discussed usefully with the interpreter before the interview itself.

- The appropriate use of formality applies particularly to the close of the discussion. Bring it to a clear ending and make sure you summarise what you see as the principal conclusions. You should give the other person an opportunity to speak of any difficulties with what you have just said. If this opportunity is taken up, deal with the issue and then go back to the process of closing the discussion.

- It may be that you can supplement the discussion with a translated version of the document you would normally hand to parents in these circumstances. Do not make any assumptions about how well that will work. It can happen that people who are not literate in English are not literate in the national language of their own countries either. In conversation among themselves they may use another language or dialect – Syhleti rather than Bengali, Mirpuri rather than Urdu and so on.

- It is really, really tiring to conduct a lengthy conversation through an interpreter. Allow for this fact in planning the rest of your day. Do not plan follow the interview with another demanding task. Book some time to relax with a hot drink or a bar of chocolate instead.

Exercise

Your setting may already have an outline 'script' of things you would want to discuss with the parents of a child who is going to attend your setting. If you do not have such a document, jot down a list of topics. *(If this is being conducted as a group exercise start by noting topics individually and then agree on a list).* Make a particular note of key words or phrases you would expect to employ.

How many of those words or phrases are you confident would be comprehensible immediately to most parents? How would you explain those you do not believe would be immediately comprehensible?

How many of those words or phrases refer to:

- arrangements relating to educational services (e.g. EYFS, SEN, Early Years Service)?
- aspects of the curriculum (e.g. knowledge & understanding of the world)?
- concepts in education (e.g. 'schema')?
- terms that might be used beyond the sphere of education, but whose meaning is not necessarily clear (e.g. 'holistic')?

How would you explain these terms to any parent? In what ways would the fact that the parent's first language was not English change the way you approached the task of explaining the work of the setting to her?

Differences in child-rearing

When a child from a different cultural background starts at your setting you need to be alert to the possibility that behaviour that might be seen as disruptive or a symptom of unhappiness may have a different meaning in the culture from which that child comes. Similarly, adults may behave in ways that surprise the child who is uncertain how to respond. For example:

- In many African cultures it is common for direct eye contact between a child and adult to be seen as impertinent on the part of the child, whereas in this country avoidance of eye contact by the child is often seen as evasive and insolent.

- Small children may be accustomed to being carried by adults in ways that are not common in this country. In many societies parents will carry a small child on the hip rather than across their upper torso.
- Formalized gestures can vary in their meaning. In parts of the Arab world shaking the head from side to side can indicate agreement not dissent (as it would normally do in England). The thumbs-up sign, which means 'OK' in many West European cultures, is an extremely obscene gesture in many Islamic countries and in some parts of the Mediterranean that were formerly under Arab rule. Similarly, in this country adults asking a child to come closer sometimes reinforce this message by a gesture using a raised finger pointing towards themselves. This is also an obscene gesture in much of the Muslim world. The use of gestures such as these will be extremely disconcerting to a child from a cultural background where they are frowned upon, and may lead to behaviour that in turn is misinterpreted as difficult or impertinent.
- The meanings attached to colours or other symbols may vary. Red means 'Danger' to most British people. It means 'Good luck' or 'Prosperity' in much of the Far East. White means purity or innocence to most Europeans, whereas in parts of Asia it is the colour that symbolises death.
- Societies where oral story-telling is still often practised are likely to have unwritten rules on the structure of narratives and the response of the audience. These may differ from those that are customary here. This aspect is particularly important for children who need the use of story-telling conventions to help them understand the differences between fiction and information-sharing (Baldock, 2006, pp.51–3). Children who respond to story-telling in ways that reflect their own cultural backgrounds rather than that of the setting may be perceived as disruptive or as failing to understand what is said. Hymes (1996) explored this phenomenon in relation to Native American children in schools in the US. Research conducted in this country might indicate similar issues with children from deeply rural parts of Africa or Asia.
- Many children will be used to eating food at home with their fingers or with implements (such as chopsticks) other than knives and forks. Guidance on the use of knives and forks is likely to be helpful to the child in the long run. The practitioner who asks the child to demonstrate alternative ways of eating is going out of her way to demonstrate respect for that child's cultural background, and giving an important lesson that everyone – even a grown-up – is learning all the time.
- A white British child handed a present that is wrapped will probably open it immediately. In Japan and some other parts of the Far East wrapped presents are not opened immediately and may never be opened. The value of the present may be small, but considerable effort

will have gone into the wrapping and it would be ill-mannered to tear it apart. If such a child is at the setting around Christmas time and it is intended to distribute small presents, this should be taken into account. The child who delays opening a package may be seen as failing to understand that a present has been given when, in fact, she is showing her appreciation of it.

It would be possible to fill a book with examples such as those just given. The point is *not* that practitioners need to learn vast quantities of material gathered by social anthropologists, but that we need to be aware of the fact that *behaviour does not always have the meaning we would usually ascribe to it.* We must consider more carefully what may be going on in the child's mind. Among the things to take into account is the fact that natural body language is more universal than formalized gestures.

Seeking the support of other children

Practitioners can be hesitant about involving other children in the process of achieving inclusion. Is this a heavy burden to impose on them? Is it a mistake to draw their attention to the fact that another child is different in some way? But peer relationships are of crucial importance to children. It is wrong to avoid involving them. Anyone who has watched young children at a holiday resort who do not speak each other's languages but get on with each other by means of gestures and facial expressions will realise how strong the impulse to make friendships is and how uninhibited children can be in overcoming obstacles caused by the lack of a shared language. More than thirty years ago, Brown (1979, p.131) noted that there was more physical contact between children in primary schools where young children came from a variety of cultural backgrounds than there was in other schools. I have no research evidence to confirm it, but my impression from contact with many settings is that it is often in the nursery that takes children from several different cultural backgrounds and provides a supportive ethos for them that children develop a concern for each other that is particularly strong and well founded.

Children told that a new arrival is different in the language she normally speaks or in some other way can usually accept that quite cheerfully. If it is not drawn to their attention by the staff, they will probably notice the difference for themselves and see it as disturbing, precisely because it has not been explained. In the period when they are developing an ability to understand that other people may have different perspectives on the world, they are very open to the idea that this may happen because of cultural or other differences. Their understanding can be enlisted by discussion with them or by such specific techniques as the use of persona dolls.

Children who come from different cultural backgrounds may also be a resource for their peers. Their explanations of aspects of their own background can be an important route for other children to understand something about the wider world.

Finally, it should be remembered that the children learn from the adults around them. If the practitioners are uncomfortable with children whose first language is not English or are different in some other way, the children will pick this up and see the difference as worrying. It is not necessary for adults to make explicitly discriminatory comments in the hearing of children for them to foster discriminatory ideas.

 Summary

The inclusion of children whose cultural backgrounds are not those of the majority at a setting is the acid test of commitment to multiculturalism. Problems that may appear to have started with the arrival of such children were probably there already. They were just concealed before that point.

Further reading

It has now become usual for the subject of inclusion to be discussed in a comprehensive manner, that is to say, taking all the factors that might impede inclusion into account.

A good introduction to the general topic of inclusion is Jenny Lindon's *Equality in Early Childhood* (2006). A recent book that focuses particularly on the issue of the inclusion of children from ethnic minorities is Sue Griffin's *Inclusion, Equality and Diversity in Working with Children* (2008).

7

The Overwhelmingly White British Setting

This chapter:

> Says something about the uneven distribution of people who are not white British across the country

> Makes the case for work relating to cultural diversity in settings where the great majority or even all of the staff and children are white British

> Describes some types of activity with children that may be particularly relevant in those circumstances

By far the greatest part of the population of the UK is white British. The precise percentage is necessarily vague. Many white British people would describe themselves as belonging to one of the nationalities within the UK (especially those who are Scottish, Welsh or Irish). Other people who are happy to describe themselves as British may be conscious and proud of a family background that is Jewish, Italian or derives from some other nationality or ethnicity that is white but not from one of the long-standing constituent nations of the UK.

The minority that is not white British is concentrated in particular parts of the country. Such people are found in greater numbers in larger towns or cities for a variety of reasons:

- Towns and cities with major docks have provided a point of entry for immigrants or refugees and asylum-seekers and they have often remained in the places where they first arrived. (This factor has become a little less significant with cheaper air travel, but still has some consequences.)

- There have usually been better employment prospects for migrant labourers in major towns and cities. This happened especially in small workshops in the early part of the 20th century, larger factories in the post-War period and more recently in the service industries.
- Universities and many Further Education establishments have been attracting increasing numbers of students from overseas.

Of course, distribution cannot be described solely in terms of urban as opposed to rural areas. Grimsby is one major urban area with comparatively few residents who are not white British. Many rural areas in East Anglia have recently experienced the arrival of large numbers of migrant agricultural workers from Portugal and other parts of the European Union. There are also examples of communities dispersing for economic reasons. For example, there are many Chinese families living in largely white British neighbourhoods because they have established small family businesses to serve the wider community (laundries in the early 20th century, Chinese restaurants and fast food outlets more recently) and they find it more practical to live on the same premises as the business.

The concentration of communities that are not white British has been partly a matter of the opportunities for employment. It is also partly a matter of people seeking social and sometimes material support when they first arrive in this country from relatives or at least people who came initially from the same regions of their countries of origin as themselves. Werbner (1995) and Anwar (1995) describe some of the ways this was working among people of Pakistani origin living in Greater Manchester in the 1990s. Adherence to a particular faith may be another factor. People who belong to faith communities that are not here in large numbers (Shia Muslims or Zoroastrians, for example) need to live in certain parts of the country if participation in shared worship is not to entail considerable travel.

The relative concentration of people from other communities has left many areas where the overwhelming majority of the population is white British, where residents may even say (though this is rarely the case in fact) that *everyone* is white. Gaine (2005, pp. 6–7) usefully describes three types of areas of this kind:

- Largely white districts within local authorities that have overall substantial minorities of people who are not white British.
- Largely white areas on the periphery of places with substantial numbers of people who are not white British (for example, the Derbyshire Peak

District, which stands between the major conurbations of Greater Manchester and Sheffield/Rotherham).

• Rural areas at some distance from those areas where minority communities are well established.

People living in the first two types of area may, of course, visit nearby city centres or out-of-town shopping precincts fairly often and have some encounters there with people from minorities they rarely meet in their own neighbourhoods. Many rural areas attract tourists and not all of those will be white British. However, the number of black and Asian people resident in Britain who visit rural areas for recreation appears to be still small. This is in spite of the fact that many of those people are themselves from rural areas and, when exchange is facilitated, find they have at least as much in common with white people working in agriculture as they do with their urban neighbours.

The question is sometimes asked whether settings in 'white' areas really need to engage in work related to cultural diversity. After all, they will rarely, perhaps never, have a child who is not white British. If they do, that child may well come from a family whose origin is in Europe, North America, Australia or New Zealand and be fairly at ease with getting to grips with British society. The settings do not, therefore, need to adjust to the different cultural needs of children in the way they might have to do in Leeds or Leicester. They may also argue that there is little point in confusing small children about what is expected of them by letting them know that in some cultures it is polite to eat with your fingers rather than a knife and fork. Better for them to have a simple message with which their minds can grapple easily.

The case for activity around cultural diversity in such areas

There are several reasons for disputing this line of argument:

• It is very rare to find an area where absolutely everyone is white British. Moreover, all the evidence is that suspicion and hostility (including criminal assaults) are most common in areas where black or Asian people are in very small minorities. I grew up in central London in the 1950s and remember the initial responses to immigrants from the Caribbean. At best there was curiosity, which made those people who were the subject of it feel uncomfortable. (One neighbour of mine, a woman from West Africa who had married an English sailor there and then come with him to London, barely left her house for several years because of the way people stared at her.) In many cases there was overt hostility directed at individuals or at whole groups. It was common outside houses where rooms were available to rent to see notices saying

'No Irish, dogs or coloureds here'. The vulnerability of relatively isolated individuals to racist abuse makes it particularly important, not less important, to tackle prejudice in 'white' areas. Such work will be more effective if it takes place before anything that might generate hostility has happened.

- Locations do not necessarily remain 'all white' forever. The semi-rural areas of South Yorkshire, which for many years had substantially white British populations (with some Irish gypsies and travellers passing through on a regular basis), have seen recent arrivals in fairly substantial numbers of Roma gypsies from Eastern Europe, migrant agricultural workers from various parts of the EU and refugees from Black African countries.

- The view that there is no problem because everyone or virtually everyone is white British simplifies the issue by seeing it in (literally) black-and-white terms. In responding to the needs of children, settings have to be alert to the ways that families, even from the same broadly described cultural background may vary among themselves. Each family has to some extent its own culture. Families that are very similar in terms of ethnicity, religion, class, the wider physical environment in which they live and so on, may still vary slightly, but significantly, in what they do about sharing family meals, giving presents, modesty in what they wear about the house, use of television, shared outdoor activities and other matters. These things can be vital when it comes to shaping responses to the child. If a family arrives at a white British setting with brown skins, an Asian form of clothing and talking to each other and their child in Tamil or Farsi, it will be obvious that there could be issues for white British practitioners about understanding their attitudes and behaviour. If the setting cannot find appropriate ways of responding to those obvious differences, then it is likely to be oblivious to more subtle differences of culture.

- All the children in a setting may be white British. This does not mean that those children will never meet and have to cooperate later in life with people who are not white British. If the acquisition of intercultural competence is left until the immediate need for it arises, it will be all the more difficult for people to adapt. The potential for inter-cultural competence has to come before someone's understanding of any other culture.

- The extent to which we have to meet and cooperate with people from radically different cultural backgrounds to our own will depend on where we live and work. It is possible for some people to live their lives with relatively little contact of that sort. However, they operate in a world where economic inter-dependence is growing and where transport and communications technology generate awareness of the scale of diversity across the increasingly inter-dependent world. If public opinion is shaped by misinformation about and suspicion of societies that are culturally different from our own, then governments are likely to make poor decisions about global affairs. We have to educate even those children who may live out their whole lives in largely white British areas of the country in citizenship that takes the whole world into account.

- We can worry too much about the ability of young children to cope with diversity. Every child who starts at school or nursery rapidly becomes aware that things are done differently at home and in the early years setting. She has to learn that her parents do not control everything (as they may seem to do inside the family home) and that different types of behaviour may be expected in different places. In most cases they display considerable sophistication in grasping and adapting to this complexity. Their ability to respond confidently to the potentially confusing variety of the social world depends on how well parents and early years practitioners help them to negotiate this task. Nevertheless, we make a serious mistake if we underestimate their potential ability to cope with differences. For them the fact that different people may eat their meals in different ways can be nothing more than another interesting, if slightly puzzling, aspect of the world.

- It is sometimes argued that it is a mistake to draw attention of children to the issue of differences between cultures. This will only alert them to the fact that relations between people of different cultural backgrounds can be characterized by tension and hostility. It is better if they are kept innocent about this matter as long as possible. This ignores the long-standing evidence that children as young as three are often aware of differences in appearance and of the fact that many in their society ascribe different values to different types of people. More recently research has demonstrated that very young children in Northern Ireland are aware of religious differences and show signs of sectarian feeling, even though outsiders would see few visible differences between people from the two communities (Connolly, 2002). The issue is already a real one for many pre-school children. Their innocence in this respect cannot be taken for granted, is not even probable. The view that it is best to leave well alone also ignores the evidence that drawing the attention of young children to the disabilities of other children and explaining them appears to encourage understanding and a willingness to help rather than prejudice (Lewis, 1995). It seems a reasonable assumption that the same will be true of differences related to cultural background.

- Work in relation to cultural diversity has been developed in response to recognition of the problem of racism. That was the historical origin. However, work on cultural diversity has a much more positive and fundamental educational purpose than that. It is vital to help the growing child understand that life does not depend on the following of established rules. Learning that some people do things differently from 'us' (whoever 'we' are in a particular context) is a valuable part of the education of the growing child and the continuing education of the adult. It need not lead to a de-valuing of our own previous experience. It is certainly not about a kind of supermarket shelf where we can pick up ideas from anywhere and apply them to our own lives on a whim. It is about recognition of the range of possibilities and the way that ideas need to develop. It is central to work with young children, not an add-on demanded by the politically correct in government or the regulatory bodies they establish.

 Exercise

If your setting is one that operates in an overwhelmingly white British area, list some of the ways in which people who are not white British are presented to your children. You should take into account:

- any work undertaken in this area by your setting itself
- any similar work undertaken by other agencies dealing with young children (Sunday School, Children's Library service and so on)
- children's TV programmes
- popular picture story books
- news items on television and in the papers
- any contact with people who are not white British that the area makes possible – including, for example, shops, restaurants and takeaways run by people whose cultural background is not white British
- experience of meeting people on foreign holidays.

Remember that, as you are dealing with young children, your focus should be on images rather than what may be said in writing.

You may not know much about some of the children's experiences. For example, your opportunities to watch young children's television may be very limited if you are in full-time work in a day care setting (childminders can have an advantage in this respect). You may need to find out a bit more about what is going on in the lives of the children with whom you are working.

What images are generated by this collection of influences? Are there any systematic distortions of reality in what is presented?

If there are systematic distortions, what steps can be taken to correct them?

Activity with children

Activities with children that can be undertaken to help them appreciate the reality of cultural diversity were discussed in Chapter 5. What is said there is as relevant to the setting in the overwhelmingly white British area as it is to settings in areas where many of the children may come from other cultural backgrounds. However, the one opportunity that may be missing for the setting operating in the kind of area discussed here is the opportunity for children to *interact* with children and adults from different cultural backgrounds. Learning about aspects of other cultures without encountering those who have such backgrounds can easily leave those cultures seeming to be merely exotic – interesting, but of little relevance. This, in turn, can reinforce rather than undermine certain types of prejudice.

There are things that can be done about this:

- Many of the things that have already been said about activities with children are especially relevant in the context of this kind of setting: the importance of not offering an overly 'traditional' view of Asian or African societies, the need to make connections with the everyday life of the children, the usefulness of involving people from the community who have personal connections with other cultures.
- Even if children have not encountered people from other cultural backgrounds where they live, they may well have done so on holiday. Build on the opportunities this fact offers. Use circle time to discuss their experience of seeing people in different types of clothing, eating different types of food, seeing writing in non-Western scripts. Some preparation is likely to be needed. Find out where children have been before initiating any discussion and consider whether any material resources will aid the learning you plan to help them develop.
- Chapter 4 spoke about twinning arrangements between settings in different countries. Such arrangements are still comparatively rare and usually involve face-to-face contact between practitioners rather than children or their parents. More could be done to extend this type of arrangement and to involve families using the service. The key thing here is that 'twinning' need not be confined to contact between settings in different countries. If a setting in an area that was overwhelmingly white British linked up with a setting that had large numbers of children who were not white British, the distances involved might be small and manageable. The two settings might even be in the same local authority. This is something with which Local Authority Early Years services or local branches of organizations such as the PLA and the National Day Nurseries Association (NDNA) should be able to help.
- The Internet offers those children old enough to have reasonably developed language skills the opportunity to encounter children from

other countries. It appears from the evidence that an overwhelming majority of older children and young adults now make regular use of social networking sites. Parents are often anxious about this and have some reason for their anxiety. There is as a result of their concerns a growing market for those sites where children and young people can exchange information and ideas but with safeguards. These safeguards include the initial access being managed by trusted adults, such as teachers, and built-in systems for preventing – or at worst responding rapidly to – abusive or otherwise inappropriate messages. Intuitive Media is one of the leading companies in this field. Their existing services are designed for children of five and over. I am not aware of any company that has tried to promote a similar service for children of 3–5 years. It is, however, evident that very young children, assisted by adults in the writing and reading of messages, could make use of a chat room designed explicitly for them. This is something that might well develop in the near future.

 Exercise

Draw up an action plan for establishing a twinning arrangement between your setting and one in a foreign country.

What will be the positive outcomes you hope to see from any twinning arrangement? What can be achieved by this kind of arrangement that could not be easily achieved by any other means?

What considerations will lead you to select the country or the setting with which to twin?

Examples might include the convenience of relatively short travel between your setting and its potential twin, the existence of particular opportunities to make contact, the fact that your town or village is already twinned with a similar area abroad so that contact with one of its early years settings can be facilitated by those responsible for the overall twinning arrangement, the ability of any of the staff or parents to speak the language of a foreign setting, the learning opportunities created by twinning with a setting in a very different country, the learning opportunities created by twinning with a setting in a country that is similar to ours.

(Continued)

(Continued)

Do you see contact between your setting and its twin as something mainly for the practitioners or as something that would also involve parents and children?

How will you set about identifying a suitable setting with which to twin? How will you establish contact? Will you, for example, use another organization to help you set up the initial communications? Which agency will this be?

Can you construct a timeframe within which the contact with the potential twin will be established and set going?

How will you evaluate the usefulness of any arrangement you manage to establish and what monitoring or review arrangements will you set up to ensure that evaluation happens?

 Summary

Cultural diversity (together with the closely associated issue of global citizenship) is as relevant to the 'all white' setting as it is to those settings where children who are not white British are to be found, perhaps even constitute the majority. A good deal can be done in this field beyond the celebration of one or two of the more colourful and lively festivals from abroad.

Further reading 📖

One of the few books that addresses the specific issue with which this chapter has been concerned is *Another Spanner in the Works: Challenging Prejudice and Racism in Mainly White Schools* by Knowles and Ridley (2005). The ideas in their book come largely from experience of work in Cumbria.

8

The Setting that is Not Primarily White British

This chapter:

> Points to the fact that there is an increasing number of settings where the majority of practitioners and families are not white British

> Asks how this should affect their responses to the issue of cultural diversity

> Asks in particular whether there are any steps such a setting needs to take to familiarize its children with white British culture

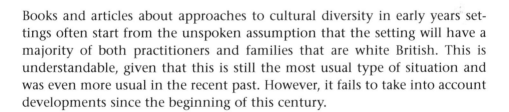

> Considers the situation of white British children when they are in the minority in a setting

Books and articles about approaches to cultural diversity in early years settings often start from the unspoken assumption that the setting will have a majority of both practitioners and families that are white British. This is understandable, given that this is still the most usual type of situation and was even more usual in the recent past. However, it fails to take into account developments since the beginning of this century.

As was said in the previous chapter, those communities that are not white British are concentrated to a considerable extent in certain urban areas. As a result, a number of schools have had large numbers of children who are not white British since the 1980s and their situation has received attention since that period. Even before that time Catholic schools in the major cities in the 1940s, 1950s and 1960s often had children from a wide range of national backgrounds, although a majority of these were white – the children of immigrants and refugees from the Irish Republic, Italy, Poland, Malta and other parts of Europe.

There was a number of schools with significant numbers of children from black and minority ethnic communities some time before there were many early years settings outside the schools system that did so. This is partly because we have had universal schooling for some time, but the growth in early years provision has been more recent. That growth had its beginnings in the 1970s, but escalated after the Labour Party won power in the general election of 1997 and introduced its National Childcare Strategy. Demand for childcare and early education grew in the period that followed, partly as a result of specific government policies designed to facilitate the development of such services, partly as a result of wider social and economic changes. The recession that began towards the end of 2008 interrupted the pattern of constant growth. In particular, it led to a drop in demand for after-school care. At the time this book was being written (in the summer of 2009) it was too soon to judge whether the interruption to expansion would become entrenched or whether it was a mere hiccup. It was also too soon to tell what impact any change of government arising from the general election of 2010 would have on early years services or the issue of cultural diversity. The expansion that had already been achieved had its impact on the customer profile for early years provision. Sure Start Children's Centres and community-run nurseries were developed in increasing numbers in those areas where substantial numbers of people were not white British. Inevitably, a small but significant number of settings came to be substantially multicultural in their composition and to have a minority, sometimes a very small minority, of white British families among their users.

At the same time there were changes in the early years workforce. For a long time the number of black and Asian practitioners in the early years field has failed to match the percentage of such people in the overall population of working age. The difficulties such people may have had in the school system provide only part of the explanation for this, since related vocational spheres have not been affected in the same way. A few years ago the most casual examination of the composition of student groups on different courses in Further Education Colleges in the major English cities would have shown a stark contrast. Many, often a majority, of those studying health and social care were black or Asian. Those studying for courses leading to qualifications issued by the Council for Awards in Children's Care and Education (CACHE) had few such students. Where they were found students of Afro-Caribbean origin outnumbered those of Asian origin. The reasons for this are unclear. The higher prestige of nursing or even social care posts over what was then usually described as nursery nursing might provide part of the explanation. Reservations in some South Asian communities about the care of children by people other than close relatives might provide another. Whatever the reason, the majority of early years practitioners were white British, even in those settings where the many of the user families were not.

This situation appears to be changing. In 2002 the Government launched an initiative to recruit more men, older people, people with disabilities and people from black and minority ethnic communities into early years work. This has probably had some impact. However, the measures taken by the Government were relatively small in scale and priority seems to have been given to the recruitment of men rather than any of the other groups identified in the initial policy statements. Some Local Authorities gave the recruitment of people from black and ethnic minority communities particular attention, initiating projects that were designed to deal with the issue. Kirklees is one of the Local Authorities whose activity in this respect has been documented (Curnow & Evans, 2004). Another is Aberdeen (Richards, 2006). To some extent the increase in the number of practitioners from black and Asian communities has probably been a self-reinforcing process. As the numbers grew it became clearer that a black or Asian practitioner need not find herself on her own in an overwhelmingly white staff group. This would presumably have made the situation more comfortable for many. It is difficult to judge how much progress is being made. The most recent figures available at the time of writing, those included in the 2007 survey of early years providers, suggest that things are moving in the right direction (Nicholson, et al., 2008, pp. 5, 82–3). However, the usefulness of the data is limited by the fact that only childminders and maintained schools were included and that some providers did not offer information on the ethnicity of their staff. The percentage of people from black and minority ethnic communities in the early years workforce still appears to be less than might be expected from the proportion such people make up of the total working-age population, but change is happening. Thus early years settings where a majority of users are not white British are increasingly likely to have a majority of the practitioners who are not white British.

The 'cultural mix' in settings where a majority are not white British can be very wide. Even if an early years unit is promoted by a faith-based organization, it may take children from several different backgrounds. A pre-school or crèche established within an Islamic centre may be attractive only to Muslim families. It may still take children of many different nationalities, including children of mature overseas students at local universities or Muslim refugees from the Balkans. The Krishna Avanti Nursery in North London, which forms part of the first Hindu faith-based school in England, takes pride in its general approach to cultural diversity and in the fact that its children are not taken exclusively from the Indian community. This is partly because it is associated with a branch of Hinduism that has been particularly successful in attracting Anglo-Saxon converts across the world. Most of the settings that have a majority of users who are not white British are not associated with particular religions or nationalities. In meeting the needs of the neighbourhoods in which they are based, they cater for people from many different communities. Indeed, this 'mix' may be one of the features that makes them particularly attractive to some parent users.

Responses to cultural diversity

Given that we now have a growing number of settings where the majority of practitioners and users are not white British, it can be asked how this influences their approach to the issue of cultural diversity.

One simple answer is that the issue is not affected at all. Such settings are, after all, governed by the same curriculum documents and other statements of official policy as are all the rest. There are, however, some respects in which their situation differs from that of settings where the majority of staff and users are white British.

There will be several advantages:

- The fact that the setting itself is multicultural in make-up will probably render it easier to address the issue of cultural diversity. The varieties of appearance, clothing, languages and scripts among the families using the centre will underline the fact that we live in a society and on a planet with many different cultures and beliefs before anyone does anything to make that point. There will be less risk that activity in the field of cultural diversity will feel like an intrusion on normality or a move away from daily activity.
- The children attending are more likely to find the world they know at home reflected in day-to-day activity at the setting. This is important. Although even young children display considerable adaptability in coping with the differences between home and setting, it can be a source of initial disorientation if the differences are too striking.
- There may be easier access to resources of various kinds. Locally-owned shops may sell many of the things that other settings have to search for at specialist outlets or resource centres – things such as non-Western clothing for children, implements for cooking and eating, musical instruments, objects of religious significance and picture story-books related to different cultural backgrounds. Parents who have specialist skills to bring (in the preparation of non-British foods, craft work or arrangements for the celebration of festivals) should find it easier to offer to do so.

- Practitioners may find it easier to make use of their understanding of their own cultural backgrounds in a setting where the staff group is representative of several cultures than they would in settings where the rest of the staff are white. The position of being the single 'representative' of or even the 'expert' about one's own cultural background can be an uncomfortable one.

There are some problematic issues that can arise:

- The fact that all or most of the families using a setting are not white British does not mean that they will be a homogenous group. There can still be some children who do not belong to the majority and they may be at risk of having their needs overlooked or their cultures not fully reflected.
- In particular, a given locality may experience tensions between different communities and these can have an impact on the atmosphere within a setting. Armed conflict continues to be a feature of our world. It is quite possible for children to be together in a setting when in parts of the world from which their families originally came members of their different communities are engaged in bitter struggles. This can be an opportunity to help towards greater understanding. Taking such an opportunity requires sensitivity and skill. The potential for damage will also be there – at least initially. Even in the absence of situations of that kind, there may be times when parents and practitioners bring reservations about other cultures to the setting. It may provide the first context in which Christians have met Muslims, Catholics have met Evangelical Christians, Sunni have met Shia.
- The child that spends some of her pre-school years in a very multicultural setting can have a great advantage. In some circumstances it can make the transition to primary school all the greater a shock. In a neighbourhood that is very multicultural the local primary school may reflect that fact even more effectively than the pre-school, nursery or children's centre. However, it is also possible that a child will move from a setting where multiculturalism is an integral part of what happens to a school where this is much less the case. This may happen especially to families where parents choose to send their children to church schools. The potential disturbance to the child should not be under-estimated, and this may be one particular reason for focusing on the process of transition.

Issues such as these do not outweigh the many advantages of the multi-cultural setting. They certainly provide no case for the argument made by some that black and minority ethnic communities should be dispersed with one consequence among others being that no early years setting would exist that did not have a majority of white British children and staff. The issues raised above simply demonstrate what might have been expected – that the need to think through activity around cultural diversity remains even in a multicultural setting. One such issue is that of what the setting is to make of white British culture (or whichever local variant of that culture applies in a particular place).

Responding to white British culture

The composition of both the staff and user groups in a setting that is located in a vividly multicultural area may make it easier to address some issues of cultural diversity. Do they make it more difficult to address the question of British culture?

Some assume that it is unlikely that a difficulty will arise. Children may live in a neighbourhood where many types of shops offer for sale clothing, foodstuffs and other everyday items that have their origins outside the UK. There may be a mosque or gudwara on the corner and the Christian church may belong to a Pentecostalist body of Caribbean or African origin rather than one of the longer-established denominations. Nevertheless, those children will probably go home to watch television programmes that reflect white culture more than any others. The shops and restaurants they encounter in the city centre will similarly reflect the majority culture. Comics and story-books will often do the same. white British culture is for better or worse all around them. Will they not just pick it up by an unplanned process of familiarization? Is any special effort required? Is there not a danger that such an effort would entail pressure to conform more closely to the dominant culture and its norms?

Clearly, it is true that children can learn a lot about white British culture from the world around them. It is also true that some approaches to explaining it could take us back to the situation where there was enormous pressure on people to adopt the culture of the dominant majority and leave behind the traditions from which their families came. (The problem was, of course, the pressure and the reactions it could sometimes cause. Many people coming to this country will be anxious to establish a British aspect to their identity in order to fit in or because there are aspects of the local culture they find attractive.) However, there are reasons for thinking that a particular effort to help children understand white British culture would be valuable:

- Children will need to grow up and survive, hopefully flourish, in a society where the mix of cultural influences will include those of the white as well as the Afro-Caribbean and Asian worlds. In fact, white British culture will continue for the foreseeable future to have a uniquely significant place. It may be an objective of policy that public institutions become more accessible in every sense to people who are not white British. It remains true that the origins of many of those institutions lie in the history of the peoples that in the course of early medieval times came to make up the population of the countries of the United Kingdom. The basis for understanding them has to be built during the foundation stage.

- White British culture did not develop in isolation or even within the confines of Western Europe. So much of it has been influenced from further abroad. The custom of drinking tea or coffee is an obvious and simple example. Much of the technology that fuelled the United Kingdom's rise to power in the period from the Tudors to Queen Victoria had its origins in the Far East. We need to find ways of presenting white British culture as an integral part of global history rather than as something quite separate from other cultures in the world. The start has to be made in this at the foundation stage. Telling young children the origin of many of the things they will encounter is one of the ways of doing this.

- The cultural background of white British people in an area may be a particular one and may not be reflected adequately in the mass media. This may be partly a matter of people who are white being themselves excluded from full participation in what is seen as their own culture because of financial disadvantage or for some other reason. It may also be a matter of more local variants on white British culture not being reflected in the representations of white British culture on television and elsewhere. Regional variations in accent and behaviour are often treated as a subject for comedy rather than as diversity to be taken seriously. Dialect poetry is usually seen as merely quaint in this country (it is much more standard in Germany, for example). Particular types of music or food may be very specifically local and under threat from a homogenous national food industry. This is as much an issue as the devaluing of cultures that have their origin outside the United Kingdom.

- There are dangers if appreciation of white British culture is not fostered in settings where other cultures have a stronger voice. We are emerging to a considerable extent from the period in which all cultures other than European, and in particular English, culture were seen as irretrievably inferior. As that emergence takes place, many of the risks that were seen at one time to be entailed in the celebration of white British culture should begin to disappear. There is a need to rescue that culture from the distorting impact of the assumption of its superiority. This will entail significant modification of it, but it is such a modification that is required rather than rejection. There is a particular element to this in Northern Ireland. There a very live and problematic question is that of how the popular culture of the Unionist community (aspects of which are no longer shared by most of the rest of the United Kingdom) can be detached from the sense of superiority to and fear of Catholic Nationalists without simply disappearing altogether.

If white British culture is to be celebrated, how is this to be done? What exactly is it that would be celebrated? Settings can celebrate Christmas and Easter as they celebrate certain other festivals. Even this is not a simple matter. In this country the marking of those festivals is now largely a matter of family activity rather than community celebration. The festivals may be rendered visible by the efforts of supermarkets and other shops to sell associated products. The celebration remains largely a private affair. How can this be reflected in the setting? Many aspects of white British culture are associated with particular parts of the United Kingdom even if they are familiar to people in the other parts. Cornish pasties and bagpipe music are just two examples. Traditional cultural activity may have no place in the outlook of most British people. Morris dancing is as far from the lives of most of the English as Middle Eastern Debkeh dancing and certainly more remote from the experience of many than Reggae.

In fact, one of the advantages of the attempt by a setting to reflect white British culture is that it will underline just how complex and problematic the concept of culture is and how much distortion can arise when the attempt is made to reflect a cultural background by pinning it down to a specific festival or one or two other aspects. Black and Asian practitioners are often asked by white colleagues to give advice on the celebration of their cultures. It would make for an interesting discussion if they were to ask their white British colleagues to tell them the best way to reflect and celebrate white British culture.

 Exercise

Take the name of the patron saint of the part of the United Kingdom to which you belong (St George, St Andrew, St David or St Patrick).

Try writing down what that saint's day means to you.

You can do this on your own or get a group discussion going on the issue or ask members of a group to each write about 250 words on that topic and then bring them together to compare the results.

The situation is likely to be different depending on the part of the United Kingdom in which you live. It may be at its simplest in Scotland and Wales where the national saints are straightforward emblems of national identity, although not necessarily significant emblems to everyone. It may be at its most complicated in Northern Ireland because St Patrick is also an important icon of the Republic. It is English people who may have the greatest difficulty. Many of them will not have the remotest idea who St George was and may resort to the Internet or some other source to find out. There will be exceptions. St George's Day is still significant to adults who are involved in the scout movement, which accords it some importance. It can also be a feature of public celebration in some rural areas. People coming from abroad – particularly from countries that were part of the former British Empire – often find it difficult to understand the fact that the nearest thing to an English National Day is not celebrated in the way they would expect.

Does your setting mark your national saint's day in some way? If so, why? If it does not, would you consider doing so? Again, what would be the reason for this decision?

If there is some aspect of British culture that you want to celebrate in your setting, you should bring to it all the questions you would bring to the decision to celebrate any other culture. Among those questions are:

- Why are we doing this?
- How will this activity link with aspects of the curriculum?
- Will we need specialist help or resources to do it?

These are questions as much for a setting where most of the practitioners and users are black or Asian and which is thinking of undertaking a particular activity to celebrate white British culture as it is for a setting where most people who are white British are thinking about an activity around a particular religious festival or music or craft work from another cultural background.

Rather than trying to think how white British culture could be best represented, try the real experts and ask the children. Are there things going on around them that they do not understand? Are there aspects of white British life of which they speak dismissively or with some element of fear? Are there things about white British culture they find interesting, but from which they feel excluded in some way? Listening to the children will tell you more about the aspects of white British culture that should be brought into the work in the setting than any source material on that culture is likely to do.

Exercise

Use circle time or meal time to discuss with the children any forth-coming event that can be seen as particularly related to white British culture. It may be something happening in their neigh-bourhood (such as a bonfire on Firework Night) or something they have seen on television (such as the State Opening of Parliament).

What is their understanding of this event and its significance? *(Don't worry too much if they get some of the facts wrong. The real issue here is their perception of what is happening.)* Are they excited about it? Does anything about it worry them? Are they completely uninterested, seeing it as something outside their own world?

Can any white British child who is there help to explain things, per-haps by talking about what her family will do during the event?

Ask them whether they would like to do anything in the setting to celebrate the event. (It is important before launching on this kind of discussion to have some idea of what might be possible, includ-ing access to relevant resources.)

If the activity goes ahead, consider how it can be part of the regular annual planning at the setting.

The inclusion of children who are white British

Potential barriers to inclusion may arise whenever a child is in a situation that is different from that of the majority in the setting. This is as true of the white British child in the setting where the great majority of children are not white British as it is of the black or Asian child in the setting where most other children are white.

There may be some tendency to overlook this because the focus has quite naturally been on the difficulties faced by many black and Asian children when they are in the minority. There will also be people who are aware that the fears expressed on behalf of white children who find themselves in a minority at school or in early years settings are often a reflection of racist hostility to anything that gives a measure of power and influence to people from black and minority ethnic communities. Public statements by teachers and others about the educational disadvantages of white children who were in schools where many children were Asians formed an important part of the increasing tensions in Bradford and other places that led to street violence in the 1980s. Given that kind of history, people may be wary of highlighting the situation of white children in situations where they are in the minority for fear of misunderstanding or exploitation of what is said by organizations of the far right.

It also has to be born in mind that the parents of the white children themselves will differ in their perception of this situation. In some cases such children will be there because their parents have made a clear decision that they want to live in an area where people come from many different backgrounds and for their child to attend a setting that reflects that characteristic of the locality. In other cases the parents may have little choice of which setting they should use and feel some discomfort about putting their child in a situation where she is part of a minority. Factors like this will obviously influence the child's ability to cope with the situation.

Practitioners need to be alert to the possibility of something going wrong rather than make assumptions that this will or will not happen. It should be evident if a child is unhappy or lacks confidence in the setting. The reasons for this need to be explored. They may have nothing to do with her minority status. If they are related to that fact, the precise nature of the barrier still needs to be understood before an effective response is possible.

- Is the child aware of any discomfort on the part of her parents or members of her wider family that she is attending such a setting? Discussion with the parents will be crucial in such a situation. The child can also be reassured to know how glad the practitioners are to have her there.
- Is she anxious because this is the first time she has encountered children who look very different from her? To be in a minority is always potentially disturbing. Many people whose family origins lie outside this country have had that experience. In a particular situation it can be the experience of a white British child. The setting should already have activities designed to help children develop pride in their individual identities and to ensure that they are not excluded in any way from the wider group. If it does, it is important to make sure that she is fully included in such activity.
- Is she cut out from some socializing with her peers because English is not the language being used by many of the children when talking among themselves? They can be engaged in talking to her in English and can help her by explaining a few phrases at least in their own language.
- Does she lack some other skill that many of the children have, such as dealing with non-Western dress or food? If so, the other children can be engaged in helping her develop her ability at those tasks.

- Is she being affected by the pride the other children take in something else they have in common (such as their religion) which the white child does not share with the majority? If so, there is a need to review what the setting is doing to enhance respect for other people's beliefs.
- Is the child now in a position where she is regarded as outside the crowd, a position that is to some extent self-reinforcing and no longer depends on the aspect of her situation that led to initial isolation? If so, a technique such as the use of a persona doll at circle time may help the other children to understand and empathise with her feelings.

All this will be familiar stuff. The techniques for overcoming barriers to inclusion are already well known. There is some risk that practitioners will not realize that a white child feels excluded simply because the problem (in so far as it has a racial aspect) is usually seen as a difficulty facing children from black and minority ethnic communities. If that happens, steps must be taken to improve practice in that respect. Having said that, I would repeat what I said earlier in this book – that my experience suggests to me that settings that are strongly multicultural in their composition are particularly good at fostering mutual understanding and sympathetic action among the children.

 Summary

This chapter has been in many ways the most exploratory in the book. The number of settings where the majority of practitioners and families are not white British is still a small one and, as a result, the specifics of their situation have not received attention. I have outlined a few issues. The development of effective practice in this kind of situation will depend to a large extent on the initiative and imagination of practitioners in such settings.

Further reading

It is because this chapter deals with an issue that has received scant attention so far that there are no obvious texts to recommend.

Conclusion

The commitment to the celebration of cultural diversity over the past thirty years or so has produced some excellent practice in early years settings as in other spheres of public service. There have also been some ham-fisted interventions and decisions that have brought the whole commitment into disrepute. When respect for other people's culture becomes timidity it ceases to be respect. Those who back away from their duty to protect children or vulnerable adults for fear that their intervention will be seen as racist are setting some people up as beyond the boundaries of the law and avoiding real engagement in a way that is itself racist. Those who try to ban the English flag or pictures of Santa Claus on the grounds it will offend minorities ascribe a failure of understanding and a lack of respect for others to those minorities in a way that is itself offensive.

Bad practice and ill-advised interventions such as those just mentioned have helped to generate over-generalized criticism of the commitment to intercultural dialogue. They help explain the unthinking assertions that multiculturalism is a failure or – worse – a menace. And while there has been good practice, there has also been mediocre practice that does not do enough to offset prejudice. The celebration of certain festivals and other gestures are not to be condemned, but they can remain mere gestures that do too little to help children cope with the multicultural world they are entering.

Those who condemn all manifestations of multiculturalism are running away from the world in which we live, a world of increasing contact between societies, economic inter-dependence and migration. This is not a new situation. Globalization began when the first clans left Africa to migrate over the Earth's surface before the dawn of recorded history. Contact between societies with different cultures has been happening for centuries. It began to grow ever more rapidly from the 16th century onwards. Technological advance will only serve to increase the scale and consequences. At the same time people all over the world are looking for frameworks in which to live that go beyond the mechanisms of the market place. Some of the manifestations of this may be unwelcome. It often takes the form of ideologically-driven strict adherence to local traditions, and those traditions can entail the unjust subordination of many. Nevertheless, the search for local identity and cultural diversity are both driven as well as opposed by globalization.

We cannot cope with these developments by:

- attempting to resurrect a traditional British culture, the features of which will be matters of controversy even among those who are white British
- wholesale commitment to a single global culture based exclusively on one version of what technological modernization entails
or
- the establishment of quite separate cultures living side by side, but with minimum communication between themselves even if open hostility is avoided.

All those three solutions to the problem of cultural diversity break down because they are all based on the idea that 'cultures' are fixed entities with clear and distinct boundaries. The contrary is the case. We always need cultural devices in order to cooperate. Shared sentiments, mutually comprehensible gestures, key icons, rules of behaviour – all these things are 'cultural' and also essential to real cooperation and communication, which cannot happen without them. However, cultures are constantly in interaction with each other and changing as a result. This has nearly always been the case. Some very isolated, small societies may have avoided outside influences and remained unchanged as a result for centuries. That was never the normal situation, and is becoming increasingly rare. Cultural diversity and the changes that result from it have become an unavoidable aspect of our lives.

This is not just something that circumstance forces us to accept. It is something to be welcomed. The attempt to understand other people who do not share the assumptions and signs that go with our culture (whichever culture that is) takes us into a new realm of understanding. It is not just the acquisition of new ideas that is at stake. It is a new sensitivity to others – something that is essential if the human species is going to survive the changes that its ingenuity has engendered.

It is in this slightly daunting context that work on cultural diversity in early years settings has to be seen. One of the great discoveries that nearly all children make in their early years is the discovery that people see things from different perspectives and that we need to understand what those perspectives are to have effective relationships with them. The early years setting is a particularly important context for opening up minds to the reality of cultural diversity. This is not just because it is important to take action against prejudice at the earliest possible stage. It is because it is in the period that lies approximately between the third and sixth birthday that children develop the understanding that lies behind all of their ability to cooperate with others. This is, therefore, the best time to help them learn how to cooperate across potential cultural barriers.

This is why the principal resource for work on cultural diversity cannot be explanations of what various religions believe or various artefacts or stories that have their origins outside white British culture. It must be in the ability of early years practitioners to understand how young children learn and what are the best ways of supporting them in that.

It also depends on the ability of practitioners to reach intelligently across cultural boundaries for themselves. If they are merely making gestures because this is what is required in the curriculum guidance, the children will spot the artificiality of the exercise and draw their own conclusions.

That ability does not come easily and can have costs. If you attempt real communication and cooperation with people whose cultural backgrounds are different from your own, then sooner or later you will get it wrong and tread on someone's metaphorical toes. And you will not always be lucky enough to do this to someone who has the perception and generosity to forgive you for it easily. This is as much a problem for someone from a minority community as it is for those who are white British.

We have one source of encouragement in this. Next time you see a recently born child, study the expression on her face. There are likely to be signs of caution, but the dominant feature will be an intense curiosity, an eagerness to learn. Perhaps before we devote time to working out what we need to teach children about the diversity of the human race, we should spend a moment wondering what we have to learn from them.

Appendix I: Resources and Further Reading

Publications for practitioners

The items for further reading recommended at the end of Chapter 5 are useful starting points for ideas on activities:

> Brightwell & Fidgin (2005) *To Begin At The Beginning*
> Garvey, Giffin & Unwin (2007) *Developing Global Learners*
> *The Child's Eye* two-DVD set on *Festivals*

Another book that provides ideas on activities with small children is:

> Milord (1992) *Hands Around the World*

However, the fact that it was published a while ago in the US may make it difficult to locate a copy.

I would also recommend:

> Taylor (2006) *Start With a Difference*

This has the interesting feature of speaking from the standpoint of an ethnic minority.

There are many books offering information on different religions.

> Cole (1991) *Five World Faiths* offers a helpful digest of information about the five major world religions.
> Alexander (ed.) (1994) *The World's Religions* is particularly comprehensive.
> Bowker (2006) *World Religions* is a more recent book and one that is lavishly illustrated.

There are books on this subject that are aimed at young children. For the most part these have children at Key Stages One and Two in mind, but they can also be helpful for work by practitioners with younger children. One good example is provided by the books in the Red Rainbow Religion collection published by Evans Brothers in London, each with a similar title (*My Sikh Faith, My Muslim Faith* and so on).

A good introduction to the story of immigration to the United Kingdom is offered by:

Winder (2005) *Bloody Foreigners: The Story of Immigration to Britain*

The history of Islam in the United Kingdom is covered in:

Ansari (2004) *'The Infidel Within': Muslims in Britain Since 1800*

A useful overall guide to cultural diversity is provided by:

Johnson (2003) *The Cultural Diversity Guide*

There are a few books that deal with the education of children from specific minority communities. Examples include:

Kahin (1997) *Educating Somali Children in Britain*
Tyler (2005) *Traveller Education*. This includes one chapter on improving access to early education for traveller children and another describing resources that can be used at the Foundation Stage and Key Stage One.

Novels

Novels often provide a good route into beginning to understand things from the perspective of someone whose cultural background is different from your own. Among the many novels dealing with the experiences of people from minority communities in this country are:

Monica Ali (2003) *Brick Lane*
Buchi Emecheta (1974) *Second-Class Citizen*
Andrea Levy (2004) *Small Island*
Marina Lewycka (2007) *Two Caravans*
Meera Syal (1999) *Life Isn't All Ha-ha, He-he*

Novels, such as those mentioned above, that give some idea of the experience of living in this country as a member of an ethnic minority tend to be about the experiences of adults and rarely concentrate on the experiences of young children or those caring for them. This limits their value in this context to some extent. They still provide a useful way of helping white British people to understand their experiences.

Books for children

The number of books suitable for use with children at Foundation Stage and Key Stage One is growing all the time. What follows is just a selection.

Some of the resource centres that are named later will be able to offer assistance with making choices.

There are many picture story-books that can be recommended. Among those that can be recommended are:

Bernard Ashley (1992) *Cleversticks*
Eileen Browne (2000) *Handa's Surprise*
Niki Daly (2000) *Jamela's Dress*
Ruth Davies (2006) *Telling Stories*
Barbara Joosse (2005) *Papa, Do You Love Me?*
David Mills & Derek Brazell (1999) *Lima's Red Hot Chilli*
Sandhya Rao (2006) *My Mother's Sari*
Na,imh bint Robert & Nilesh Mistry (2002) *The Swirling Hijaab*

Several of these are already well known, reflecting the fact that they are very engaging and based on a clear understanding of what young children need from stories. Some of them now have associated games, posters or Big Book versions (particularly useful for story-telling with groups of more than two children). The book by Ruth Davies includes stories from different countries and also has advice on story-telling and on activities that can be built on the foundation of those stories.

The BBC website has a section on stories from around the world for young children: www.bbc.co.uk/cbeebies/storycircle/worldstories

There are some good collections of nursery rhymes from around the world that you can add to the standard ones that are probably already in use in your setting:

Asian Nursery Rhymes (by Itchykadana) in Bengali, Gujerati, Panjabi and Urdu in the original versions and English translations, published by Mantra in 1996. Unfortunately, this book is out of print, but you may be able to track down a copy in a public library.
Floella Benjamin (1995) *Skip Across the Ocean*

As in the case of different religions, there were until fairly recently few non-fiction books addressing issues related to other aspects of cultural diversity and aimed at pre-school children, although it was often possible with careful planning to make use of books aimed at primary school children. There are now more of these.

A particularly good example is:

Beatrice Hollyer (1999) *Wake Up, World! A Day in the Life of Children Around the World*. It features children from the UK, the US, Brazil, Russia, Vietnam,

Australia and India. The fact that it presents children from both 'developed' and 'developing' countries is a particularly strong aspect, subverting the notion that cultural diversity is about how 'we' look at Asia, Africa and Latin America. The photographs are excellent. There is also a photo-activity pack *Your World, My World* compiled by Teresa Garlake and published in 2001 by Oxfam that is based on the book.

Other examples include:

Emma Brownjohn (2002) *All Kinds of Bodies*. This is part of a series with similar titles *'All Kinds of …'*. The whole series can be recommended.
Lisa Bruce & Stephen Waterhouse (2001) *Engines, Engines* is a counting rhyme in an Indian setting.
Lisa Easterling (2007) *Our Global Community Games*
Cindy Gainer (1998) *I'm Like You, You're Like Me* is a picture book celebrating similarities and differences between children around the world. The same author has also published a guide with helpful advice to adults on how to talk about the book with children and design follow-up activities.
Beatrice Hollyer (2004) *Let's Eat* is about food enjoyed by children from five different countries.
Thando McLaren (2005) *My Day, My Way* gives accounts of a day in the life of children from four different countries.
Catherine McNamara (2003) *Nii Kwei's Day* describes a day in the life of a Ghanaian boy told in photographs; it has the advantage that this is a story about an African living in a modern city.
Ifeoma Onyefulu (2000) *Ebele's Favourite* is about children's games in Nigeria, some of which have equivalents in British games.
Kate Petty (2007) *Around the World Hair* describes different hairstyles around the world.
Jo Readman & Ley Honor Roberts (2004) *The World Came to My Place Today* about the origins in other countries of many everyday products; it is a good basis for activities.
Gwenyth Swain (1999) *Eating*, describes different types of food eaten in different countries.
Melanie Walsh (2004) *My World, Your World* is an excellent book for illustrating differences and similarities in the lives of children from around the world.

Music

Most of the larger CD shops will have sections on so-called 'world' music. Many of the CDs available are produced by the World Music Network, which is associated with the Rough Guides to travel: www.worldmusic.net

The principal company offering music from around the world for young children is the American firm Putumayo: www.putumayo.com

Posters

Some posters come as part of the package with picture story-books along with other materials. One example is offered by the posters that accompany the two-DVD set on festivals by Child's Eye Media.

Probably the most widely used poster is *Hello* published by Mantra. It presents greetings in a range of languages.

Other posters that can be recommended include:

> *Everyone Smiles in the Same Language* from Trend Enterprises
> *Friendship Posters*, set of six in the MILK collection published by
> Festival Shop (www.festivalshop.co.uk)

Sources of advice and resources

There is a number of development education centres across the country (not all of them using that title). Your nearest one will be able to provide you with advice and access to resources. They vary among themselves in the extent to which they cater specifically for the needs of practitioners working in early years settings, but even those that do less in this field than some others should still prove a useful source of assistance.

You can find your nearest centre from the following national organizations:

> Development Education Association (England) – www.dea.org.uk
> International Development Association of Scotland (IDEAS) – www.
> ideas-forum.org.uk
> Cyfanfyd (Wales) – www.cynfanfyd.org.uk
> Centre for Global Education (Northern Ireland) – info@centreforglobal
> education.com

Other organizations where resources can be found include:

> Articles of Faith (Bury, Lancashire, supplies artefacts relating to major
> world religions) – www.articlesoffaith.co.uk
> Books & More (Bradford, supplies books and other resources relating to
> cultural diversity and world religions and black history covering all

areas of the curriculum at primary and secondary levels) – www.books-and-more.co.uk

Eduzone (London, general educational suppliers whose resources include ones particularly relevant to cultural diversity) – www.eduzone.co.uk

The Parrotfish Company (Maldon, Essex, offers a wide range of resources on the subject matter covered in this book) – enquiries@parrotfish.co.uk

Primary Colours (Huddersfield-based organization that provides a number of services, including teachers' packs and consultancy arrangements related to cultural diversity. Possibly their most original contribution lies in the interactive theatrical events they put on in schools and elsewhere. Much of their material is intended for older primary school children, but they do offer services related to Foundation Stage and KS1 as well) – www.primarycolours.net

Soma Books Ltd (London, specializes in materials from India) – crafts@somabooks.co.uk

Starbeck Educational Resources (Ripon, North Yorkshire) – www.starbeck. com

Sterns (London, source for world music on CD and DVD) – www.sternsmusic. co

TTS Group Ltd (Kirkby-in-Ashfield, Nottinghamshire, educational suppliers with stock designed for early years) – www.tts-shopping.com

Chapter 3 made reference to products available from Simulation Training Systems. Their website is www.stsintl.com Their postal address is PO Box 910, Del Mar, CA 92014, US.

You should also be able to look to the ethnic minority education service in your Local Authority for advice and possibly for access to resources.

Appendix II: The Development Education Centre of South Yorkshire and its Cultural Mentor Service

As was said in the Preface, many of the ideas in this book come from the work of the Development Education Centre in South Yorkshire (DEC(SY))and its Cultural Mentor Service.

DEC(SY) was established in 1984 and is a registered charity (no.517354). Its basic objective is to work with teachers and others involved in education throughout South Yorkshire to promote understanding of development issues and a global perspective in the curriculum. It is one of a number of such bodies across the country (not all of them calling themselves Development Education Centres). The organization is affiliated to a national network, the Development Education Association, and to a regional body, the Yorkshire and Humberside Global Schools Association.

DEC(SY) has a small number of paid staff who – together with volunteers – engage in several kinds of work, including training and information sessions for teachers and others, the production of booklets and resource packs on various issues and the management of several projects. It is based in Scotia Works, a building in the centre of Sheffield that is shared by a number of voluntary organizations with interests in international cooperation and education. It uses some of the space there as a resource centre offering books addressed to professionals in education, picture story-books for children, CDs, films, posters and artefacts which are available for sale or on loan.

There has sometimes been in the past an assumption that development and global education issues are not suitable subjects for young children. DEC(SY) is one of several DECs that have argued for several years that the foundations for an appreciation of the serious issues involved in global citizenship have to be laid at an early stage. From the early 1990s its resources were being used successfully by early years settings.

In the year 2000, members of the Pre-School Learning Alliance and the National Day Nurseries Association got together with representatives of DEC(SY) and the Young Children's Service in Sheffield's Education Department to consider new ways of promoting an appreciation of cultural diversity in early years settings in the city. These discussions led in 2001 to the launching of the Cultural Mentor Service within DEC(SY) under the umbrella of the Early Years Development & Childcare Partnership (EYDCP) in Sheffield. The basic idea was that more use should be made of the knowledge that some practitioners had of particular cultures, usually because they came from those cultural backgrounds themselves. They would be given the opportunity to visit settings other than their own to advise and support colleagues there with activities designed to foster better understanding of the communities from which they came. The EYDCP provided funds for cover for those people when they were visiting other settings and the funding of a staff member within DEC(SY) who was to coordinate this work.

The scheme did not go as well as had been hoped. It proved difficult to identify enough practitioners with the necessary knowledge and when they were identified releasing them for this work was not always easy even if funding for cover was available. As a result of this experience the Cultural Mentor Service was altered in several ways:

- The idea of recruiting people working in settings was dropped and replaced by the establishment of a small team of 'Cultural Mentors'.
- As well as working in settings, the team designed and ran a number of short courses, the most substantial of these entailing 20 hours class contact time, 10 hours individual tutorial time and self-directed study and practice within settings.
- The scheme, which had at first dealt exclusively with pre-school day care settings, expanded into work with childminders, summer play schemes, after-school clubs and parent support groups.

There was another development. The original project had envisaged people with expertise going into settings to help their practitioners understand cultural backgrounds with which they were not familiar. The team that was appointed saw a need to get beyond this and address the issue more fundamentally. Somewhat to their surprise, practitioners were asked during visits to settings or at training sessions to identify their own cultural background. As Hlabera Chirwa, one of the team, expressed it, 'You cannot approach another culture in an open and friendly way until you are confident about your own cultural identity'. The idea of getting people to think about their own cultural identities putting English culture on the same footing as others may have come as a surprise at first, but it has proved very invigorating in practice. Practitioners, students and parents of young children have all spoken warmly of the impact that the work of the Cultural Mentors has had on them and the way that it has enabled them to re-examine and develop their approach to cultural diversity.

My experience of working with this team of people provides the basis for much of what is said in this book.

For further information on DEC(SY) visit www.decsy.org.uk

References

Abbe, A., Gulick, L.M.V. & Herman, J.L. (2007) *Cross-cultural Competence in Army Leaders: A conceptual and empirical foundation*. Washington, DC: US Army Research Unit.

Aboud, F. (1988) *Children and Prejudice*. Oxford: Blackwell.

Ackroyd, P. (2002) *Albion: The Origins of the English Imagination*. London: Chatto & Windus.

Alexander, P. (ed.) (1994) *The World's Religions*. Oxford: Lion.

Ali, M. (2003) *Brick Lane*. London: Doubleday.

Allen, C. (2006) *God's Terrorists: The Wahabi Cult and the Hidden Roots of Modern Jihad*. New York: Perseus.

d'Ancona, M. & Brown, G. (eds) (2009) *Being British: The Search for Values that Bind the Nation*. London: Random House.

Ansari, H. (2004) *'The Infidel Within': Muslims in Britain Since 1800*. London: Hurst.

Anwar, M. (1995) 'Social Networks of Pakistanis in the UK: A Re-evaluation' in A. Rogers, & S. Vertovec, (eds) *The Urban Context: Ethnicity, Social Networks and Situational Analysis*. Oxford: Berg.

Asley, B. (1992) *Cleversticks*. London: Collins.

Astington, J.W. (1994) *The Child's Discovery of the Mind*. London: Fontana.

Auernheimer, G. (2007) *Einführung in die Interkulturelle Pädagogik*. Darmstadt: Wissenscahftliche Buchgesellschaft.

Bagguly, P. & Hussain, Y. (2005) 'Flying the Flag for England? Citizenship, Religion and Cultural Identity among British Pakistani Muslims' in T. Abbas (ed.) *Muslim Britain: Communities Under Pressure*. London: Zed Books.

Baldock, P. (2006) *The Place of Narrative in the Early Years Curriculum: How the Tale Unfolds*. London: Routledge.

Benjamin, F. (1995) *Skip Across the Ocean*. London: Frances Lincoln.

Bowker, J. (2006) *World Religions: The Great Faiths Explored and Explained*. London: Dorling Kindersley.

Bragg, B. (2006) *The Progressive Patriot: A Search for Belonging*. London: Banton.

Brightwell, J. & Fidgin, N. (2005) *To Begin At The Beginning*. Poole: Development Education in Dorset (DEED).

Brown, B. (2001) *Combating Discrimination: Persona Dolls in Action*. Stoke-on-Trent: Trentham.

Brown, D.M. (1979) *Mother Tongue to English: The Young Child in the Multicultural School*. Cambridge: Cambridge University Press.

Brown, H. (1998) *Unlearning Discrimination in the Early Years*. Nottingham: Trentham.

Browne, E. (2000) *Handa's Surprise*. London: Walker.

Brownjohn, E. (2002) *All Kinds of Bodies*. London: Taufo.

Bruce, L. & Waterhouse, S. (2001) *Engines, Engines*. London: Bloomsberg.

Bruner, J.S. (1963) *The Process of Education*. New York: Vintage.

Byram, M.S. (2008) *From Foreign Language Education to Education for Intercultural Citizenship: Essays and Reflection*. Cleveland: Multilingual Matters.

Camilleri, C. & Cohen-Emerique, M. (1989) *Chocs de cultures: Théories et enjeux pratiques de l'interculturel*. Paris: Editions l'Harmatton..

Carroll, T. & O'Connor, A. (2009) All about bi-lingualism. *Nursery World*, 7 May, 17–22.

Cashmore, J.A. & Goodnow, J.J. (1986) Influences on Australian parents' values: Ethnicity versus socio-economic status. *Journal of Cross-Cultural Psychology*, 17, 441–481.

Chalta, M. (2005) Diversity, creativity and imagination in the early years. *Early Education*, 45, Spring, 7–10.

Clark, M.M. & Waller, T. (eds) (2007) *Early Childhood Education & Care: Policy and Practice.* London: Sage.

Cohen-Emerique, M. (1999) Le choc culturel. *Revue Antipodes*, 145, 11–2 .

Cole, M. (1998) 'Culture in development' in M. Woodhead, D. Faulkner and K. Littleton, (eds) *Cultural World of Early Childhood.* London: Routledge.

Cole, W.O. (ed.) (1991) *Five World Faiths.* London: Cassell.

Connolly, P. (2002) *Too Young To Notice? The Cultural and Political Awareness of Three- to Six-Year-Olds in Northern Ireland.* Belfast: Community Relations Information Centre.

Connolly, P. & Huskin, K. (2006) The general and specific effects of educational programmes aimed at promoting awareness and respect for diversity among young children. *International Journal of Early Years Education*, 14(2), 107–26.

Cooper, A., Hetherington, R., Baiston, K., Pitts, J. & Spriggs, A. (1995) *Positive Child Protection: A View From Abroad.* Lyme Regis: Russell House.

Cosh, J. (2002) Speaking Our Language. *Nursery World.* 19 December, 24–5.

Curnow, N. & Evans, M. (2004) Minority Report. *Nursery World*, 22 April, 10–11.

Daly, N. (2000) *Jamela's Dress.* London: Frances Lincoln.

Datta, M. (2000) *Bi-linguality and Literacy: Principles and Practice.* London: Continuum.

Davies, N. (2008) *Flat Earth News.* London: Chatto & Windus.

Davies, R. (2006) *Telling Stories.* Lancaster: Global Link.

Department for Children, Education, Lifelong Learning and Skills (DCELLS) (DCSF) (2008a) *Framework for Children's Learning for 3 to 7-year-olds in Wales.* Cardiff: Welsh Assembly Government.

Department for Children, Education, Lifelong Learning and Skills (DCELLS) (DCSF) (2008b) *Welsh Language Development.* Cardiff: Welsh Assembly Government.

Department for Children. Schools & Families (DCSF) (2007) *Guidance on the Duty to Promote Community Cohesion.* London: HMSO.

Department for Children, Schools and Families (DCSF) (2008a) *Statutory Framework for the Early Years Foundation Stage.* Nottingham: HMSO.

Department for Children, Schools and Families (DCSF) (2008b) *Practice Guidance for the Early Years Foundation Stage.* Nottingham: HMSO.

Department for Education & Skills (DES) (2003) *Every Child Matters.* London: HMSO.

Department for International Development, Department for Education & Skills and Qualifications and Curriculum Authority (2005) *Developing the Global Dimension in the School Curriculum.* Glasgow: DfID.

Derman-Sparks, L. (1993) Revisiting multicultural education: What children need to live in a diverse society. *Dimensions of Early Childhood*, 22(1), 6–10.

Easterling, L. (2007) *Our Global Community Games.* London: Heinemann.

Emecheta, B. (1974) *Second-Class Citizen.* London: Allison & Busby.

Foot, P. (1965) *Immigration and Race in British Politics.* London: Penguin.

Fox, K. (2004) *Watching the English: The Hidden Rules of English Behaviour.* London: Hodder & Stoughton.

Fukuyama, F. (1992) *The End of History and the Last Man.* Harmondsworth: Penguin.

Gaine, C. (2005) *We're All White, Thanks: The Persisting Myth about 'White' Schools.* Stoke-on-Trent: Trentham.

Gainer, C. (1998) *I'm Like You, You're like Me.* Minneapolis, MV: Free Spirit.

Gallego González, P. (1998) Interculturidad: un proceso formativo entre culturas. *Servicios Sociales y Política Social*, 44, 55–68.

Gardner, H. (2001) *Intelligence Reframed*. New York: Basic Books.

Garlake, T. (2001) *Your World, My World*. London: Oxfam.

Garvey, V., Giffin, H. & Unwin, R. (2007) *Developing Global Learners: Supporting the global dimension in early years foundation stage settings*. Sheffield: Development Education Centre for South Yorkshire (DECSY).

Gilroy, P. (1993) *The Black Atlantic: Modernity and Double Consciousness*. London: Verso.

Gimeno Sacristán, J. (2000) *Educar e conviver na cultura globa: As exigências da cidadania*. Sao Paulo: Edições Artmed.

Gordon, G. (2007) *Towards Bicultural Competence: Beyond Black and White*. Stoke-on-Trent: Trentham.

Greenblatt, S.J. (1990) *Learning to Curse: Essays in Modern Culture*. New York: Routledge.

Griffin, S. (2008) *Inclusion, Equality and Diversity in Working with Children*. Harlow: Heinemann.

Gundara, J.G. (2000) *Interculturalism, Education and Inclusion*. London: Sage.

Halliday, F. (2003) *Islam and the Myth of Confrontation* (revised edition). London: Tauris.

Hendry, J. (2008) *An Introduction to Social Anthropology: Sharing Our Worlds* (2nd edition). Basingstoke: Palgrave Macmillan.

Heyden, J., de Gioia, K. & Hadley, F. (2003) *Enhancing Partnerships and Networks with Non-English Speaking Families in Early Childhood Services: Final Report*. Sydney: Government of New South Wales.

Hollyer, B. (1999) *Wake Up, World! A Day in the Life of Children Around the World*. London: Frances Lincoln.

Hollyer, B. (2004) *Let's Eat*. London: Frances Lincoln.

Huntington, S.P. (1996) *The Clash of Civilisations and the Remaking of the World Order*. London: Simon & Schuster.

Hymes, D. (1996) *Ethnography, Linguistics, Narrative Inequality: Towards an Understanding of Voice*. London: Taylor & Francis.

Itchykadana (1996) *Asian Nursery Rhymes*, illustrated by Anita Chowdry and chosen by Sanjirinee. London: Mantra.

Janmohamed, S.Z. (2009) *Love in a Headscarf: Muslim Woman Seeks the One*. London: Aurum.

Johnson, E. (2003) *The Cultural Diversity Guide*. Southampton: Meridian Broadcasting.

Jones, E. (1998) *The English Nation: The Great Myth*. Stroud: Sutton.

Joosse, B. (2005) *Papa, Do you Love Me?* San Francisco, CA: Chronicle Books.

Kahin, M.H. (1997) *Educating Somali Children in Britain*. Stoke-on-Trent: Trentham.

Kirby, F. (2006) China Syndrome. *Nursery World*, 11 May, 13–2.

Knowles, E. & Ridley, W. (2005) *Another Spanner in the Works: Challenging Prejudice and Racism in Mainly White Schools*. Stoke-on-Trent: Trentham.

de Korne, H., Byram, M.S. & Fleming, M. (2007) Familiarising the stranger: Immigrant perceptions of cross-cultural interaction and bi-cultural identity. *Journal of Multiligual and Multicultural Development*, 28(4), 290–307.

Lane, J. (1999) *Action for Racial Equality in the Early Years*. London: National Early Years Network.

Laot, J. (2006) *La méthode des chocs culturels: Sur la voie de l'action interculturelle*. Brussels: Femmes Prévoyantes Socialistes.

Lerner, D. (1958) *The Passing of a Traditional Society: Modernising the Middle East*. London: Macmillan.

Levy, A. (2004) *Small Island*. London: Headline Books.

Lewis, A. (1995) *Children's Understanding of Disability*. London: Routledge.

Lewycka, M. (2007) *Two Caravans*. London: Fig Tree.

Lindon, J. (2006) *Equality in Early Childhood: Linking Theory and Practice*. London: Hodder Arnold.

Lluch, X. (2009) *Societat I multiculturitat: Una perspectiva educativa.* Barcelona: Fundació Jaume Bofill.

Malik, K. (2008) *Strange Fruit: Why Both Sides are Wrong in the Race Debate.* Oxford: Oneworld.

Matsumoto, D., LeRoux, J.A., Robles, Y. & Campos, G. (2007) The Intercultural Adjustment Potential Scale (ICAPS) predicts adjustment above and beyond personality and general intelligence. *International Journal of Intercultural Relations,* 3, 747–759.

McLaren, T. (2005) *My Day, My Way.* London: Tango.

McNamara, C. (2003) *Nii Kwei's Day.* London: Frances Lincoln.

Mercer, A. (2000) Pride of place. *Nursery World,* 30 November, 12–3.

Miles, D. (2005) *The Tribes of Britain: Who Are We? And Where Do We Come From?* London: Weidenfeld & Nicolson.

Milord, S. (1992) *Hands Around the World: 365 Creative way to Build Cultural Awareness and Global Response.* Charlotte, VT: Williamson.

Mills, D. & Brazell, D. (1999) *Lima's Red Hot Chilli.* London: Mantra.

Moñivas Lázaro, A. (1998) Multiculturidad (Ciencia y Sociedad). *Servicios Sociales y Política Social,* 44, 9–32.

Moodian, M.A. (2008) *Contemporary Leadership and Intercultural Competence.* London: Sage.

Na, imh bint, R. & Mistry, N. (2002) *The Swirling Hijaab.* London, Mantra.

Najmudii, R. (2007) 'A Confused or Rich Identity?' in N. Arbabzadah (ed.) *From Outside In: Refugees and British Society.* London: Arcadia.

Nicholson, S., Jordan, E., Cooper, J. & Marsh, J. (British Market Research Bureau) (2008) *Childcare & Early Years Providers Survey: 2007.* London: Department for Children, Schools & Families.

Northern Ireland Council for the Curriculum, Examinations and Assessment (1997) *Curricular Guidance for Pre-School Education.* Belfast: Department of Education for Northern Ireland.

O'Brien, F. (1973) *The Poor Mouth,* translated by P.C. Power. London: Hart-Davis MacGibbon.

Omaar, R. (2006) *Only Half of Me: Being a Muslim in Britain.* London: Viking.

Onyefulu, I. (2000) *Ebele's Favourite.* London: Frances Lincoln.

Parekh, B. (2000) *Rethinking Multiculturalism: Cultural Diversity and Political Theory.* London: Macmillan.

Paxman, J. (1999) *The English: A Portrait of a People.* London: Penguin.

Pérez, A. (2000) *La cultura escolar en la sociedad neoliberal.* Madrid: Ediciones Morata.

Petty, K. (2007) *Around the World Hair.* London: Frances Lincoln.

Portera, A. (2006) *Globalizzazione e pedagogia interculturale: Interventi nella scoula.* Trento: Edizione Erickson.

Ramadan, T. (1999) *To be a European Muslim: A Study of Islamic Sources in the European Context.* Leicester: The Islamic Foundation.

Rao, S. (2006) *My Mother's Sari.* New York: NorthSouth Books.

Readman, J. & Roberts, L.H. (2004) *The World Came to My Place Today.* London: Eden Project.

Richards, G. (2006) Found in Translation. *Nursery World,* 13 April, 16–7.

Risager, K. (2000) The Teacher's Intercultural Competence. *Sprogforum,* 6(18), 14–20.

Robinson, K. & Jones Diaz, C. (2001) *Diversity and Difference in Early Childhood Education: Issues for Theory and Practice.* Milton Keynes: Open University Press and McGraw Hill.

Rubiol, G. (2004) *Turquiá entre Occidente y el Islam: Una historia contemporánea.* Barcelona: Viena Ediciones.

Said, E. (1978) *Orientalism: Western Conceptions of the Orient.* London: Vintage.

Sardar, Z. (2008) *Balti Britain: A Journey Through the British Asian Experience.* London: Granta.

Sarwar, G. (2004) *British Muslims and Schools* (3rd edition). London: Muslim Educational Trust.

Schmidt, A.J. (1997) *The Menace of Multiculturalism*. Westport, CT: Praeger/Greenwood.

Scottish Consultative Council on the Curriculum (1999) *Curriculum Framework for Children 3 to 5*. Edinburgh: The Scottish Office.

Sen, A. (2006) *Identity and Violence: The Illusion of Diversity*. London: Allen Lane.

Siraj-Blatchford, I. (1994) *The Early Years: Laying the Foundations for Racial Equality*. Nottingham: Trentham.

Siraj-Blatchford, I. (2000) *Supporting Identity, Diversity and Language in the Early Years*. Buckingham: Open University Press.

Smidt, S. (2006) *The Developing Child in the 21st Century: A Global Perspective on Child Development*. Oxford: Routledge.

Southern, R.W. (1962) *Western Views of Islam in the Middle Ages*. Cambridge, MA: Harvard University Press.

Spence, J. (1998) *The Chan's Great Continent: China in Western Minds*. Harmondsworth: Allen Lane.

Steger, M.B. (2003) *Globalisation: A Very Short Introduction*. Oxford: Oxford University Press .

Super, C.M. & Harkness, S. (1998) 'The development of affect in infancy and early childhood' in M. Woodhead, D. Faulkner and K. Littleton, (eds.) *Cultural Worlds of Early Childhood*. London: Routledge.

Swain, G. (1999) *Eating*. Minneapolis, MN: Lerner.

Swann Report (1985) *Education For All: The Report of the Committee of Enquiry into the Education of Children from Ethnic Minority Groups*, Cmnd, 9543. London: Her Majesty's Stationery Office.

Syal, M. (1999) *Life Isn't All Ha-ha, He-he*. London: Doubleday.

Tassoni, P. (2003) So to Speak. *Nursery World*, 23 January, 12–3.

Taylor, J. (2006) *Start with a Difference*. London: Jewish Council for Racial Equality.

Turner, M. (1997) 'Working in partnership: parents, teacher and support teacher together' in E. Gregory, (ed.) *One Child, Many Worlds: Early Learning in Multicultural Communities*. London: Fulton.

Tyler, C. (2005) *Traveller Education*. Stoke-on-Trent: Trentham.

Uwins, J.A. (2008) *Parents are not a homogenous group: a case study of partnership with black African parents and the reflection of their children's cultural identities in the nursery*. Dissertation submitted for MA in Early Childhood Education, University of Sheffield.

Vevers, S. (2006) Making Friends. *Nursery World*, 17 August, 10–11.

Walker, C.J. (2005) *Islam and the West: A Dissonant Harmony of Civilisations*. Stroud: Sutton.

Walsh, M. (2004) *My World, Your World*. London: Corgi.

Ward, V. (2007) *Who Cares About Britishness? A Global View of the National Identity Debate*. London: Arcadia.

Welsh Assembly Government (2006) *Education for Sustainable Development and Global Citizenship*. Cardiff: Welsh Assembly Government.

Werbner, P. (1995) 'From Commodities to Gifts: Pakistani Migrant Workers in Manchester' in A. Rogers & S. Vertovec (eds) *The Urban Context: Ethnicity, Social Networks and Situational Analysis*. Oxford: Berg.

Winder, R. (2005) *Bloody Foreigners: The Story of Immigration to Britain*. London: Abacus.

Author Index

Subject Index

Exciting Early Years and Primary Texts from SAGE

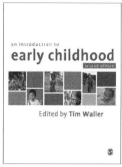

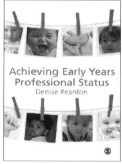

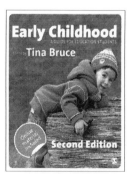

15201945R00090

Printed in Great Britain
by Amazon.co.uk, Ltd.,
Marston Gate.

CONTENTS

1 *The Mule Track*
1918
Oil on canvas
60.9 × 91.4
(24 × 36)
Imperial War
Museum, London

PAUL
NASH

David Boyd Haycock

British Artists

Tate Publishing

For Nicholas Kahn

Acknowledgements

I am very grateful to Nicola Bion and Richard Humphreys for commissioning
this book, and to John Jervis for his excellent work in editing it for publication;
to Claire Gouldstone for her fine work on the picture research, and to Richard
Dawes and my anonymous reader for their valuable improvements to the final text.
All have been a pleasure to work with, and their help in completing the book has
been inestimable.

First published 2002 by order of
the Tate Trustees
by Tate Publishing, a division of
Tate Enterprises Ltd,
Millbank, London SW1P 4RG
www.tate.org.uk

© Tate 2002

Reprinted 2007, 2011

British Library Cataloguing in
Publication Data
A catalogue record for this book is
available from the British Library

ISBN 978 1 85437 436 3

Distributed in North America by Harry
N. Abrams, Inc., New York
Library of Congress Control Number:
2002112228

Concept design James Shurmer
Book design Caroline Johnston
Printed in China by Prosperous Printing

Front cover: *Wood on the Downs* 1930
(fig.30, detail)

Back cover: *We are Making a New World*
1918 (fig.22, detail)

Frontispiece: *Self-Portrait* 1922;
The British Museum, London

Measurements of artworks are given in
centimetres, height before width,
followed by inches in brackets

INTRODUCTION

As a painter, illustrator and critic, Paul Nash was at the forefront of British art in the first half of the twentieth century. He is frequently described as an 'essentially English' artist, and it is true that he had his earliest influences in the nineteenth-century Romantic tradition of William Blake, Samuel Palmer and Dante Gabriel Rossetti. But he also sought to shake what he considered the conservative, myopic English establishment of the 1920s and 1930s, to bring it to its senses after the futile destruction of the Great War, and to help it recognise the thrilling potential of continental modernism. After his powerful anti-war works of the Western Front in 1917–18 (fig.1) Nash went on to defend Picasso, to experiment with abstraction and to embrace Surrealism. Yet in January 1943 he objected to the recent inclusion of one of his paintings in his friend John Piper's book *British Romantic Artists*, asking: 'Romantic art what is that? I turned the pages wondering more and more. Romantic? this? that? Constable, Steer, Sickert *Romantic* painters? ... when all is said I do not like the word Romantic applied to that which in its best and truest expression in English art should be called Poetic.'[1]

So it is true that as a painter Nash ceaselessly returned to the inspiring poetry of the English landscape, a landscape which so captivated him as a child. He believed that in English painting, behind the 'frank expressions of portrait and scene', there existed 'an imprisoned spirit'. This spirit was 'the source, the motive power' which animated all English art. 'If I were asked to describe this spirit,' he wrote in the 1930s, 'I would say it is of the land; *genius loci* is indeed almost its conception. If its expression could be designated I would say it is almost entirely lyrical. Further, I dare not go.'[2] The idea of the *genius loci*, the 'genius' or 'spirit' of a place, is a profound one in Western landscape history. It is a suggestion of vitality, of beauty, of the subtle interaction of Man, Nature and the imagination. It is the notion that drives much of Nash's art, from his early drawings and watercolours to his final oil paintings. It was a reality that lay behind the ordinary, it was the super-reality he discovered in Surrealism in the 1930s. It was what existed beyond the 'deceptive mirage' of Nature through which Turner had broken, 'to a reality more real' which lay beneath.[3]

It is this process of search and discovery that will unfold across the pages of this biography. And, as I shall show, it is war as well as landscape that binds Nash's career, that provides the boundaries and stimulus to his life's achievement. Nash would draw attention to the dual aspects of his war work, those of landscape and fantasy, in the essay 'Art and War', published in May 1943, three years before his death. There he expressed his admiration for Paolo Uccello's fifteenth-century painting *The Battle of San Romano* (fig.2), in the National Gallery, London. He noted how it was 'customary to speak of the Uccello battle as paradoxically peaceful. I do not find it so altogether ... above

all, for me the most convincing character of reality is the *unreal* quality of the scene. It is like a battle in a dream, fought out among green hills and flowering hedges. I remember the tall grasses and the wild flowers that nodded over the gaping trenches in front of Ypres in 1917.'[4]

As Nash had predicted, he found the true subject of his great talent and unique imagination once again in a world war. But when Nash writes of war it is not simply the two great wars Britain fought with Germany in 1914–18 and 1939–45. It is also humanity's ongoing war with Nature, with the seasons and elements that advance, grow, retract and destroy. And it is also our personal, spiritual war with the ever-present, dreamlike spectre of death. One of Nash's earliest imaginative drawings, the wonderful *Angel and Devil* of 1910 (fig. 3), deals with these powerful conflicts. He included lines of his own verse to accompany the picture:

> A place of gibbet-shapen trees and black abyss
> Where gaunt hills brooded dark and evil
> Girdled by dense wet woods and rushing streams
> A dread place only seen in dreams
> In which there is no history but this
> That on yon' stony shouldered tor
> An angel fought a devil.

For early in his career Nash also had pretensions to be a poet or playwright. Though these ambitions would never be realised, our perception of Nash's vocation is assisted by his often lyrical letters, by his journalism and by his hugely informative but unfinished autobiography, *Outline*. Assisted by this remarkable narrative, Nash's story as an artist is also a psychological story, a personal exploration of the spiritual journey from birth to death. In the opening pages of *Outline* he records some of his earliest dreams. One of these, he

2 Paolo Uccello
(1397–1475)
*The Battle of San Romano c.*1450–60
Tempera on wood
182 × 320
(71⅝ × 126)
National Gallery, London

3 *Angel and Devil* 1910
Watercolour, ink and pencil on paper 35.6 × 26.7 (14 × 10½)
Victoria and Albert Museum, London

explains, 'consisted, simply, of flying or floating, usually downstairs and round about the top of the hall'. Or sometimes he would find himself 'in other places, unknown country perhaps', leaping to great heights and then floating to the ground, 'like a leaf on the still air ... All my life, from time to time, I have enjoyed this mysterious, exciting experience.'[5] Psychoanalysts have identified this dream of weightlessness as a 'repetition' or memory of our earliest intra-uterine existence, when we floated in the amniotic fluid of the womb, at one with our universe and with no weight to carry.[6] Tellingly, Nash's dream of flight is paralleled by another early dream, a nightmare in which he would find himself 'in a tunnel which was either closing in or had narrowed imper-ceptibly, and I was trapped, horribly, unable to squeeze through or to back out'.[7] Nash, it seems, was close to the emotions and forgotten horrors of his birth. Of course, these recollections came late in his life, when flight had also become closely connected to death, to the soul's journey into the afterlife.

Nash was a survivor of the slaughter of the Great War, writing in a period hugely influenced by the work of Sigmund Freud, so it is unsurprising to find these strange strands in his writing as well as his painting. Therefore, as much as possible, I will let Nash speak, let him use his own words to explain his work and to chart his journey towards his last 'aerial creatures', in which he finally appeared to fulfil his lifetime's ambition of physical flight.

1

EARLY VISIONS AND POEMS

First Places

Paul Nash was born in Kensington, London, on 11 May 1889, the eldest child
in a moderately wealthy middle-class family. His father, William Harry Nash,
was a barrister, and his mother Caroline was the daughter of a Royal Navy
captain. Despite his urban upbringing Nash would always be happier in the
countryside, and it was from the country, not the town, that his family origi-
nated. His father had grown up at Langley Marish, in Buckinghamshire, and
in *Outline* Nash recorded the deep impression his first visit to his grandfather's
house made on him: 'It was like finding my own home, my true home, for
somehow it was far more convincing than our so-called home in London. I
realised, without expressing the thought, that I belonged to the country. The
mere sight of it disturbed my senses. Its scenes, and sounds, and smells intox-
icated me anew.'[1] A short childhood stay with an aunt and uncle at Yateley, in
Hampshire, awoke in him his first love of winter landscapes. He recollected
'the brittle ice pools with their dark thin rushes on the common, the rich
weather stains and bruises on the dripping trees in the deep lanes which led up
to the Flats, the colour of faded, rotting paling in the pure distilled beam of the
winter sun – these I absorbed'.[2]

But even in London Nash discovered quiet spots where Nature seemed to
weave a special magic. He called them 'places', and the first he fell upon was a
dislocated corner in the formal landscapes of Kensington Gardens. As he
explained it, 'There are places, just as there are people and objects and works
of art, whose relationship of parts creates a mystery, an enchantment, which
cannot be analysed.' His quiet nook of Kensington Gardens revealed itself in
its subtle, uncertain difference from the rest of the park: 'it was like a wild
streak in a well-brought-up family, a break away from tradition. Simply, it was
not the same as the rest.' (In its way it was, of course, Nash himself.) As Nash
grew up and discovered new 'places' and began to record them in drawings
and paintings 'it was always the inner life of the subject rather than its characteristic lineaments which appealed to me, though that life, of course, is
inseparable, actually, from its physical features'. As he explained, 'the secret of
a place lies there for everyone to find, though not, perhaps, to understand. I
shall tell of places infinitely far removed from each other in character.'[3] As we
shall see, these 'places' included the prehistoric sites of the Wittenham
Clumps and the Avebury stone circles, the sea wall at Dymchurch, and the
trenches of Passchendaele. Yet in each of these Nash was trying not only to
find its essence, the essence of the landscape, but the essence of the artist as
well. The sensitive observer inevitably projects his own emotion on to the landscape, and finds in its shapes and spaces his own 'inner life'.

In spite of their son's precocious sensitivity, Nash's parents decided that he should follow in his maternal grandfather's footsteps, and he was educated for a career in the Navy. Enrolled first at St Paul's School in London, he was then coached at a special school in Greenwich for the Naval Entrance Examination. Nash, however, displayed a spectacular inaptitude for mathematics, and failed the exam. In fact his whole experience of formal education was one of failure. He was not happy at school, a situation made worse when he became a boarder in 1901 after his parents left London for Iver Heath, in Buckinghamshire. At school he felt his freedom had been stolen from him: 'In fact I think it is fair to say that in those years I suffered greater misery, humiliation and fear than in all the rest of my life.'[4]

He left school in 1906 with no idea of what he could do for a career, but suggested to his father that he might earn his living 'as a black and white artist or illustrator of some kind'. This proposal seems to have come somewhat out of the blue: Nash gives little evidence of having been interested in art or drawing before this. Though an aunt had been friends with the Victorian landscape painter and nonsense poet Edward Lear, and her drawing room 'was full of his dry, luminous water-colours', Nash had had little other exposure to the art world. But his father happily accepted his proposal and in fact 'everything was done to launch me on this precarious career'.

4 Dante Gabriel Rossetti (1828–1882) *Dantis Amor* 1860 Oil on mahogany 74.9 × 81.3 (29½ × 32) Tate, London

Regions of Air

So it was that in December 1906 the seventeen-year-old Nash started attending classes at Chelsea Polytechnic. Then, in the autumn of 1908, he began evening classes at the London County Council School of Photo-engraving and Lithography in Bolt Court, Fleet Street. There he remained for another two years, commuting to London every day from Iver Heath and studying for a career as a commercial artist. But instead of profiting from this training 'and becoming a slick and steady machine for producing posters, show cards, lay-outs and other more or less remunerative designs, I fell under the disintegrating charm of the Pre-Raphaelites, or, rather, of Dante Gabriel Rossetti'.[5] Principally a watercolourist, Rossetti (1828–1882) was one of the pre-eminent names in Victorian art and poetry (fig.4). In 1910 Nash wrote that he would rather see one of Rossetti's paintings 'than that of any other artist. Whatever sense of beauty or line I may have or may develope I seem to owe to him. And I have only to look at his designs to feel a burning desire to create something beautiful.'[6] Those familiar only with Nash's work from after 1917 may find this early influence something of a surprise.

Yet, under the influence of Rossetti's pseudo-medieval romanticism, Nash now began to write poetry, and then plays. Cycling home to Iver Heath from the railway station he would cross a bridge over the River Alderbourne. Here he seemed to hear voices, and 'Henceforth, my world became inhabited by

5 *Our Lady of Inspiration* 1910 Ink and chalk on paper 22.9 × 17.2 (9 × 6¾) Tate, London

6 Samuel Palmer
(1805–1881)
*The Harvest Moon:
Drawing for 'A
Pastoral Scene'*
c.1831–2
Pen and ink and
gouache on card
15.2 × 18.4 (6 × 7¼)
Tate, London

images of a face encircled with blue-black hair, with eyes wide-set and luminous, and a mouth, like an immature flower, about to unfold.' This remote face
was 'lit only by some other radiance which poured out of the eyes in their
steady gaze – unaware of the mundane world; certainly unaware of me'.[7]
And then, almost inevitably, he discovered William Blake (1757–1827), another poet-painter of ecstatic, visionary status. And he also discovered the work
of Blake's dedicated disciple Samuel Palmer (1805–1881) (fig.6), whose own
'monstrous moons' and 'exuberance of stars' hanging in the night sky above
English pastoral scenes would find their place in Nash's work too.[8] These
were idiosyncratically British influences. Though Nash resisted the label of
'Romantic', he clearly partakes of an artistic expression closely connected to
a spiritual attachment to place and landscape.

   And reading Blake's poetry inspired him to 'open my eyes and look about
me, above all, to look up, to search the skies'. He began to form a habit of what
he called 'visual expansion' into Blake's 'regions of air'. 'I believed that by a
process of what I can only describe as inward dilation of the eyes I could
increase my actual vision. I seemed to develop a power of interpenetration
which disclosed strange phenomena. I persuaded myself I was seeing visions.
These often took the form of faces and figures in the night sky.'[9] Such experiences inspired some of his earliest works, including *Our Lady of Inspiration* and
Vision at Evening (figs.5, 7). Though he was also at this time writing letters full
of unrequited love to a cousin, the death of his mother in February 1910 after
a long illness was no doubt a psychological influence on these enigmatic drawings. While playing down the impact of her death in the published version of
Outline, in an excised section he wrote of how, when thinking of her, he was

'overwhelmed with misery and anxious distress as at the reminder of something dreaded'.[10]

Under his new, Romantic influences, Nash's still quite juvenile work received some significant and beneficial recognition. The most long-lasting of these early admirers, as well as an important friend and correspondent for the rest of Nash's life, was the poet and playwright Gordon Bottomley. Born in Yorkshire in 1874, Bottomley was an 'invalid' from his late teens. After moving to the Lancashire coast he wrote verse and plays influenced by Rossetti and William Morris. He would come to critical attention with the publication of 'King Lear's Wife' in Edward Marsh's *Georgian Poetry* (1913–15). In 1910 a neighbour lent Nash a limited-edition copy of Bottomley's one-act play *The Crier by Night* (1902). It reminded him of his own imaginative experiences, 'my familiar world of darkness, the voice by the Alderbourne and the giantesses of the night skies'. Inspired by the play's events, Nash made a few drawings in the book. Impressed, the neighbour sent the book back to Bottomley, who later reflected that the drawings 'were remarkable for a nascent but already powerful imagination and an interesting originality of technique'.[11]

A friendly correspondence quickly developed, though Nash was soon complaining to Bottomley that his drawing was 'rotten bad. You see the gods have given me a head full of golden pictures and precious little natural ability to carry them out – and the impatience of a fire horse!'[12] Bottomley wrote back encouraging Nash in both his drawing and his poetry, suggesting the Slade School of Fine Art in London as a useful place for him to improve his drawing. 'I think you are going to do the real thing, if you work faithfully,' wrote Bottomley, 'and someday I am going to be happy that I was one of the first to see it in you.'[13]

Encouragement such as this was reinforced by the recognition Nash was receiving from other quarters. In 1910 Selwyn Image, soon to become Slade Professor of Fine Art at Oxford University, was invited to an exhibition of students' work at Bolt Court. He was an acolyte of the great Victorian art critic

John Ruskin and, according to Nash, 'the last conspicuous pre-Raphaelite before the second advent in the person of Stanley Spencer.'[14] Image picked out for particular praise Nash's pen-and-ink drawing illustrating Rossetti's poem 'The Staff and Scrip'. He invited Nash to tea, which marked his entry 'into another world' – the home of an aesthete. Image's house was filled with the 'austere craftsmen-like designs' of the William Morris tradition, and in later years Nash's interest would extend to interior design. Nash's work was also admired by the painter William Rothenstein, an original member of Walter Sickert's Fitzroy Street Group and future principal of the Royal College of Art. Like Bottomley, Rothenstein recommended the Slade. When Nash explained that he could not expect his father to pay for the classes, Rothenstein declared, 'Well, then, why not make them for yourself?'[15]

So Nash set about earning the Slade fees by designing bookplates and illustrations (fig.8). This led to a meeting with the Irish poet W.B. Yeats, whose book of poems *The Wind Among the Reeds* Nash hoped to illustrate. He visited Yeats with a collection of his visionary drawings, finding him 'sitting over a small dying fire'. He 'probed me with a few languid questions, peering at the drawings the while and smiling at me with an amused air which I found disconcerting. "Did you really see these things?" Yeats asked.' In the presence of 'the master of visions', Nash declared that yes, he had. Yeats's publishers, however, 'were not favourable to the proposition'.[16] But despite the failure of this scheme, by October Nash had earned enough money for the fees, and was enrolled at the Slade.

Nash's drawing teacher at the Slade was the irascible Henry Tonks, who, in 'cold discouraging tones', accepted him into the school. 'It was evident he considered that neither the Slade, nor I, was likely to derive much benefit.'[17] Nash was alarmed to discover how 'backward' his own drawing skills were, but once he had got used to the 'beautifully mad' Tonks's sarcastic manner he found him a good teacher. He learnt, he said, more in the first fortnight there than in the previous five years. But rather than a 'temple of art', Nash found the Slade to be 'more like a typical English Public School seen in a nightmare'.[18] Nonetheless, as he had hoped, he soon made a number of friends. These included such future luminaries of British art as Stanley Spencer, Christopher Nevinson, Ben Nicholson (with whom he became close), Edward Wadsworth and Dora Carrington.

As Nash wrote in *Outline*, the Slade at that time was 'seething under the influence of Post-Impressionism'. In 1910 and 1912 the painter and critic Roger Fry had staged two exhibitions of continental art at London's Grafton Galleries. The first, which centred on work by Manet, Gauguin, Van Gogh and Cézanne, had, in Nash's words, 'caused quite a disturbance'. The Post-Impressionist style marked a radical restatement of the new in modern art. Almost overnight the conservative British art world was faced with a break with tradition that had been evolving for some thirty years in France. Nash recorded that one critic, Sir Claude Phillips of the *Daily Telegraph*, 'the most honest and uncompromising of them all, threw down his catalogue upon the threshold of the Grafton Galleries and stamped on it'. But this exhibition, Nash went on, 'was nothing to what followed the second opening. It seemed, literally, to bring about a national upheaval.' The second Post-Impressionist exhibition was dominated by the works of Picasso and Matisse. These appeared brash and crude to English eyes, the continental artists rejecting traditional notions of representation and asserting their own, strongly subjective viewpoint on the world. Fry wrote in his catalogue that these artists 'do not seek to imitate form, but to create form; not to imitate life, but to find an equivalent for life' – a phrase which would later appear in Nash's work.[19]

Inevitably the professors at the Slade 'did not like it at all', but they could not prevent its influence upon their students – though they tried. Tonks called on their 'sporting instincts' and asked them to stay away from the show. But as far as Nash was concerned, Post-Impressionism 'made no difference either way'. He later admitted he was left as untouched by the second exhibition as he had been by the first: 'I remained at the point I had reached', and he continued to make his drawings of 'visions'.[20]

Going in for Nature

In fact Nash's memory let him down when he wrote these remarks in his autobiography, as by the time of the second Post-Impressionist exhibition he had already left the Slade. He had been there for little more than a year, and despite

9 *The Three in the Night* 1913
Watercolour, ink and
chalk on paper
52.7 × 34.3
(20¾ × 13½)
Private Collection

his initial advances felt he had made little real improvement in his drawing skills. Tonks had told him he was 'like a man trying to talk who has not learnt the language', and Nash reflected that he left the school 'without having learnt to draw in the accepted sense'.[21] He struggled with figure drawing, and it would never be his strong point. It was in Nature that he was finding his true inspiration, and in trees in particular, which, with their sensuous but mysterious personalities, become symbolic substitutes for the human female figure. He could draw a tree in front of him as he 'felt' it. 'I did not find it difficult to draw this tree, as I had found the models at the Slade difficult to draw,' he explained.[22] But help was at hand. Another of Nash's influential new patrons was the painter and former Slade Professor at Oxford Sir William Blake Richmond. Richmond's late father was the portrait painter George Richmond, who had been one of the Ancients, the group of young acolytes and friends of Nash's hero, William Blake. It was Sir William who now recognised Nash's talent for landscape, and suggested he should 'go in for Nature'. Nash recalled that he had 'only a vague comprehension of his meaning, but out of curiosity I began to consider what Nature offered, as it were, in raw material. How would a picture of, say, three trees in a field look, with no supernatural inhabitants of the earth or sky, with no human figures, with no story?'[23] (fig.9) By the summer of 1912 he could tell Bottomley that he was trying to paint trees 'as tho they were human beings ... because I sincerely love & worship trees & know they *are* people & wonderfully beautiful people'.[24]

Nash now began to discover that the landscape was theme and subject enough in itself, and to Bottomley's regret he began to shed his Pre-Raphaelite figures. He realised he could follow his own formula, and that, as the Post-Impressionists had shown, in art there are no rules, and in a picture shadows and reflections can go any way you want them to. And 'going in for Nature' meant further experience with 'places'. One of the first of these new places,

10 *Bird Garden* 1911
Watercolour, ink and
chalk on paper
38.7 × 33.7
(15¼ × 13¼)
National Museum
and Galleries of
Wales, Cardiff

freed from his earlier visions, was the view from the morning-room in his father's house at Iver Heath. This he called 'the Bird Garden' (fig.10). 'It was undoubtedly the first place which expressed for me something more than its natural features seemed to contain, something which the ancients spoke of as *genius loci* – the spirit of a place'. In the dramatic way it seemed to respond to light, the Bird Garden appeared sometimes to take on 'a startling beauty, a beauty to my eyes wholly unreal. It was this "unreality", or rather this reality of another aspect of the accepted world, this mystery of clarity which was at once so elusive and so positive, that I now began to pursue and which from that moment drew me into itself and absorbed my life.'[25] This pursuit was effectively now to become his life's work.

Another important 'place' discovered at this time was the Wittenham Clumps, a pair of shallow, rounded hills topped with trees that rise above the flat lands of the Thames Valley in what was then north-west Berkshire (fig.11). Seated on one of the hilltops is a small prehistoric fort, which adds to their sense of remote human history. In a letter of September 1911 Nash described these 'grey hallowed hills crowned by old old trees, Pan-nish places down by the river wonderful to think on, full of strange enchantment ... a beautiful legendary country haunted by old Gods long forgotten'. To Nash, who had travelled abroad only once, to northern France, they were 'the Pyramids of my small world'.[26] Indeed, pyramids were the subject of one of the earliest of his

11 *Wittenham Clumps* c.1913 Watercolour, ink and chalk on paper 30.8 × 39.7 (12⅛ × 15⅝) Tullie House Museum & Art Gallery, Carlisle

12 *The Pyramids in the Sea* 1912
Ink and watercolour
on paper
32.4 × 29.2
(12¾ × 11½)
Tate, London

mature drawings (fig.12), a strange night-time vision in which the dunes of the Egyptian desert are turned mysteriously into black waves of water.

Although figures are absent from many of these landscapes, the places in Nash's work rarely existed without the intervention – the very presence even in their absence – of human activity. This is clearly seen in another of his drawings from this period, *The Wanderer* (fig.13). A distant figure disappears into the trees, leaving a subtle trail where it has walked through the long stalks of summer grass. For Nash, returning now to the land as a painter was a return to the rustic world of his forebears: 'What better life could there be – to work in the open air, to go hunting far afield over the wild country, to get my living out of the land as much as my ancestors ever had done.'[27] The youthful drawings of this innocent, bucolic period remain some of his finest achievements. He would later look back on them with understandable nostalgia.

First Successes

In November 1911 Nash moved from Iver Heath to a bedsit in Chelsea. Here he found 'life warm, tingling and inspiring all about me', his eyes opening to

London's 'inner beauty'.[28] In the autumn of 1912 Sir William Richmond helped to arrange a meeting between Nash and Arthur Clifton, manager of the Carfax Gallery, then one of the most distinguished and exclusive art venues in London. Though it usually exhibited only Old Masters or the latest work from Paris, Nash persuaded Clifton to include some of his drawings on one of the walls. For a first exhibition it was a happy success, with William Rothenstein appearing and purchasing a drawing, *The Falling Stars*. A year later, in November 1913, Nash held a very successful joint exhibition with his younger brother, John Nash (1893–1977), at the Dorien Leigh Gallery in South Kensington. The twenty-year-old John, a trainee journalist, was also interested in becoming a professional artist, and his brother encouraged him, though, significantly, he advised him against studying at an art school. John was thus largely self-trained, but went on to earn his own considerable reputation as a landscape painter and illustrator (fig.25). The visitors to the brothers' exhibition included the collectors Charles Rutherston and Michael Sadler, who both bought pieces, and Spencer Gore, president of the Camden Town Group, a breakaway faction of modernist English artists. Gore took six of Paul's paintings and six of John's for a show in Brighton entitled *An Exhibition of English Post Impressionists and Cubists*. 'This is amusing to us,' wrote Paul: 'so we're Post Impressionists and Cubists are we?'[29]

Roger Fry was another enthusiastic visitor to the London show. Nash told Bottomley that Fry 'was obviously *very* pleased with our work & stayed some time talking & inspecting'.[30] He also heard later that Fry had seen his drawings at the New English Art Club's public exhibition 'and liked them more than anything else there'. By February 1914 Nash had been invited by Fry to join the Omega Workshops, which had been launched the previous July. He was certainly very interested in the idea of artists establishing themselves in business, 'producing drawings, paintings, decorated furniture, etc'.[31] But he was cautious of Fry, wary of his potential influence over his work. Nash was still all for going his own way, and though he assisted Fry with his restoration of the Mantegnas at Hampton Court Palace, he made little contribution to Omega.

But clearly things were going well for the ambitious young man. He and John were both elected to the Friday Club, which included Fry, Duncan Grant and Vanessa Bell of the influential Bloomsbury Group. They were also invited to exhibit their work in Leeds, and at the exhibition *Twentieth Century Art: A Review of Modern Movements* at the Whitechapel Art Gallery in London. And as well as these successes, Paul had become engaged to an attractive young Oxford graduate and suffragette, Margaret Odeh, whom he had met at a friend's studio in March 1913. By early August of 1914, following a visit with Margaret to Cumbria and Yorkshire, he felt that he had 'given a jump right away from "Nash trees"'.[32] He was on the verge of something new – commercial success. But that same month the market for drawings and paintings evaporated. Britain was suddenly at war with Germany and the Austro-Hungarian Empire.

13 *The Wanderer c.*1911
Watercolour, ink, chalk and pencil on paper 47 × 35.6 (18½ × 14)
The British Museum, London

2

THE VOID OF WAR

No Ordinary War

The arguments that brought armed conflict to Western Europe for the first time since the Franco-Prussian War of 1870–1 had been brewing for years. They were many and complex. Sparked on 28 June 1914 by the assassination in Sarajevo of the heir to the Austrian throne by a Bosnian-Serb nationalist, they culminated on 4 August with Germany's invasion of Russia, Belgium and France. For Nash, 'the whole business is most bloody stupid'.[1] Many would come to agree with him, though not before millions had died. Later Nash's wife wrote that the 'impact of War seemed quite unreal to both of us, and it interrupted a new and lovely life which we had planned during that year, a life which was to be devoted to an intensive research and development of his work as an artist'.[2] Nash's first inclination was for joining the Red Cross or 'gathering in the harvest or guarding the Railway'. He was 'all against killing anybody' and had no keenness to train as a soldier; the war was simply an intrusion on his developing career. But feeling that he would inevitably get 'dragged in' sooner or later, on 10 September he enlisted for home service as a private in the Artists' Rifles, part of the London Regiment of Territorials.

His experience of army training was not as awful as he had feared, and he was still able to draw and paint, and to exhibit new work in London. He and Margaret also decided against the long engagement they had planned, and on 17 December 1914 they married in London, at St Martin-in-the-Fields, beside the National Gallery in Trafalgar Square. They would live in Margaret's flat in Judd Street, at the north end of Bloomsbury, overlooking the grand façade of St Pancras Station.

As it turned out, the next two years on home service were relatively uneventful for Nash, though he soon longed to go to the front: 'I should hate the slaughter – I know I should but I'd like to be among it all it's no ordinary war.'[3] By 1916, after the massacre of that summer's disastrous offensive on the Somme, the British Army could no longer rely on volunteers or home service alone to make up its numbers. With the war grinding on relentlessly and no end in sight, conscription was introduced and Nash undertook officer training. In December he was gazetted second lieutenant in the Hampshire Regiment. He landed in France on 22 February 1917 and joined the 15th Battalion on the Ypres Salient.

Nash remained alert to the natural beauties of this new world. Marching up to the front line, he discovered surprising sites among the destruction – spring flowers blooming everywhere, green buds on the trees in a shell-destroyed wood still 'reeking with poison gas', where a nightingale sang.

14 Paul Nash in
1918
Tate Archive

'Ridiculous mad incongruity!' he told Margaret. 'One can't think which is the more absurd, the War or Nature.' Fortunately for Nash, this was a quiet time in the line, and he felt happier now he was in the trenches and no longer waiting for action: 'It sounds absurd, but life has a greater meaning here and a new zest, and beauty is more poignant.'[4] He continued to draw, making sketches of the blasted woods, a ruined church, a scarred hill and 'the trenches under a bloody sort of sunset, the crescent moon sailing above'. A month later he was writing, 'Oh, these wonderful trenches at night, at dawn, at sundown! Shall I ever lose the picture they have made in my mind.'[5] Yet there was a strangeness too to this 'monstrous land'. The front line was a 'nightmare' where nothing seemed real.[6]

As his time at the Front continued, and as he grew closer to his men, Nash's attitude to the war hardened. In May he wrote home that they were all 'sad and sick with longing for the end of this awful unending madness. I cannot get things straight at all. What is God about? ... The cause of war was probably quite futile and mean, but the effect of it is huge.' Yet, as if girding himself and his wife for the forthcoming offensive, he assured her that he still felt he was 'one with my native land'.[7] Then, on the night of 25 May, a week before the new assault was to be launched, in the darkness Nash fell from a parapet and into a trench, breaking a rib on the way. By 1 June he was back in London. Meanwhile the war continued without him, and a few days later the 15th

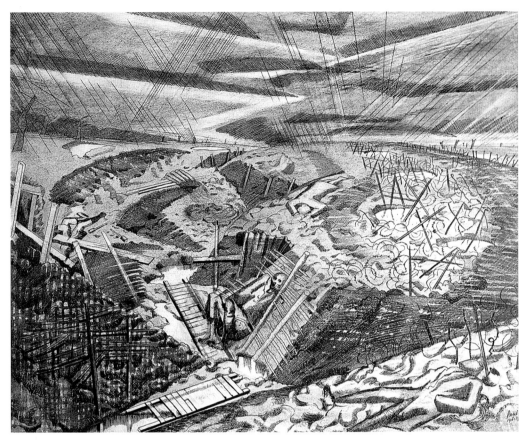

Hampshires attacked Hill 60, where many of his fellow officers and men were duly slaughtered (fig.19). As he acknowledged, his escape 'was a queer lucky accident', and one that quite possibly saved his life.[8]

15 *After the Battle*
1918
Pen and watercolour
on paper,
46.3 × 59.6
(18¼ × 23½)
Imperial War
Museum, London

War Artist

Back in London Nash resumed his drawing in safety and comfort. At the end of June he exhibited at the Goupil Gallery a series of twenty drawings of the Ypres Salient, which were well received. Nash was pleased by this success, and with the critical recognition it received. However, he told Bottomley he was aware that he still needed more time to study Nature before she would 'yield her mysteries. Sometimes I am desperate at my impotence.' But he was seeing 'so much more now: the world is crowded with the most marvellous things; everywhere I see form & beauty in a thousand thousand diversities'. This included the figure of his wife, and he was frustrated again in his 'longing to draw people which is causing me much pain and despair'.[9] In the figure drawings that do survive, as well as in some of the letters of this period, there is evidence of a more erotic edge to his sexuality. The youthful visions of damsels in the sky have vanished, to be replaced, through the impact of war, by a recognition of the reality of human nature – in both its brutality and its sensuality.

Yet there was still a tameness to his early drawings of the war. Nash's work remained largely unmarked by the real violence and tragedy of the conflict. His experience in the trenches in the spring of 1917 had been too limited, too uneventful – it is quite possible that he had not even seen a dead body. But in July he met up again with a former Slade colleague, Christopher Nevinson. Nevinson had seen action serving as an ambulance driver with the Red Cross, but was now working as an Official War Artist. Even before the war he had been closely involved in two major artistic movements that had largely passed Nash by: Futurism, born in Italy under the inspiration of Filippo Marinetti, and its English cousin, Vorticism, led by the controversial painter and writer Wyndham Lewis. Marinetti had visited England in 1910, 1912 and 1914, during which time he had exhibited works by members of the movement and delivered lectures on its fantastic ideals. Futurism was all about modernity, about sweeping away the stultifying past and eulogising the present in the anarchic form of machines, fast-moving motor cars and aeroplanes, and glorifying the destructive effects of war. Nevinson was the only English convert to Marinetti's cry for a new art that would be 'strong, virile and anti-sentimental'. But Lewis made a similar call in his rebellious magazine *Blast*, which first appeared in July 1914 and contained the Vorticist Manifesto. Lewis also wanted

16 Christopher Richard Wynne Nevinson (1889–1946)
Flooded Trench on the Yser 1915
Oil on canvas
50 × 61 (19⅝ × 24)
Private Collection

an iconoclastic new art that would reflect the state of modern, industrialised England. Vorticist art was strongly geometric in form, intense in colour, abstract and powerful. Though not obsessed with war in the way the Futurists were, in its destructive intensity *Blast* still prefigured the forthcoming struggle. Indeed, the magazine included a reproduction of Lewis's recent monumental canvas *Plan of War*.

Nash had seen the magazine, sending a copy to Gordon Bottomley, whose Victorian tastes predictably left him unimpressed. Nor did Vorticism appear to have made much of an impact on Nash, who was more interested in Nature than in machines. But Nevinson, who had come to reject Marinetti's adulation of war in the face of its stinking reality, showed the movement's forceful influence to excellent effect in his early paintings of the conflict. *Returning to the Trenches* (1914–15), *La Mitrailleuse* (1915) and *Flooded Trench on the Yser* (1915) (fig.16) were quickly heralded in Britain and France as major pieces of war art. Nash, too, was impressed. Towards the end of March 1917 he had asked Margaret to send him a copy of Nevinson's drypoint etching *Ypres After*

17 *The Orchard*
1917
Watercolour, ink and pencil on paper
57.1 × 45.7
(22½ × 18)
Tate, London

the First Bombardment (1916). 'I should like to have it if possible,' he explained. 'It is part of the world I'm interested in.'[10] The sight of ruined houses behind the front line was 'wonderful', and he wrote, 'I begin to believe in the Vorticist doctrine of destruction almost.'[11] Nevinson later helped teach Nash lithography, and under his guidance the pointed, zigzag style of Vorticism started to make an impression. Though its full impact would not appear until Nash's great oil paintings of the following year, *The Orchard* (fig.17), a watercolour painted on a visit to Gloucestershire around this time, does reveal some of this new influence. Though a pastoral scene, the picture retains a sense of unease in its rigorous lines and sharp angularity, with the barbed-wire fence separating the artist from the lines of trees in their military ranks. Psychologically, it is a troubled picture, promising tranquillity but revealing disturbance.

A Bitter Truth

At the end of August 1917 Nash was posted to a reserve battalion at Gosport, near Portsmouth. He was now attempting to get sent to the Front as an Official War Artist. He had a number of influential supporters, including the collector Edward Marsh, as well as Rothenstein, Fry and Tonks. But some officials were not so certain. Campbell Dodgson, one of the government's advisers on potential war artists, described Nash as 'decidedly post-impressionist, not cubist, but "decorative", and his art is certainly not what the British public will generally like'.[12] The politician and author John Buchan, who was then a director at the Ministry of Information, agreed. But he told the government's Director of Propaganda that they should appoint Nash nevertheless: 'There is a tremendous consensus of opinion about his work.'[13]

Nash was duly assigned on 12 October 1917, and was soon in Flanders, now as an official observer with servant and chauffeur-driven car. Nevinson's vision of the conflict had been softened by his appointment as a war artist, but Nash's was now bitterly emboldened. General Headquarters wanted him to operate from behind the lines, away from the fighting, but he would have none of it. Using 'nothing but brown paper and chalks' to make his sketches, he insisted on 'getting as near to the real places of action as it was possible to go'.[14] By the time of his return to the trenches it was mud-drenched winter, and the Third Battle of Ypres – better known as Passchendaele – had been struggling hopelessly through quagmire for three bloody months. The front line, which now saw the first use of mustard gas by the Germans, was a worse place even than the nightmare Nash had left behind in March. And it was an abomination that the jingoistic British press was failing to represent it in all its awful truth.

Nash recorded his impressions of this slaughterhouse in a long, impassioned letter to his wife on 16 November 1917:

> I have seen the most frightful nightmare of a country more conceived
> by Dante or Poe than by nature, unspeakable, utterly indescribable. In
> the fifteen drawings I have made I may give you some vague idea of
> the horror, but only being in it can ever make you sensible of its

dreadful nature and of what our men in France have to face. We all have a vague notion of the terrors of a battle … but no pen or drawing can convey this country – the normal setting of the battles taking place day and night, month after month. Evil and the incarnate fiend alone can be master of this war, and no glimmer of God's hand is seen anywhere. Sunset and sunrise are blasphemous, they are mockeries to man, only the black rain out of the bruised and swollen clouds all through the bitter black of night is fit atmosphere in such a land. The rain drives on, the stinking mud becomes more evilly yellow, the shell holes fill up with green-white water, the roads and tracks are covered in inches of slime, the black dying trees ooze and sweat and the shells never cease. They alone plunge overhead, tearing away the rotting tree stumps, breaking the plank roads, striking down horses and mules, annihilating, maiming, maddening, they plunge into the grave which is this land; one huge grave and cast up on it the poor dead. It is unspeakable, godless, hopeless. I am no longer an artist interested and curious, I am a messenger who will bring back word from the men who are fighting to those who want the war to go on forever. Feeble, inarticulate, will be my message, but it will have a bitter truth, and may it burn their lousy souls.[15]

With this angered objective, Nash returned to England in December with more than '50 drawings of muddy places'.[16] He began to work them up into paintings for a one-man exhibition at the Leicester Galleries in May 1918. It was called *Void of War*, a title possibly inspired by Blake. In September 1917 Nash had made three illustrations to Blake's poetic tale of destruction 'Tiriel', and he may also at this time have read his more famous poem 'Milton', with its lines from 'Book the Second':

> O Immortal? how were we led to War the Wars of Death?
> Is this the Void Outside of Existence, which if enter'd into
> Becomes a Womb? & is this the Death Couch of Albion?
> Thou goest to Eternal Death & all must go with thee.

In the context of an all-out war that seemed destined to end only when the last man had died, Blake's words are highly appropriate.

Significantly, before this new exhibition Nash's work had largely taken the form of pen-and-ink drawings embellished with watercolour. This in itself was a potentially powerful medium, producing striking images of the field of battle such as *After the Battle* and *Wire* (figs.15, 18). Nash's attempts at lithography under Nevinson's tuition also resulted in noteworthy images, such as a rare work focusing on human activity, the rain-drenched avenue of *Men Marching at Night* (fig.20). But in early 1918 he finally started work with a new medium, oils. The results, exhibited at the Leicester Galleries, such as *Void* (fig.21) and the bitterly, ironically titled *We are Making a New World* (fig.22), were immediately successful. Unlike his other early oil paintings, which 'practically grew on the canvas', this last work was closely based on a drawing, *Sunrise: Inverness Copse*. The one exceptional difference is that in the final

18 *Wire* 1918
Ink, watercolour and chalk on paper 47.6 × 62.2 (18¾ × 24½)
Imperial War Museum, London

19 *The Landscape, Hill 60* 1918
Ink, watercolour and chalk on paper 39.3 × 49.5 (15½ × 19½)
Imperial War Museum, London

20 *Men Marching at*
Night 1918
Lithograph
51.4 × 41.9
(20¼ × 16½)
Imperial War
Museum, London

painting the mass of brown cloud has become blood red, as if Nature bleeds over this shattered landscape of broken trees – trees which, of course, represented for Nash living personalities. This is a landscape of pitiable emotion. Devoid of human figures, but overflowing with the impact of human action, it is an unmerciful evocation of the devastation and pointlessness of the war. It is widely hailed as one of the greatest painted images of the conflict.

In July Nash told Bottomley that these efforts at oils had been 'a complete experiment you know – a piece of towering audacity I suppose as I had never painted before'.[17] His inexperience with the medium can be seen, but he proudly added that two paintings had immediately been purchased for the nation, with *Void*, one of his most popular works, bought by the Canadian government. The critics were equally impressed. Herbert Read, who served with distinction on the Western Front, wrote that on first seeing Nash's work 'I was immediately convinced' that he 'could convey, as no other artist, the phantasmagoric atmosphere of No Man's Land'. For Read, Nash revealed the war's 'outrage on Nature – the Nature which had been so delicate and sensuous to New English eyes'.[18] For Nash's friend and biographer Anthony Bertram, his were 'the only true war pictures. They *were* the war, equivalents for the war and not reports on it. They were the soldier's experience and not the journalist's or the touring artist's.'[19]

The Menin Road

While at the Front in November, Nash had been able to track down his brother, who was now a sergeant in the Artists' Rifles and had seen action during the Passchendaele offensive. He pulled strings at the Ministry of Information, and was able to get him enrolled as an Official War Artist. John returned home to England in January 1918, and after the success of Paul's *Void of War* show the brothers were commissioned to paint major works for the Imperial War Museum. They rented a shed at Chalfont St Peter in the Buckinghamshire countryside to use as a studio, establishing themselves and their wives there in June. As Nash told Bottomley the following month, 'folded as we are in the luxurious green country', their minds were still 'perpetually bent upon those scenes' they had witnessed in France and Belgium. 'Well it is on *these* I brood for it seems the only justification of what I do now – if I can help to rob war of the last shred of glory the last shine of glamour.' He felt very serious about 'this big picture', and planned to give it 'all I can muster'.[20]

21 *Void* 1918
Oil on canvas
71.4 × 91.7
(28⅛ × 36⅛)
National Gallery of
Canada, Ottawa

22 *We are Making a New World* 1918
Oil on canvas
71.1 × 91.4
(28 × 36)
Imperial War
Museum, London

23 John Nash
Over the Top 1918
Oil on canvas
79.3 × 107.3
(31¼ × 42¼)
Imperial War
Museum, London

For this commission Nash painted *The Menin Road* (fig.24), a huge canvas of some five and a half square metres. Again broken trees play an important part in the structure of the painting, and heavy shafts of sunlight penetrate the gloom. But here in the middle ground, among the zigzagging trenches, there are soldiers, dwarfed by the dismembered landscape around them. Nash told Bottomley in April 1919 that *The Menin Road* was 'by far the best thing I have yet done', and it is certainly an impressive work.[21] Around the same time as he was painting this monumental masterpiece his brother was working on the equally powerful *Over the Top* (fig.23). This depicts a diversionary attack by the Artists' Rifles on 30 December 1917 in which John had participated. He later recalled that it was 'pure murder' and he was lucky to escape untouched.[22] Though John was, like Paul, a keen painter of landscapes – strongly hinted at in the strong reds of the earth in the trench and the massed clouds on the horizon – this painting focuses on the individual's experience. It too is a forceful rendition of war, and it is remarkable to think of the two men working together in the quiet English countryside on these tableaux of death and devastation – a period of seclusion that also produced John's tranquil evening landscape, *The Cornfield* (fig.25).

The Nashes remained working at Chalfont St Peter until early 1919, though the war had ended on 11 November 1918. The endless fighting had at last ground down the morale of the German and Austrian people, and with defeat at the Front inevitable and revolution at home foreseeable, the Kaiser had abdicated and fled to neutral Holland. The Allies had wanted total victory at any cost, and they would now make certain Germany paid a full and heavy penalty for starting the war. This punishment, meted out in the heavy-handed Treaty of Versailles, would lay the seeds of further and far worse troubles in the future. These would in turn set the context for Nash's final artistic triumphs. Meanwhile, at

24 *The Menin Road*
1918–19
Oil on canvas
182.8 × 317.5
(72 × 125)
Imperial War
Museum, London

Chalfont St Peter he became embroiled in an affair with another man's wife. This established a pattern of short-lived relationships and philandering that continued into the late 1930s. Nash found married life difficult, having acknowledged his prenuptial mistrust of it in an understandably omitted line in the draft of *Outline*: 'We should be tied up, we should be tied down, fidelity was impossible, boredom inevitable.'[23] In order to survive, through the 1920s the couple would spend a lot of time apart. But on this early occasion Margaret took her culpable husband with her back to London. In February he was finally released from the Ministry of Information, and then by the Army. After the success of his battlefield paintings he would now face new struggles: what he pithily called the 'struggles of a war artist without a war'.[24]

25 John Nash
The Cornfield 1918
Oil on canvas
68.6 × 76.2
(27 × 30)
Tate, London

3

MAKING A NEW WORLD

The Critic

Inevitably the horrors of the Great War changed Nash. In prefatory remarks excised from the published version of *Outline*, he wrote how, up to

> the close of 1917, even in spite of the war, my life had run a more or less smooth and happy course; but with the last phase of the war and my participation in it as an official artist on the Western Front, a change began to take place. Thenceforth the whole savour of living, and the nature of my work seemed directly affected. I was launched into a turbulent sea where the dramatic adventures of life and art were breaking anew.[1]

Though he continued to display his wit and humour, after 1918 he was also more serious, more driven in his career as an artist, sometimes to the exclusion of his wife and his friends. He suffered increasingly from periodic bouts of depression, what his brother called 'the Nash blackness'. He was cast adrift by the return to life as a peacetime artist: what should he do now? What kind of a life could he make for himself and for Margaret? How would they live? Though they had a reasonable private income, they also had middle-class expectations, and money would be a struggle for much of the rest of Nash's life.

The next ten years is thus an unsettled story of peripatetic ramblings, mostly between London and the south coast of England, with occasional journeys abroad. It is a sometimes cloudy picture of a life lived on the move, of health worries and of Nash's struggles to develop for himself an avant-garde style and identity while still retaining the tenets of the English landscape tradition. This was the troubling conundrum he now sought to answer: was it possible to be British, and to still be modern? He wasn't alone in his dilemma. The war had caused a crisis in European culture and society: what were the values that had been fought for, what did the future hold? Where could modern art go now? This is the decade that saw publication of radical new literature such as James Joyce's *Ulysses* (1922), T.S. Eliot's *The Waste Land* (1922) and Virginia Woolf's *To the Lighthouse* (1927). But how would the pictorial arts respond?

Nash attempted to find an answer, but his early supporters, in particular Bottomley and Rothenstein, became increasingly uneasy about the new direction his paintings took. Bottomley had always believed Nash should never have dropped figures from his pictures, even though this was never his strong point. Rothenstein, meanwhile, felt Nash was drawing away from direct representation from Nature, though Nash assured him that this was not the case.

Perhaps more correctly, both Bottomley and Rothenstein felt their friend was leaving behind his English Romantic roots, with its own origins in the Renaissance tradition. This was perhaps true. Bottomley wrote that Nash 'thinks he can more quickly get to where he wants to be if he uses new traditions from France instead of old ones from Italy. And he won't; and he doesn't need to.'[2] This, then, was a period of dilemma for Nash. Should he follow his own vision, as he had at the Slade, or should he continue further down the path of continental modernism? Either way, he was largely going it alone. The Bloomsbury Group did not care much for his work, and his former ally Fry became particularly hostile, attempting to have him excluded from the London Artists' Association. Nash was alienating many of his old friends in his ambition to follow his own course.

One of the first new directions he took was into art criticism. He was a competent and lively writer, but not always a great critic. There was frequently an uncertainty or confusion as to what his ideas really were, for he did not always express himself clearly. However, much more than many of his contemporaries, over the next two decades, in a variety of journals and magazines, Nash became an important advocate of the modern movement in British art, and his writing and criticism provide an invaluable angle on his own work. In 1931 he would declare: 'To perceive through the images and monuments of man some glimmering of an ordered plan, some movement of a rhythm animating the universe, this must be the impulse of the modern writer upon Art who is not content to remain a critic.'[3] Nash held a low opinion of the British public in general, and of its attitude to modern art and design in particular. It was, he felt, his job to enlighten the average citizen to its powerful potential. In his earliest art criticism he restated his belief that the artist should be socially and culturally active. Artists were not to lock themselves away and work in isolation, for the world was 'entering an age of co-operation, and the artist must be asked to contribute to the plans of public buildings and better housing. The artist with his special feeling for form, colour and design is best qualified to add beauty to utility, and waken the public to the possibilities of their environment.'[4] This would be a difficult and challenging task, for the popular attitude to art remained starkly conventional.

The Sea

A critical event in 1919 was Nash's first visit to Dymchurch, on the Kent coast between Rye and Folkestone. The sea wall there would become one of his new 'places' (fig.26). He would later reflect on how, in his early, pre-war years as an artist, he had known 'nothing of the sea or the magical implication of aerial perspective across miles of shore, where waves alternately devour and restore the land'.[5] An early inspiration for Nash had been Blake's sublime poem to his friend and patron Thomas Butts, with its visionary evocation of seas and yellow sands, where the grains, along with every element of Nature, 'Are men seen afar'.[6] At Dymchurch, as on the Western Front, Man and Nature met in conflict, the two fighting it out, neither side ever quite able to overpower the other. This experience harked back not only to the war, but also to Nash's early

vision of *The Pyramids in the Sea* of 1912 (fig.12), and it had a deep psycho-logical effect on him. He felt that the paintings, drawings and etchings he executed here were the most important he undertook during this period. The powerful emotion many of them reveal was also influenced by another experience of mortality. At Dymchurch in 1919 Nash had met Claud Lovat Fraser, an ambitious artist and designer only a year younger than himself. They had quickly become good friends, but in June 1921 Fraser died suddenly, deeply affecting Nash. The death of his mother had rendered a powerful effect on Nash's work, as had the deaths of many friends and colleagues during the war. Later, in 1925, Margaret suffered a miscarriage, and death would seem to haunt him for the rest of his life. It is from death that his most powerful themes are drawn. In 1928 he told Margaret, 'I cannot realise what after-life can mean. The mind reels at the thought of absolute perfection. It does not lie within human conception. Somehow to be born again seems to me the ideal but how, in what form?'[7] Like the search for a distinctly modern British art, this search for the perfection of the afterlife and rebirth would be a driving motive for much of Nash's subsequent career.

Over the next few years the Nashes spent much time on the south coast, either at Dymchurch or at Iden, near Rye, in East Sussex, close to Walland and Romney Marshes. Nash described this landscape lyrically in 1923: 'The Marsh and this strange coast. The forms with their black magenta and orange colourings. The ancient Marsh churches. The lovely wooded canal under the hills and the hills themselves overlooking a land so fair and fantastic.'⁸ This coast became the scene for a whole series of paintings. Some of them, such as *Winter Sea* (fig.27), begun in 1925, would be the most powerful and successful Nash would produce in these two decades of experiment and uncertainty. But Nash was not alone in this flight from the city. Though his own love affair with the English countryside had started long before the war, the 1920s saw a distinct trend among British artists to return to Nature. Ben Nicholson, who was also struggling to find a new form of representation, visited Nash at Dymchurch and painted the same coastline, while Vanessa Bell and Duncan Grant painted pictures of the Sussex landscape and Fry escaped to Provence to work. Two of Nash's most promising future students at the Royal College of Art, Edward Bawden and Eric Ravilious, likewise turned to the countryside for inspiration, and celebrated a rural life in Essex. This was very much a retreat from the modern, in the same way that Palmer and the Ancients and William Morris had withdrawn from industrial, modernising England in the nineteenth century. If Nash's new British art was to be modern, it was modern only in the sense of style, and not in substance.

27 *Winter Sea*
1925–37
Oil on canvas
71.2 × 96.6
(28 × 38)
York Art Gallery

28 *Winter Wood*
1922
Wood engraving,
14.7 × 11.4
(5¾ × 4½)
The Whitworth Art
Gallery, University of
Manchester

Illustrator, Designer, Teacher

An early admirer of Nash's post-war work was T.E. Lawrence, then as now
better known as Lawrence of Arabia. In 1921 he bought *Coast Scene* for his
room in the Colonial Office, hoping it might startle his moribund employers
into life. Lawrence later asked Nash if he would provide illustrations based on
Lawrence's own photographs for his account of the wartime Arabian campaign. Nash was uncertain about working from someone else's pictures, but
when he saw them he decided it was 'going to be great fun – what a place!
Petra the city of the Dead! O what a dream!'⁹ His illustrations subsequently
appeared in *The Seven Pillars of Wisdom* in 1926. Book illustration became an
area in which Nash now increasingly worked, partly as a way simply to make
money, and between 1918 and 1932 he illustrated some eighteen books. In
1920 the Society of Wood Engravers was formed, and Nash became a member.
Like the retreat to rural subjects, wood engraving was a return to an older,
simpler artistic style which appealed to numerous artists between the wars.
Ravilious, Bawden and Nash all embraced it, and it had an influence on their
painting too. In 1922 Nash published *Places*, his most concerted attempt at
'the dual expression' he had once praised in Rossetti and Blake – that is,
the dual expression of the poet-painter. He did everything for the book except
print it – he designed the cover, cut its seven wood engravings and the
lettering, and wrote the text. The title page described these engravings as

29 *Still Life* 1927
Oil on canvas
91.4 × 71.1
(36 × 28)
Leeds City Art
Gallery

'illustrations in prose'. *Winter Wood* (fig.28) develops the conceit that a row of trees makes an avenue through the woods as an aisle in a church: 'In Winter Wood the wet mould is fragrant,' runs the accompanying text, 'soft is the touch of leaves, footsteps tread noiselessly all these dim tenuous aisles.' Ford Madox Ford told Nash he thought these descriptions 'largely nonsense'. Nash accepted this, though he told Bottomley, 'if they are largely nonsense they are more or less decorative nonsense'.[10]

Another subject he developed was still lifes of flowers. But these are often flat, rather pale and insipid paintings (fig.29). There is little drama to them. His best work continued to be his landscapes, such as *Chilterns under Snow*, painted in 1923. As we noted in the first chapter, the autumn and winter months had long appealed to Nash. As early as November 1910 he had told Bottomley of the 'glorious' joy he felt in these seemingly gloomy seasons: 'The mass of people go about saying "how mournful, how sad" I never did sympathise with them these are the jolly days. I want to make a picture of great bowed trees against a wide sky of clouds with all the birds suddenly flying up from the field & all the yellow leaves falling down & the shafts of the sun turning them all golden I pray I can do it.'[11] In *Chilterns under Snow*, as, in a different way, in *Winter Sea*, and in his views of the Wittenham Clumps of the 1940s, we experience Nash's love of the darker, sparer tones of the bare English landscape. Sometimes this limited palette is taken too far – indeed in 1931 the sculptor Jacob Epstein described Nash's paintings as 'anaemic'.[12] Nash's landscapes thus differ significantly from his brother's, such as *The Cornfield* (fig.25), with their bright, cheerful, summer colours. Yet he is often able to surprise with a painting such as *Wood on the Downs* (fig.30). Based on a drawing made in spring from a spot near Ivinghoe Beacon in north Buckinghamshire, it is a particularly successful work from this often difficult, indecisive period. It is a return, almost, to the undulating forms of *We are Making a New World*. But here is tranquillity, the grass is green, there is the white of the chalk downs, the full forms of the trees in first leaf. It is a happy, confident painting.

As well as his writing, illustrating and painting, Nash became involved in theatre and textile design, including designs for dress material and rugs, and he later made occasional commercial designs for glass, ceramics and wood. He also now began teaching for the first time. Between October 1920 and the summer of 1923 he taught at Rothenstein's art college in Oxford, and in

30 *Wood on the Downs* 1930
Oil on canvas
71.1 × 91.4
(28 × 36)
Aberdeen Art Gallery

September 1924 he was appointed an assistant in the School of Design at the Royal College of Art, working a day and a half a week. He was a teacher very much in the modern mould, who seemed to have forgotten his own Romantic roots – one former student later remarked that Nash gave them 'a feeling that art began with the Post-Impressionists'.[13]

But these responsibilities, necessary if he were to survive financially, put a strain on him. After paying a visit to his sickly father in the autumn of 1921 Nash had collapsed, and drifted in and out of consciousness for a week. He was taken to the London Hospital for Nervous Diseases, where he was told by a specialist that he was suffering from emotional shock 'starting from the period of his work as a War Artist, and ending in the emotional shock of his father's illness.'[14] He was told to rest, and to avoid strenuous work. This was but an early sign of difficult times to come.

Travels

The trips which Nash and his wife made to the Mediterranean coast over the next few years were often for the purpose of improving his health. At Christmas 1924 they travelled to Paris, and then in early 1925 to Cros-de-Cagnes, on the Côte d'Azur. In March they went on to Italy, visiting Genoa, Pisa, Siena and Florence. They did not stay long, as they were both disturbed by the rise of Fascism there. Though troubled by poor weather, when the sun did appear Nash was moved by the sense of light and colour. He wrote to his brother of the 'Lovely grey blues, pinks, grey greens, infinite gradations of tones of yellows, creams & whites especially in the buildings. The buildings excite me no end.'[15] The memorable paintings from these continental trips are few, but one of the finest is surely *Blue House on the Shore* (fig. 31), in which we also see the

31 *Blue House on the Shore c.* 1930–1
Oil on canvas
41.9 × 73.7
(16½ × 29)
Tate, London

32 Giorgio de
Chirico (1888–1978)
*The Uncertainty of the
Poet* 1913
Oil on canvas
106 × 94 (41¾ × 37)
Tate, London

influence of the great Italian painter Giorgio de Chirico (fig. 32). In 1928 there
was an exhibition of de Chirico's work at Tooth's Gallery in London. Revealing
the insularity of the post-war British art market, this was the first significant
London exhibition of a major contemporary continental artist since the
Matisse and Picasso shows at the Leicester Galleries in 1919 and 1921. For
Nash, de Chirico was a visionary, and was – along with Matisse, Picasso and
Fernand Léger – one of the four major influences on modern art. As we shall
see in the next chapter, de Chirico was a leading inspiration for the Surrealists,
and Surrealism would be a forceful influence on Nash through the 1930s and
1940s. But we already start to discern its new influence in the late 1920s. In
Northern Adventure (fig. 33), a view of St Pancras Station in London, and in
Landscape at Iden (fig. 34), both from 1929, we see clear hints of de Chirico's
passion for architecture and for curious juxtapositions of seemingly unrelat-
ed objects. These are odd paintings, with their uninhabited landscapes. Where
have the people gone, the people who have left behind these strange scaffolds
and neatly stacked piles of wood? What is the symbolism of the snake that
weaves through the fence, or the disjointed window that points at the sky?
Both paintings are almost like deserted stage sets with side screens and back-
drops, revealing the influence of Nash's earlier interest in theatre.

But again this influence of de Chirico is a sign of Nash's uncertainty, of his
search for a new direction. Iden had provided him with the inspiration of the
south coast, but he now needed something new. In April 1928 he told Margaret of his feeling that they should leave Sussex, but where to go to next he
did not know. 'I am very puzzled what to do. I want to expand yet I do not see
my way.'[16] This feeling of personal crisis was exacerbated by the death of his

33 *Northern Adventure* 1929
Oil on canvas 91.4 × 71.1 (36 × 28)
Aberdeen Art Gallery

34 *Landscape at Iden*
1929
Oil on canvas
69.8 × 90.8
(27½ × 35¾)
Tate, London

father the following February. But with money from the sale of the house at Iver Heath, the Nashes journeyed again to France in 1930, along with their friends Ruth Clark and Edward Burra, a soon-to-be-successful young painter from Rye, 'an eccentric talented delicate creature, extremely amusing'.[17] On this trip Nash and Burra both became keenly interested in Surrealist painting. Nash in particular welcomed 'the release of the dream' that Surrealism seemed to offer. Now he had found something he could work with. In this respect the trip was a great success. But on another level it was a dangerous failure. Nash developed bronchitis, which would increasingly damage his already delicate health. Margaret blamed it on exposure to poisonous gas in the Passchendaele trenches in 1917. Though this seems unlikely, through the next decade Nash's health declined further, and he was often debilitated by a crippling asthma. But he also found new directions. The 1930s would thus be a decade of profound contrasts.

4

UNIT ONE AND SURREALISM

First Attempts to Fly

Despite his discoveries during the 1930 vacation, Nash was not won over to Surrealism immediately. For a while he continued to experiment with another major development in modern European art, abstraction. In the 1920s and 1930s proponents of abstraction such as Piet Mondrian and Joan Miró sought unity and clarity in their painting through the use of geometric shapes and the relationship between objects and colours. The most notable and successful British acolytes of abstraction would be Nash's friends Ben Nicholson and the sculptor Barbara Hepworth. Its influence on Nash can be seen in the scaffolding structure in the foreground of *Northern Adventure* (fig.33), which he considered one of his earliest forays into the world of abstract forms. He also wrote about the movement, somewhat uncertainly, in his art criticism, having in late 1930 become the art critic for the *Week-end Review*, and then in 1931 the art critic for the *Listener*, a post he shared with Herbert Read, then the leading writer on modern art in Britain. Nash admitted in 1935 that he found abstraction a 'bewildering expression'. In the early 1930s he had experimented quite vigorously with the style, but he soon recognised that such experiments as *Voyages of the Moon* of 1930 and *Kinetic Feature* of 1931 (fig.35) were largely unsuccessful.

However, he did not depart from abstraction totally empty-handed. In his short essay 'Aerial Flowers', published in 1945, he explained how these paintings were his 'first attempts to fly'. At Passchendaele, Dymchurch and Romney Marsh he had cast about 'for different ways and means of expression'. After ten years these searches had led him to these 'tentative experiments in abstract design'. But although he confessed to making 'no headway in this direction either, my exercises tended to increase the range of my perception. I began, for instance, to explore in depth by new methods to re-value colour relationships and practice with more subtlety the acute problem of poise. I realize now that these were actually my first attempts to fly. Once the traditional picture plan was abandoned in favour of design in space the true equivalent was virtually established. Imaginatively, in a pictorial sense, I was airborne.' However, the symbols of this new, abstract world did not suit Nash: 'the renunciations my new state required bored and discouraged me'.[1] He was called back to his symbols of old, of Nature and 'the hard cold stone, the rasping glass, the intricate architecture of trees and waves, of the brittle sculpture of a dead leaf'.[2] Yet he did not wholly reject abstraction, for he found that it had helped to liberate him from the forces that had tied him to what he called 'the terrestrial plane'. Now he could experiment with confidence: 'I could never be frightened by the law of gravity quite to the same degree again.'[3]

35 *Kinetic Feature*
1931
Oil on canvas
66 × 50.8 (26 × 20)
Tate, London

But while Nash now possessed a new-found confidence and direction, these were hard times to be an artist, and he depended on writing for much of his income. (A 'sort of second rate Roger Fry' he jokingly called himself in 1931.[4]) His oil paintings were not selling particularly well – a consequence of the depressed economic climate. 1926 had seen the General Strike, and 1929 the Wall Street Crash. Nevertheless, in December 1930 the Nashes moved into a large house in Rye, with a terraced garden and a view over the marshes and out to sea. Nash's friends here would include the novelists Radclyffe Hall, E.F. Benson and Sheila Kay Smith, as well as the American poet Conrad Aiken, and Edward Burra, who lived close by. Aiken became an important influence, Margaret later writing that he 'revived Paul's natural love of poetry and helped to bring out in Paul's work a surer form of poetic expression'.[5] The poet wrote of Nash's 'love of beauty that was oddly both animal and mineral'. He could be, he wrote, 'as soft as a cobweb or the flesh of a woman, or as hard as one of the flints in the *Nest of Wild Stones*'. Yet Aiken feared that his friend had intentions towards his flighty wife, describing him as a 'philanderer and rogue to beware of'.[6]

In America

In 1931 Nash was invited to be the British representative on the International Jury at the Carnegie Exhibition in Pittsburgh, Pennsylvania. He had declined the same offer in 1929 as it would have interrupted his work; this time he accepted, though he was reluctant and uncertain about the undertaking. Paris, not New York, was still the focal point of the international avant-garde. It was the Second World War that destroyed this hub, and only then, after many of Europe's best artists had fled to the United States, would New York become the new centre of the modernist movement. For Nash, who had been reading a book about the gangster Al Capone, America in the age of prohibition was a dangerous, unattractive place. 'What kind of men are these?' he wrote to Margaret before their voyage out. 'The war was dreadful enough but it was fought bravely and in a sort of mistaken idealism but to take life for beer – my God. I think I shall vomit from New York to Pittsburgh and back.'[7]

And America was equally unsure of what to expect of Nash. An early press release in the *Pittsburgh Sun-Telegram* (written, according to Nash, 'by some not very well-informed lady with an inadequate command of language') explained that he had first come to attention through his war work. Since then, however, 'his peace-time paintings have been logical performances but anti-climax to that dread picture "The Menin Road"'. While his still lifes and seascapes 'command respect', they were, the same critic thought, 'utterly divorced from life'.[8] This was harsh criticism, and it stung Nash, but it was not wholly without truth, as he must have realised.

Once in New York, however, Nash was not interested in meeting the country's fine artists. He wanted to meet its comic artists. He was strongly drawn to American humour, in particular cartoonists such as Walt Disney, George Herriman, creator of the *Krazy Kat* cartoon strip, and the artists of the *New Yorker*, whom he praised in an article in *Week-end Review*. James Thurber, a

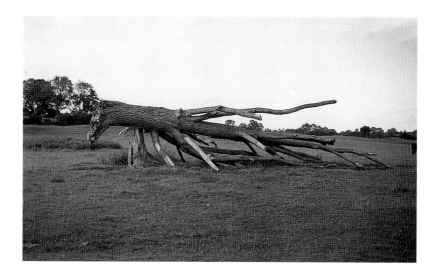

comic artist Nash was keen to meet, recalled that at that time there was 'no one in England, or anywhere else outside the States, who knew our comic art so well, or appreciated it so heartily'. Thurber also noted that in New York Nash's 'utter absorption in the unique and the unusual overcame all other emotions'.[9] One feature he was inevitably drawn to in the Manhattan landscape was the skyscrapers, to which there was nothing remotely similar in Europe. He spoke of his feeling that, through these beautiful, enormous buildings, New York was 'in search of harmony. It is trying to find beauty in solidity ... This aspect of New York indicates the passing of sentimentalism. It indicates that New York is attempting to face nature and its future alone.'[10]

As a present for this trip, Margaret bought her husband a pocket Kodak camera. He used it for the rest of his life, and it became a very valuable tool. As his asthma worsened and it became harder for him to sketch for any length of time out of doors, the camera provided him with the aid of what he called another 'eye'. It recorded rapidly and 'with beautiful precision'. Nash would increasingly produce his landscape paintings from photographs, not sketches, and found that he 'developed something like a new consideration of landscape pictorially'.[11] He became quite an accomplished photographer, particularly of landscapes and curious objects in those landscapes (fig.36). The late masterpiece *Totes Meer* (fig.50) would be but one example of this new relationship between photographer and painter.

Unit One

In October 1931, shortly after his return from America, Nash was involved in the exhibition *Recent Tendencies in British Painting* at Tooth's Gallery in London. It included his painting *Kinetic Feature*, and there he had also seen 'collected together, the pictures of artists who had been working out, apart, ideas which, either by conception or the idiom of their expression, or often because of both qualities, were separated from the main trend of contemporary

English art'. It was clear to him for the first time that 'the majority of these artists were somehow allied in purpose'. The exhibition was the inspiration for a new group whose formation Nash announced in a letter printed in *The Times* on 12 June 1933. They stood, he declared, 'for the expression of a truly contemporary spirit, for that thing which is recognised as peculiarly *of today* in painting, sculpture and architecture'.[12] The group called themselves Unit One, and their headquarters was the Mayor Gallery in London's Cork Street. Another inspiration was the Pre-Raphaelites, 'in the sense that those artists were a brotherhood, [and] these are a unit: a solid combination standing by each other and defending their beliefs'.[13] The members of Unit One were the painters John Armstrong, Edward Burra, John Bigge, Tristram Hillier, Ben Nicholson, Edward Wadsworth and Nash; the sculptors Barbara Hepworth and Henry Moore; and the architects Wells Coates and Colin Lucas. As Herbert Read explained in his introduction to the book *Unit One* (1934), which contained a collection of statements by each of the members, the name had been chosen because 'though as persons, each artist is a *unit*, in the social structure they must, to the extent of their common interests, be *one*'.[14] It appeared that a combination of one for all and all for one was the only way modernism could become a legitimate force in English art.

In April 1934 the Mayor Gallery held an exhibition of Unit One's work, which was later shown in Liverpool, Manchester, Hanley, Derby, Swansea and Belfast. Though Nash was the driving force, he, along with most of the group, did not sit easily with its expressed ideals. In his letter to *The Times* he had explained that what the members stood for was 'decidedly at variance with the great Unconscious School of Painting', and that they also seemed 'to be lacking in reverence for Nature as such'. Nash's friend Anthony Bertram believed that 'no artist has ever made a statement which so completely misrepresented his own deepest imaginative pursuit'.[15] So, with even Nash deceiving himself as to the objectives of Unit One, and expressing what was effectively a false unity, it is unsurprising that the group crumbled early in 1935. It would in fact be in that 'great Unconscious School of Painting' – Surrealism – that Nash discovered his true outlet. As he told Herbert Read in 1942, 'I did not find Surrealism, Surrealism found me.'[16]

'Urne-Buriall' and Avebury

But before moving on to Surrealism, we must step back a few years. The need to make a living meant that in the early 1930s Nash had to find an eclectic range of commercial jobs. In a one-off commission in 1932 he designed a bathroom for the Austrian dancer Tilly Losch, wife of the art collector Edward James – a beautiful creation of glass, steel and neon lighting (fig. 37). But his most successful commercial work was with the oil company Shell-Mex. The firm's advertising manager, Jack Beddington, brought in contemporary artists, of whom Nash and Graham Sutherland were the most famous, to work on advertising designs. In an article in the *Listener* Nash praised Beddington's campaign for 'consciously or unconsciously ... discharging an aesthetic responsibility to the public'.[17] It was an excellent project, and it included

a series of Shell guidebooks to the counties of England, which was put under
the editorship of the poet John Betjeman. Nash would later be invited to write
the guide to Dorset, an idiosyncratic work which was published in 1936
(fig. 38).

   Another commission, which proved even more fertile ground for Nash's
imagination, was an invitation to illustrate work by the seventeenth-century
antiquary and physician Sir Thomas Browne. He chose the two metaphysical
essays 'Urne-Buriall' and 'The Garden of Cyrus', and it is easy to see their
appeal, with their mystical themes of death, the afterlife and the strange
ancient symbolism of the quincunx. One of the lines in 'Urne-Buriall' inspired
the painting *Mansions of the Dead* (fig. 39), which would mark an important
turning-point in Nash's work. Nash later realised that Browne 'must have

been thinking of tombs *under the earth*' when he wrote these lines. But to the
artist they had 'suggested only aerial habitations where the soul like a bird or
some such aerial creature roamed at will perching now and then on these
convenient structures in the clouds or in the pure upper air'.[18] Furthermore,
his work on 'Urne-Buriall' was a valuable preparation for the discovery of
another new 'place', this time in rural Wiltshire.

In July 1933 the ailing Nash went on holiday to Marlborough with his
friend Ruth Clark. From there they made a day trip to nearby Avebury. Less
famous than Stonehenge, but older and so extensive that the site embraces an
entire village within its circumference, the prehistoric stone circles and
avenues at Avebury have a strange power to enrapture the first-time visitor.
Inside a large, encircling trench and bank of earth dug from the downland
chalk stand enormous sarsen stones. A short distance away rises Silbury Hill,
the largest man-made prehistoric monument in Europe. Clark recorded that
when Nash first saw the Avebury stones he was immediately 'excited and fascinated ... His sensitiveness to magic and the sinister beauty of monsters was
stirred, and he long contemplated the great mass of their forms, their aloof-
ness, their majesty, the shadows they cast on the green, the loveliness of their
harsh surfaces and the tenderness of their colouring. He seemed to have found
renewed vitality in this countryside and in these ancient symbols.' Suddenly
Nash was once more 'charged with purpose. His strength was equal to the

39 *Mansions of the Dead* 1932
Pencil and watercolour on paper 57.8 × 39.4 (22¾ × 15½)
Tate, London

quest he was minded to follow.'[19] He wrote to his wife, 'If anything will preserve my interest in landscape from a painter's point of view, it will be this
country.'[20]

Avebury, the 'hallowed remnants of an almost unknown civilization',[21] like
the Wittenham Clumps, spoke of the ancientness of Britain. And it also spoke
of the brutal changes being wrought on that landscape during the inter-war
years. This landscape and its historical associations were proving of considerable interest to a number of other British artists, including Sutherland, Piper
and Ravilious. Once again it fascinated Nash, as it had in his youth. He

55

Prospect of the Temple on Overton Hill. 8 July 1725.

TAB. XXI.
P.40.

The Hahpen. or head of the Snake. in ruins.

40 William Stukeley
(1687–1765)
'Prospect of the
Temple on Overton
Hill 8 July 1723'
Engraving from
*Abury: A Temple of
the British Druids*,
published 1743

41 *Equivalents for
the Megaliths* 1935
Oil on canvas
45.7 × 66 (18 × 26)
Tate, London

42 *Landscape of the Megaliths* 1937 Watercolour on paper 50.2 × 75.6 (19¾ × 29¾) Albright-Knox Art Gallery, Buffalo, New York

obtained a copy of *Abury: A Temple of the British Druids*, written by the eighteenth-century antiquary William Stukeley. Stukeley had conceived of Avebury as an immense serpent temple built by post-diluvian Druids, with the avenues of stones which lead from the central circle representing a huge hieroglyphic symbol of the Christian Holy Trinity (fig.40). It was a vivid if ultimately unhistorical conception of the past such as this that captivated Nash, and one that 'yielded material for pictures'. And Stukeley had been an influence on that old hero of Nash's, Blake. Alongside Browne, Stukeley and Blake, Nash, with his *Equivalents for the Megaliths* (fig.41), become one in a chain of writers and artists capturing and reinterpreting the mystical heritage of the British landscape. Yet he was at the same time attempting to rise above this influence, and to see the stones almost as abstract qualities alone. He explained to the friend who bought *Equivalents for the Megaliths* that he had wanted to 'avoid the very powerful influence of this antiquarian suggestion, and to insist only upon the dramatic qualities of a composition of shapes equivalent to the prone or upright stones simply as upright or prone, or leaning masses, grouped together in a scene of open fields and hills. Beyond that resolve the picture cannot be traced, logically. It developed inevitably in its own way.'[22]

As the art critic Myfanwy Evans wrote in her influential magazine *Axis* in the early winter of 1937, Nash had 'no interest in the past as *past*, but [in] the accumulated intenseness of the past as *present*'.[23] He hated the modern human intrusion on history, and disliked archaeology. He felt that after the restoration of Avebury undertaken in the early 1940s the 'primal magic of the

57

stones' appearance was lost'. When he visited the excavations at the prehistoric Maiden Castle in Dorset, he was not interested in the archaeological discoveries being made, but in that place's 'awful beauty', and the relationship of objects in its landscape. At Maiden Castle he saw the sun beating down 'on the glinting white bones' of human skeletons. Some, he wrote in an article for *Country Life* entitled 'Unseen Landscapes', seemed to be 'the nests of giant birds; the gleaming skulls like clutches of monstrous eggs. It was a place, with these scattered groups of fantastic nests and long raised ledges on the open hills.'[24] As is clear, by the time these remarks on monsters were written, in the spring of 1938, Nash's eyes had been fully opened to Surrealism, with its powerful recognition of the odd and the strangely juxtaposed.

The Surrealist

Nash's desire to move to Wiltshire was never fulfilled. Leaving Rye, he and Margaret eventually returned to London, before setting off in November 1933 on a long trip to the south of France, Gibraltar and north Africa. Their intended destination had been Spain, but the political situation there, which was eventually to descend into violent civil war between the Republican government and the Fascist army led by General Franco, had meant a change of destination. And Nash was, again, taken ill with his bronchial complaint. On their return to England in June 1934 the couple moved to a cottage in Romney Marsh. Again he was captivated by this 'everlasting lovely' landscape. And here he made his first Surrealist discovery, an *objet trouvé*, 'a superb piece of wood sculpture (salvaged from the stream) like a very fine Henry Moore'.[25] This piece would be exhibited as *Marsh Personage* at the first International Surrealist Exhibition, which took place in London in 1936.

Surrealism arrived late to England. It had been born in Paris in 1924 out of the ashes of the self-destructive Dada movement, itself a radical intellectual and artistic response to the madness of the Great War. The First Surrealist Manifesto, penned by the French poet André Breton, united the writings of Sigmund Freud on the unconscious with the radical legacy of French writers such as the Marquis de Sade, the Comte de Lautréamont and Guillaume Apollinaire, and lionised the strange art of Gustave Moreau and de Chirico. The English writer David Gascoyne explained in 1935 that 'the avowed aim' of the Surrealist movement was 'to reduce and finally to dispose altogether of the flagrant contradictions that exist between dream and waking life, the "unreal" and the "real", the unconscious and the conscious'.[26] For Nash, it was 'the pursuit of the soul, the attempt to trace the "psyche" in its devious flight, a psychological research on the part of the artist parallel to the experiments of the great analysts'.[27] For many of the British artists and writers involved in Surrealism, it also had its English roots. For Gascoyne, Surrealism could not be limited to any one particular time or place. He pointed to the 'strong surrealist element' to be found in the works of Shakespeare, Coleridge, Blake, Edward Lear and Lewis Carroll.[28] British Surrealism was, to both its critics and its champions, a new Romantic movement. It was, however, also largely stripped of its revolutionary cadences.

43 *Harbour and Room* 1932–6
Oil on canvas 91.4 × 71.1 (36 × 28)
Tate, London

As a source of artistic inspiration, it was a godsend to Nash. However the International Surrealist Exhibition, which he helped organise and which included works by, among many others, Max Ernst, Salvador Dalí and Joan Miró, had a mixed reception. Though the *Daily Telegraph*'s critic described it as 'London's most sensational art-show for many years', the *Daily Mail* found the whole thing 'thoroughly decadent and unhealthy'. The 'ordinary man or woman', it declared, 'will have some difficulty in discerning any motive beyond eccentricity in apparently meaningless paintings and other "works of art" done in buttons, nails, shoelaces and rusty nibs'.[29] The *Sunday Times*, however, affirmed that, of the British contributors, Nash was 'by far the most distinguished'.[30] The exhibits of the acknowledged 'English Surrealist-in-Chief' included the painting *Harbour and Room* (fig.43), a curious, dreamlike juxtaposition inspired by seeing the sea reflected in the mirror of a French hotel room.

By the time of the exhibition the Nashes had moved to Swanage, on the Dorset coast. But Nash grew to dislike the town, which he described in an article entitled 'Seaside Surrealism', and in the summer of 1936 they moved to a large house in Hampstead, north London. Here Nash started work on another of his major Surrealist works, *Landscape from a Dream* (fig.44). Though this was admired by Breton, and is often considered one of the best works of British Surrealism, there is something rather flat and uninspired about the painting. It has little of the strangeness of the odd reflections and extraordinary juxtapositions of the Belgian Surrealist René Magritte (who dubbed Nash 'the Master of the Object'). Nor does it possess the mysterious wonder of the paintings

44 *Landscape from a Dream* 1936–8
Oil on canvas
67.9 × 101.6
(26¾ × 40)
Tate, London

45 Max Ernst
(1891–1976)
The Entire City 1934
Oil on paper laid on
canvas 50.2 × 61.3
(19¾ × 24⅛)
Tate, London

of the German Surrealist Max Ernst, whom Nash so admired (fig.45). Nash
had written in 1933 of Ernst's troubling, 'disconcerting associations of birds
and flowers, suns and forest – suns which look like targets, forests which more
resemble trees'. The influence of Ernst is apparent in *Landscape from a Dream*
and *Pillar and Moon* (fig.47), though the results are tamer and rather lifeless.
Nostalgic Landscape (fig.46), with its Dymchurch backdrop, was begun in 1922,
but Nash reworked it in 1938 under the Surrealist influence, presumably
inserting the strange architectural feature which now sits incongruously on
the sea wall, its corridor suggestive of a new, subterranean landscape that is
to be entered. In 1936 Nash had a passionate but brief affair with the Surrealist artist Eileen Agar, and there is a hint of this troubled romance in these
works of the second half of the decade. He hoped, albeit unsuccessfully, to
rediscover in Agar the muse he had once found in Margaret.

In Hampstead the Nashes were drawn into a wide network of European
artists. The troubles in Spain in 1934 had been but one indication of the terri-
fying events that were shortly to explode in Europe. Another clear sign of the
developing crisis was the steady trickle into England of continental artists and
intellectuals. The Nazi Party had come to power in Germany under the leadership of Adolf Hitler in 1933. Almost immediately they had implemented
their fascist ideology, persecuting all cultural, social and racial 'degenerates',
including communists, homosexuals, gypsies, Jews and avant-garde artists –
be they painters or jazz musicians. They closed the visionary Bauhaus art and
design school, and its founder, the German architect Walter Gropius, fled to
England in 1934. That same year another of the Bauhaus team arrived, the
Hungarian designer Marcel Breuer, as well as the German-Jewish architect

47 *Pillar and Moon*
1932–42
Oil on canvas
50.8 × 76.2
(20 × 30)
Tate, London

Erich Mendelsohn. The Hungarian artist László Moholy-Nagy followed in 1935, the Russian sculptor Naum Gabo in 1936 and Sigmund Freud and Mondrian in 1938. While some moved on to the United States, many either passed through or settled in Hampstead, where the coterie of British avant-garde artists and writers included Nash, Moore, Nicholson, Hepworth and Read.

But the cosiness of this new home would not last long. In 1938 the Venice International Biennale included a retrospective of Nash's works in oil and watercolour, but by the end of the following summer Britain was once again at war with Germany and Austria, and soon with Italy also. Ironically, war would complete the full circle of Nash's development as an artist, and offered him the opportunity of his last great flourish.

opposite
46 *Nostalgic Landscape* 1922–38
Oil on canvas
71.1 × 50.8
(28 × 20)
New Walk Museum
and Art Gallery,
Leicester

5

FURTHER ADVENTURES
IN FLIGHT

The War of Machines

Though the new war with Germany would bring him discomfort and upheaval, it gave Nash the opportunity to return to those themes that in 1917 and 1918 had helped him make his name as an avant-garde artist: conflict, death and the ruined landscape. As he told his brother in November 1941, 'I reckon myself very fortunate to have found a second time true inspiration in the subject of war.'[1]

The Nashes' first act of the war, however, was to uproot themselves from Hampstead. The threat of aerial bombardment seemed imminent to Margaret, and they left London for the relative safety of Oxford, eventually settling in a ground-floor garden flat at 106 Banbury Road. This would be Nash's last home. Almost immediately he founded the Arts Bureau in Oxford for War Service, which he hoped would help make the best use of the talents of artists (including architects, painters, sculptors, writers and musicians) for the war effort. He mooted his ideas to Sir Kenneth Clark, Director of the National Gallery. Clark was encouraging, but although the Bureau included among its numbers such eminent names as Lord David Cecil, John Betjeman and John Piper, it was not a success. As Nash told Bottomley, 'When the war began I was badly eclipsed. I stopped painting & writing & invented a new job for myself, a wild affair which was near being the end of us since it turned out a monster that devoured time energy and all our spare money.'[2]

But only a few months after the German invasion of Poland in September 1939 Nash also made enquiries about again becoming an Official War Artist. As Clark, who became Chairman of the War Artists Advisory Committee (WAAC), explained, the first purpose of the scheme was 'to provide a memorable record of the war and all its associated activities'. This, wrote Clark in his typical style, was best achieved by artists because they were 'more sensitive and observant than ordinary people', and 'certain important but fleeting emotions aroused by the war can only be given permanence through the medium of art'.[3] The men commissioned by the WAAC to record the conflict included such significant names as Moore, Piper, Spencer, Sutherland and Ravilious (who would lose his life in an air crash in Iceland in 1942). But Nash would not be any run-of-the-mill documentarist. His Surrealist legacy and all he had worked for as a painter through the 1930s could never permit that. He asked Clark if he 'could be given official facilities for recording monsters. I believe I could make something memorable. Monsters include ... tanks, aeroplanes, blimps, mechanical personages of all kinds. I see these things as the protagonists of the war. This is the War of Machines and they have taken on human and animal appearance.'[4] To his great credit, Clark, who could easily have been deterred by such high-falutin, Surrealist ideas, recognised Nash's potential to represent aerial scenes. On the basis of his 1932 painting *Mansions of the Dead* (fig. 39) – and to his own considerable surprise and pleasure – Nash was commissioned to the Air Ministry.

Ironically, Nash's chronic asthma meant that his lifelong ambition of flight would never be physically realised. But he visited airfields and crash sites and gathered all the photographs, newspapers and illustrated weeklies he could muster, trawling them for images of the war. His first completed work was a series of watercolours of downed German bombers, with the collective title *Marching Against England*. These crash paintings were the direct legacy of the standing stones of Avebury and his Surrealist paintings and photos of objects in the landscape (fig. 36). As Herbert Read wrote in 1944, for Nash 'The wrecked airplane was one more monolithic object, fallen unexpectedly from the sky, but endowed with an additional mystery, ominous and deathly.'[5] This is at its most obvious in *Bomber in the Corn*, where a blood-red sun, low on the horizon, casts an eerie glow over a circle of tangled wreckage, while an 'avenue' of debris leads off into the distance among the golden cornfields. But also in *Under the Cliff* (fig. 48) we witness the powerful symbolism of the white cliffs of the English coast absorbing the fractured tail of a German Heinkel. Nash explained that he was 'fascinated' by the 'incongruous disasters befalling the Luftwaffe aircraft day by day; crashing into the cornfield or tearing

48 *Under the Cliff*
1940
Watercolour on paper
38 × 56 (15 × 22)
Ashmolean Museum, Oxford

up the seashore, burning themselves away in the summer coverts, disturbing the pheasants and so on'.[6] Ben Nicholson actually told Nash that he thought these watercolours were 'far more convincing and natural Surrealism ... than when you import some large stones or wooden forms into the foreground as in peacetime'.[7] The WAAC was also delighted by the pictures, considering them 'the best work sent in so far by any war artist'.[8]

Surprisingly, however, the Air Ministry took a dim view of the paintings.

Left
49 Wrecked aircraft at Cowley Dump, 1940
Tate Archive

Below
50 *Totes Meer (Dead Sea)* 1940–1
Oil on canvas
101.6 × 152.4
(40 × 60)
Tate, London

Nash recorded that he was 'made to feel that to make a picture of the wreck of an enemy machine on the ground was rather like shooting a sitting bird'.[9] So *Marching Against England* was followed by a tamer series of watercolours of British bombers, both on the land and in action. Though these were well received and 'highly thought of' by both the WAAC and the RAF airmen whose planes they depicted, they do not have the same sense of power – or indeed beauty – as Nash's crashed aircraft. And he was soon expressing his own dissatisfaction with his war work. He felt 'it seemed too detached to be followed whole-heartedly at that moment of history'. By the summer of 1940 the British Expeditionary Force had been evacuated from Dunkirk, and the Low Countries and France had fallen to the Germans. Dogfights now raged in the skies over southern England, and invasion seemed imminent. Nash acknowledged that he had already come 'face to face with the odious word Propaganda. Well, why not,' he asked himself. 'It was useless to deny that pictorial propaganda had immense possibilities.'[10]

In August 1940 he visited a dump for wrecked German aircraft at Cowley, on the outskirts of Oxford, where he made sketches and took numerous photographs (fig.49). After this visit he started work on his first oil painting as a war artist, and *Totes Meer (Dead Sea)* (fig.50) proved to be his finest painting of the decade and also probably the most famous oil painting of the whole conflict by any British war artist. On submitting the finished work to the WAAC in March 1941, he was careful to stress that it was 'based on an actual scene', and explained the origin of the painting:

> The thing looked to me, suddenly, like a great inundating sea. You
> might feel – under certain circumstances – a moonlight night for
> instance, this is a vast tide moving across the fields, the breakers
> rearing up and crashing on the plain. And then, no; nothing moves, it
> is not water or even ice, it is something static and dead. It is metal piled
> up, wreckage. It is hundreds and hundreds of flying creatures which
> invaded these shores ... By moonlight, the waning moon, one could
> swear they began to move and twist and turn as they did in the air.'[11]

He added that the white owl which can be seen to the right of the picture swooping down and 'flying low over the bodies of the other predatory creatures' was not so much a symbol but more to complete the functional, aesthetic requirements of the picture. Nonetheless, it does add an important symbolic touch, the hunter surveying the hunted, and reminds us that this is still essentially a landscape. This was, again, one of Nash's 'places'. It was a Romantic encounter with man-made ruins. He wrote too of his sensation that the Cowley dump was haunted: 'I do not mean the wraiths of lost pilots or perished crews were hovering near, it was nothing so decidedly human, but a pervasive force baffled yet malign hung in the heavy air.'[12]

Aerial victory

Clark described *Totes Meer* as 'most beautiful – the best war picture so far I think'.[13] But despite Clark's enthusiasm (an enthusiasm fully justified by the critical acclaim that met public exhibition of the painting at the National Gallery in May 1941), in December 1940 Nash's appointment with the Air Ministry ended. He reflected ruefully upon this in a letter to Bottomley: 'The Airmen liked my pictures, not so the Air Ministry ... Our Relations became somewhat strained eventually but then they baled me out at about 20,000 ft. as it were.'[14] With the support of both Clark and the more 'enlightened' Advisory Committee, however, Nash was soon found a post at the Ministry of Information. This, while providing him with expenses, was without a fixed salary, making him again dependent upon sales. As he told Bottomley, 'So long as they buy I don't mind but everything is very precarious.' In fact sales of his work went very well during the war years. It continued to be exhibited abroad under the auspices of the British Council, and by 1944 he was in the happy situation of selling work almost as fast as it was shown, 'for the first time in my life'.[15] By the end of the war Nash was firmly established at the forefront of modern British painters.

But in the early 1940s the financial picture was not so rosy. The Nashes' situation was not helped by their ever-failing health, and Nash was clearly depressed. 'Personally I never expected to survive so long,' he told Bottomley ruefully in April 1941. 'I imagined that if war came that would be the end of everything. Well it hasn't turned out like that, but I cannot see any future. It would be different if we had health but we're just a couple of old crocks.'[16] In May his London gallery, Tooth's, was bombed and he lost several drawings, including 'one of the best I'd done alas – and no photograph'. He found he couldn't get on with his work, he couldn't get on with his book, he was 'just a mental mess'.[17]

Despite working under these heavy physical and emotional strains, in his first canvas for the Ministry of Information Nash would attempt something radical and new. By October 1940 it was clear that the RAF had outfought the Luftwaffe. The threat of invasion was lifted and the Germans turned their attention to 'blitzing' London. In the famous words of the Prime Minister, Winston Churchill, 'Never in the field of human conflict has so much been owed by so many to so few.' Nash now sought to represent that conflict in paint. As he explained, *Battle of Britain* (fig.52) was

> an attempt to give the sense of an aerial battle in operation over a wide area and thus summarise England's great aerial victory over Germany. The scene includes certain elements constant during the Battle of Britain – the river winding from the town and across parched country, down to the sea; beyond, the shores of the Continent, above, the mounting cumulus concentrating at sunset after a hot brilliant day; across the spaces of sky, trails of airplanes, smoke tracks of dead or damaged machines falling, floating clouds, parachutes, balloons. Against the approaching twilight new formations of the Luftwaffe, threatening.[18]

It would be an evocative and successful painting, but Nash knew he was attempting something difficult. In October 1941 he told Clark, 'I don't know what you will say about this picture. I took a chance and I am almost ready to believe it has come off. But in the last few days I could not feel quite satisfied.'[19] But his fears were unnecessary: Clark was again impressed. He told the artist: 'I think in this and *Totes Meer* you have discovered a new form of allegorical painting. It is impossible to paint great events without allegory, but unfortunately we no longer accept symbols like those which satisfied the classical painters, and you have discovered a way of making the symbols out of the events themselves.'[20] Like *Totes Meer*, in January 1942 *Battle of Britain* was exhibited to the public, along with the work of other war artists, and was

52 *Battle of Britain*
1941
Oil on canvas
121.9 × 182.8
(48 × 72)
Imperial War
Museum, London

again well received. *The Times*'s critic noted the new style of the painting, and the fact that the 'soft colouring' and 'rather confusing design' of Nash's more recent work had gone. 'Here the colour effect is intense and dramatic.'[21]

53 *Defence of Albion*
1942
Oil on canvas
121.9 × 182.8
(48 × 72)
Imperial War
Museum, London

A Ministry of Imaginative Warfare

We have already noted Nash's recognition of the importance of art as propaganda in the new war against Germany. In the spring of 1941 he expressed his belief that 'This is, before all else, a war of the imagination.' He also recognised the strength of the German propaganda machine, which, he believed, had 'captured the imagination' of the world. But, he wondered, 'where is *our* imagination, have *we* no ideas, nothing up our sleeve – or better still, can't something be found in our *head*? And why not? Why not a Ministry of Imaginative Warfare? ... What is needed immediately is a counter-imaginative thrust which by its suddenness and novelty will strike at the mind as no armoured or explosive blow will at the counter-armoured body.'[22] He told his brother that he felt a responsibility to make 'a good picture first but if possible a picture to make you feel good (or, if you're a Nazi, not so good)'.[23] For despite his return to the subject of armed conflict, Nash's attitude to the Second World War differed significantly from his attitude to the First. Then, in the face of the endless, pointless slaughter, his personal and artistic vision had become increasingly pacifist. But his response to the later war was much more aggressive. He hated Hitler and the Nazis, both their fascist belligerence and anti-avant-garde aesthetic. In their now infamous exhibitions of *'entartete Kunst'* ('degenerate art') the Nazis had pilloried and then sold or destroyed the work of such supreme modernists as Chagall, Gauguin and Picasso, as well as that of the Surrealists de Chirico and Ernst. Though unable to fight the Nazis as a man, Nash could still fight them as an artist.

However, his next attempt to do this in oil, a 'portrait' of a Sunderland flying boat of the Coastal Command in action off Portland against a German U-boat and entitled *Defence of Albion* (fig.53), was not a great success. He wrote himself that he had 'despaired of it many times'[24] and the *Manchester Guardian* criticised it for its 'surely self-conscious, synthetic allegory'. But the critic did add that this was 'a failure in the grand manner. Not many other artists are ambitious enough to come a really spectacular cropper.'[25]

Nash was also experimenting with collage, the cut-and-paste technique he had learnt as a Surrealist. He told Clark how for several weeks over the winter of 1941–2 he had been unable to paint and had found himself 'spending most of my hours doing nothing but brood upon Hitler'. This brooding produced a short series of collages entitled *Follow the Führer* (fig.54). Nash explained that the importance of collage was that it 'allowed actual photographic images ... of Hitler's horrible head ... You see, I believe Hitler to be the embodiment of evil just now but his physical personality is an image at once terrible and absurd.' The 'whole idea of the series' was that 'they should be extensively reproduced'.[26] It was in this format – mass-produced images – that he really saw his work succeeding as propaganda. But despite the success abroad of collage

54 *Follow the Führer, Over the Snows* 1942
Chalk, watercolour and collage
38.1 × 55.9 (15 × 22)
Imperial War Museum, London

propaganda, for example that of the anti-fascist German artist John Heart-field, Britain was still not prepared at this date to respond to such Surrealist juxtapositions. For this reason Nash's quick-witted collages have, sadly, never become as well known as his oil paintings.

55 *Landscape of the Vernal Equinox* 1944
Oil on canvas
63.5 × 76.2
(25 × 30)
Scottish National Gallery of Modern Art, Edinburgh

Aerial Flowers

After 1942's *Defence of Albion* Nash did not work on another large-scale war painting for some two years. This fact reflects his declining health, his concern with his artistic vision and his preoccupation with other, more personal projects. Increasingly after 1940, Nash was aware that he did not have long to live. He complained to a friend in June 1942 that 'Life just gets mingier and mangier – we dwindle, the lights dim, the shadows creep nearer.'[27] In a despondent letter to Burra in September he wrote that he and Margaret were 'so indescribably falling apart ... It is so boring. So often we want to die. I can't explain.'[28] This melancholy outlook had a deep influence on his attitude to his work and to his whole career as an artist. He was looking both back to his achievements and ahead at how posterity would judge him.

But work on his autobiography, begun in the late 1930s, had trailed off, as if somehow he did not know how to recapture or describe his life since 1918. He would write in the preface to *Outline* that his 'whole vision' of the path of the book had been 'eclipsed by the abrupt darkness' of the outbreak of the new war.[29] In looking back, however, he rediscovered his interest in Rossetti and the Pre-Raphaelites, as well as the early stimulus of the Wittenham Clumps. From November 1942 he began visiting the house of a friend on Boar's Hill, a short distance from Oxford. From here he had, with the aid of binoculars, a clear view of the Clumps. These hills had been an important influence on him as a young artist. He now returned to them as an imaginative subject. The following year he would remark that 'through field-glasses one sees a landscape that one can see in no other way',[30] and this method of 'remote viewing' had a clear impact on his paintings from this final period, substantially foreshortening the depth of field. This may be seen most obviously in *Landscape of the Vernal Equinox* and *Landscape of the Summer Solstice* (figs.55, 56), both views of the Wittenham Clumps. Nash described the former painting (which was soon bought for the Queen's collection) as 'a landscape of the imagination'. Equal weight, he explained, was given to the colours and influence of the setting sun and the rising moon, and, through the spring equinox, 'the *fact* of equal day and night' was presented.[31]

56 *Landscape of the Summer Solstice* 1943
Oil on canvas
71.8 × 91.6
(28¼ × 36)
Felton Bequest, 1952
National Gallery of
Victoria, Melbourne

57 *Flight of the Magnolia* 1944
Oil on canvas
50.8 × 76.2
(20 × 30)
Tate, London

And these landscapes are also a response to the war, as the Dymchurch paintings had been a response to his experiences in the Passchendaele trenches. Their sense of place is truly heightened by their wartime context, the sense of a land and a way of life under threat. This is a patriotic, nostalgic experience, highlighted in the work of other WAAC artists, particularly Piper and Sutherland. It is an experience that finds its fulfilment in the important but underrated Neo-Romantic movement of this period, of which Nash was a significant progenitor. These landscapes are truly English, in the way that the landscape scenes of Samuel Palmer which had impressed Nash as a young man are quintessentially English. They are at once real and recognisable, yet suffused with a strong, idiosyncratic sense of fantasy

And there is another influence working on these paintings. In the early summer of 1943 he browsed through Sir James Frazer's *The Golden Bough*, attracted by its exploration of ancient myth. Frazer (1854–1941) was one of the first anthropologists, and his book was a vast comparative study of mankind's beliefs and institutions, containing extensive discussions of such things as fertility rites, sacrificial kings and dying gods, and analysis of the primitive mind. It was hugely influential on literary and artistic minds of the 1920s and 1930s. As well as these solstice and equinox landscapes, for which Nash ventured the term 'transcendental', his flower paintings benefited from Frazer's influence. He called them his 'strange new pictures. Giant flowers blooming among the clouds or sailing down the night skies like falling stars.'[32] A surreal moment in his garden added to his experience. He was busy 'breaking off the dying, dark, ethereal flowers of a favourite poisonous plant when I heard

– Last night heavy and medium hellebore bombed the mountains of the Moon.[33] He attempted to reproduce this curious fantasy in collage, but the emotions it stimulated in his imagination are best found in the bizarre painting *Flight of the Magnolia* (fig.57). Flowers in these final paintings become a metaphor and a symbol for his own encroaching demise. His American friend James Thurber explained how Nash 'was able to face the awful and too early discontinuance of his vital life, largely by persuading himself that the experience of death was akin to flowers aerially borne, a kind of eternity of fragrant and gentle drifting'.[34]

War Victim

Inspired by his landscape work and his strange visions of flight, Nash returned to a commission for the WAAC with a strongly experimental painting, *Battle of Germany* (fig.58). He told Clark in September 1944: 'I have risked much in it. If it comes off it might be the best thing I have done of any kind.'[35] The painting, which was based on careful study of official records, depicted an RAF moonlit-night bombing raid over Germany. Like *Battle of Britain*, Nash explained to the Committee, the painting was 'wholly an imaginary scene', but one containing various phenomena which he considered to be 'constant in such battle dramas', such as the 'great column of black smoke slowly spreading over the sky'. With its 'arbitrary' forms and colours and its 'chromatic percussion', which he intended to 'suggest explosion and detonation', Nash anticipated confusion from the critics over the painting. But he could not

58 *Battle of Germany* 1944
Oil on canvas
121.9 × 182.8
(48 × 72)
Imperial War
Museum, London

have reckoned with even Clark's puzzled response: 'alas, I can't understand it – even with your admirable text to enlighten me ... I can only tell you truthfully my own feelings in front of it, which were apologetic bewilderment and incomprehension.'[36]

It was the last painting Nash undertook for the WAAC. *Battle of Germany* was simply too Surrealist for the Air Ministry. By May the following year the Nazis were defeated and the war in Europe was over. But Nash was complaining, 'I am quite distraught these days. Life becomes increasingly difficult, the struggle intensifies, never eases.' Although he was able to continue working on his 'Sunflower' oils, he pondered over his unfinished autobiography, reflecting on his artistic career. He told Bottomley, 'When I came to look into the early drawings I lived again that wonderful hour. I could feel myself making those drawings – in some ways the best I ever did to this day. And because of this I suddenly saw the way to finish my "life" – half of which you have read & been so generous about – I feel I could make a complete thing by taking it up to 1914 – just up to the war. After that it was another life, another world.'[37]

The 'life' was never finished. By October 1945 Nash was too ill to work, and early in 1946 he suffered an acute attack of pneumonia, which put his weakening heart under even greater strain. In April he wrote to Bottomley, reflecting that it was 'slightly unreal sometimes to be alive[.] I was, apparently by all accounts so near being dead. In fact I have no right, I am told, to be what I very nearly am, quite recovered ... Really, I'm a war victim, Gordon! I painted so many outsize pictures for the M[inistry] of I[nformation] that the strain crocked up my heart.'[38] Despite the optimistic ring to this letter, Nash died in his sleep – from heart failure – on 11 July 1946. Margaret described it as his *'merciful & peaceful* journey to other worlds & spheres of the mind – I am heartbroken'. He was buried in the churchyard at Langley Marish in Buckinghamshire, alongside four generations of his family, 'those fine ancestors who made him love England'.[39]

One of Nash's last pieces of writing to be published, the essay 'Aerial Flowers', had appeared in *Counterpoint* magazine in 1945. There he had revealed: 'But it is death I have been writing about all this time and I make no apology for mentioning it only at the end, because anything written here is only the preliminary of my theme ... Death, about which we are all thinking, death, I believe, is the only solution to this problem of how to be able to fly. Personally, I feel that if death can give us that, death will be good.'[40] Only in death could he finally take wings and fly.

Notes

PN Paul Nash

GB Gordon Bottomley

MN Margaret Nash

Introduction

1 Tate Archive, 12 January 1943.

2 Bertram, p.183.

3 Ibid.

4 Nash, 'Art and War', *World Review*, May 1943.

5 *Outline*, p.27.

6 See Michael Balint, *Thrills and Regressions*, New York 1959.

7 *Outline*, p.26.

Chapter One: Early Visions and Poems

1 *Outline*, p.46.

2 Ibid., p.41.

3 Ibid., pp.35–6.

4 Ibid., p.54.

5 Ibid., pp.75–6.

6 PN to GB, late April 1910, *Letters*, p.4.

7 *Outline*, p.78.

8 Nash, 'Aerial Flowers', p.3.

9 *Outline*, pp.79–80.

10 King 1987, p.9.

11 *Letters*, p.xi.

12 PN to GB, 9 April 1910, *Letters*, p.1.

13 GB to PN, 2 August 1910, ibid., p.8.

14 *Outline*, p.81.

15 Ibid., p.87.

16 Ibid., pp.87–8.

17 Ibid., p.89.

18 Ibid., pp.89–90.

19 Spalding 1986, p.39.

20 *Outline*, p.93.

21 Ibid., p.110.

22 Ibid., p.110.

23 Ibid., p.105.

24 PN to GB, August 1912, *Letters*, p.42.

25 *Outline*, pp.106–7.

26 Bertram 1955, p.69; Nash 1949, p.122.

27 *Outline*, p.122.

28 PN to GB, 22 November 1911, *Letters*, pp.26–7.

29 Quoted in Bertram 1955, p.76.

30 PN to GB, 27 December 1913, *Letters*, p.68.

31 Quoted in Bertram 1955, p.75.

32 Bertram 1955, p.77.

Chapter Two: The Void of War

1 PN to Eddie Marsh, 'Bloody August 1914', Bertram, p.85.

2 *Outline*, p.177.

3 PN to Emily Bottomley, October 1914, *Letters*, p.76.

4 PN to MN, 7 March 1917, *Outline* p.187.

5 PN to MN, 6 April 1917, ibid., p.194.

6 PN to MN, 26 April 1917, ibid., p.198.

7 PN to MN, 12 May 1917, ibid., pp.202–3.

8 PN to GB, August 1917, *Letters*, p.85.

9 PN to GB, *c.*23 August 1917, *Letters*, p.86.

10 PN to MN, late March 1917, *Outline*, p.192.

11 PN to MN, 21 March 1917, Tate Archive.

12 Imperial War Museum, Nash file, 18 October 1917.

13 Bertram, p.94.

14 PN, Imperial War Museum, Nash file.

15 PN to MN, 16 November 1917, *Outline*, pp.210–11.

16 Bertram 1955, p.95.

17 PN to GB, 16 July 1918, *Letters*, p.98.

18 Read 1948, pp.8–9.

19 Bertram, p.99.

20 PN to GB, 16 July 1918, *Letters*, p.99.

21 PN to GB, April 1919, ibid., p.103.

22 Cork, p.196.

23 Draft of *Outline*, Tate Archive 7050.2.

24 *Outline*, p.218.

Chapter Three: Making a New World

1 Draft of *Outline*, Tate Archive 7050.2.

2 GB to PN, 12 December 1919, *Letters*, p.116.

3 *New Witness*, 7 February 1931.

4 Ibid., 23 May 1919.

5 Draft of *Outline*, Tate Archive 7050.2.

6 *Outline*, p.79–80.

7 PN to MN, 1928, King, p.125.

8 PN to Percy Withers, 15 May 1923, King, p.109.

9 PN to GB, 12 September 1922, *Letters*, p.156.

10 PN to GB, 31 December 1922, ibid., p.163.

11 PN to GB, 15 November 1910, ibid., p.13.

12 King, p.156.

13 Bertram, p.114.

14 King, p.102.

15 Bertram, p.114.

16 PN to MN, April 1928, King, p.122.

17 PN to Percy Withers, 11 April 1930, King, p.146.

Chapter Four: Unit One and Surrealism

1 *Outline*, pp.260–1.

2 'For, but not With', *Axis*, 1 January 1935.

3 *Outline*, p.261.

4 PN to GB, 19 December 1931, *Letters*, p.207.

5 MN, Victoria & Albert Museum.

6 Bertram, p.171; King, p.135.

7 PN to MN, no date, Paul Nash Trust.

8 King, p.148.

9 Bertram, pp.172–3.

10 Interview in *New York Herald Tribune*, 19 September 1931.

11 Nash, advertising notice for *Fertile Image*.

12 *The Times*, 12 June 1933.

13 *Listener*, 5 July 1933.

14 Read, *Unit One*.

15 Bertram, p.183.

16 King, p.166.

17 *Listener*, 20 January 1932.

18 PN to Hartley Ramsden, 4 June 1941, Bertram, p.196.

19 Bertram, p.216.

20 Bertram, p.217.

21 PN to Lance Sieveking, 4 May 1937, Bertram, p.243.

22 Ibid.

23 Bertram, p.237.

24 *Outline*, p.231.

25 PN to Clare Neilson, 6 August 1934, Bertram, p.220.

26 David Gascoyne, *A Short Survey of Surrealism* (London 1935), p.x.

27 *Listener*, 5 July 1933.

28 Gascoyne, p.132.

29 *Daily Telegraph*, 12 June 1936; *Daily Mail*, 12 June 1936.

30 *Sunday Times*, 21 June 1936.

Chapter Five: Further Adventures in Flight

1 PN to John Nash, ?November 1941, Bertram, p.256.

2 PN to GB, late March 1941, *Letters*, p.220.

3 *Artists' International Association Bulletin* 68, December 1941.

4 PN to Clark, Tate Archive, Clark Archive, uncatalogued.

5 Read 1948, p.16.

6 *Outline*, p.263.

7 Nicholson to PN, 25 June 1943, Tate Archive.

8 Imperial War Museum, War Artists Archive, minutes 14 August 1940.

9 *Outline*, p.263.

10 Undated notes, quoted in Hall, p.29, Tate Archive.

11 PN to E.M.O. Dickey, Secretary of War Artists Advisory Committee, 11 March 1941, Imperial War Museum, War Artists Archive.

12 Tate Archive 7050.3925, *The Writings of Paul Nash*, BBC radio broadcast.

13 Clark to PN, 15 March 1941, Imperial War Museum.

14 PN to GB, 17 April 1941, *Letters*, p.219.

15 PN to Percy Withers, 9 May 1944, Bertram, p.262.

16 PN to GB, 17 April 1941, *Letters*, p.218.

17 PN to Ruth Clark, 20 May 1941, Bertram, pp.254–5.

18 Nash, n.d., Imperial War Museum, War Artists Archive.

19 PN to Clark, 16 October 1941, ibid.

20 Clark to PN, 22 October 1941, ibid.

21 *The Times*, 23 January 1942.

22 PN to Dickey, undated letter, ?April 1941, Imperial War Museum, War Artists Archive.

23 PN to John Nash, ?November 1941, Bertram, p.256.

24 PN to Clark, 29 April 1942, Tate Archive, uncatalogued.

25 *Manchester Guardian*, 29 May 1942.

26 PN to Clark, Tate Archive, Clark Archive, undated and uncatalogued.

27 PN to Clare Neilson, 29 June 1942, Bertram, p.259.

28 PN to Edward Burra, 11 September 1941, Bertram, p.259.

29 *Outline*, p.19.

30 Sieveking, p.81.

31 Tate Archive 7050.3925, *The Writings of Paul Nash*, BBC radio broadcast.

32 PN to Clare Neilson, 8 June 1944, Tate Archive.

33 *Outline*, p.264.

34 Bertram, p.225.

35 PN to Clark, 2 September 1944, Imperial War Museum, War Artists Archive.

36 PN, 1 October 1944, and Clark to PN, 30 October 1944, Tate Archive.

37 PN to GB, late July 1945, *Letters*, p.219.

38 PN to GB, early April 1946, *Letters*, p.266.

39 MN to GB, 14 July 1946, *Letters*, pp.267–8.

40 *Outline*, p.265.

Bibliography

Abbott, Claude Colleer and Anthony Bertram (eds.), *Poet & Painter. Being the Correspondence Between Gordon Bottomley and Paul Nash, 1910-1946*, London 1955

Bertram, Anthony, *Paul Nash. The Portrait of an Artist*, London 1955

Cardinal, Roger, *The Landscape Vision of Paul Nash*, London 1989

Causey, Andrew, *Paul Nash*, Oxford 1980

Causey, Andrew, *Paul Nash's Photographs: Document and Image*, London 1973

Cork, Richard, *A Bitter Truth: Avant-Garde Art and the Great War*, New Haven and London 1994

Digby, George Wingfield, *Meaning and Symbol in Three Modern Artists: Edvard Munch, Henry Moore, Paul Nash*, London 1955

Eates, Margot (ed.), *Paul Nash: Paintings, Drawings and Illustrations*, London 1948

Hall, Charles, *Aerial Creatures: Paul Nash*, London 1996

Haycock, David Boyd, *A Crisis of Brilliance: Five Young British Artists and the Great War*, London 2009

King, James, *Interior Landscapes: A Life of Paul Nash*, London 1987

Nash, Paul, 'Aerial Flowers', Oxford 1947

Nash, Paul, *Outline: An Autobiography and Other Writings*, with a preface by Herbert Read, London 1949

Read, Herbert, *Paul Nash*, 3rd ed., edited by Sir Kenneth Clark, in *Penguin Modern Painters* series, Harmondsworth 1948

Robinson, Leonard, *Paul Nash: Winter Sea: The Development of an Image*, York 1997

Rothenstein, John, *Modern English Painters*, vol.2, London and Sydney 1984

Sieveking, Lance, 'Paul Nash', in *The Eye of the Beholder*, London 1957

Spalding, Frances, *British Art Since 1900*, London 1986

Copyright Credits

Photographic Credits

Index